To Jack

Please accept this book in celebration
of the Fiftieth Anniversary
of the Gene B. Glick Company.

I hope you enjoy it.

Gene Glick

Born to Build

Born to Build

The Story of the Gene B. Glick Company

Gene Glick

Guild Press of Indiana
Carmel, Indiana

 Published in the United States by Guild Press of Indiana, Inc., Carmel.

Library of Congress
Catalog Card Number
97-74000

ISBN 1-57860-005-7 (hardcover)
ISBN 1-57860-012-X (paperback)

Printed in the United States of America

Text design by Sheila Samson

This book is dedicated to my loving wife and wonderful partner of fifty-plus years, Marilyn Koffman Glick, in celebration of our golden wedding anniversary as well as the fiftieth anniversary of the founding of the Gene B. Glick Company.

Without Marilyn's vision, wise counsel, tremendous work, and unfailing support in every aspect of life it could not have been written. I quote the words of poet Roy Croft, which I used to mark our twentieth wedding anniversary and are as true to me today as they were then:

I love you because you
Are helping me to make
Of the lumber of my life
Not a tavern
But a temple: Out of the works
Of my every day,
Not a reproach
But a song.
I love you
Because you have done
More than any creed
Could have done
To make me good
And more than any fate
Could have done
To make me happy.

It is a salute, too, to our four daughters, Marianne, Arlene, Alice, and Lynda, their husbands, and their children, whose encompassing love warms us every day.

And this dedication extends to our loyal colleagues; as has been written, "No man is an island . . .," which thought is as true in every business enterprise as it is in poetry. We acknowledge and honor this debt with tremendous gratitude.

Contents

Preface

THE IRASCIBLE Samuel Johnson observed that "no man but a blockhead ever wrote except for money." Since it's immediately obvious that this book will never make *The New York Times'* nonfiction bestseller list, Johnson's view is not the underlying inspiration for it.

So why did I write it? For several reasons, all of which I thought were valid, with the reader either establishing or rejecting that belief. It will be your call.

One of my reasons for writing this is that it would inform, perhaps inspire, establish some history, and, I hope, entertain with some humor. I didn't want to write the kind of book that once you put it down, you couldn't bear to pick it up again!

On a personal level, it was to tell our children and their children and their children's children more about what we did and how we did it, and a bit more about the times in which we lived. I have always wished I knew more about the lives of my ancestors.

In the business world we hope that laying out what amounts to a case history of what can be accomplished, starting from scratch, will not only be of interest to someone with an entrepreneurial bent, but might be an inspiration to anyone wishing to make the attempt to follow a dream. And from a purely academic point of view, I hope this book will be an explanation to the student of how an idea grew to become a major force in an entire industry.

Among other merits, we know it will inform our colleagues, present and future, of the basic tenet on which the organization was built and how it prospered: that dedicated service by people of excellence would be recognized in the marketplace. It should become obvious that teamwork of those sharing a mission is the basis of success of an organization formed of people with vision and integrity.

The suggestion has been made to me many times through the years to write this book, but every time the thought crossed my mind, with great self-control I would lie down until the thought passed.

But several years ago, with the fiftieth anniversary of the company approaching, I understood what value the history would have, and I faced up to the task, which has been monumental. It has taken far more time than anticipated, more work than we thought possible, and has admittedly been a source of exasperation at times.

So the question arises: would you start the effort again? And the answer is a resounding "Yes"! Memories were stirred, factors of success were revealed, and the underlying value of the project was very much reinforced.

Have I achieved these goals in this volume? I must leave that judgment with you, the reader, having done the best I could, but I hope that you will find at least some parts of our goals to be of interest as you browse through these pages.

ACKNOWLEDGMENTS

Frank Basile first proposed writing our company history as early as 1987, and again in 1992. As I told Frank just a few months prior to the publication of this book, I was glad he persevered until I finally agreed to do it, but I was not certain I'd be pleased with the result.

Besides Frank, there obviously are many people to thank, without whose work the book would not have been possible, and their contributions must be gratefully acknowledged.

I want to thank Bill Beck for the countless hours he spent interviewing me and others. He asked the right questions to elicit the most appropriate and interesting information. And I think he kept this dictum in mind very well: "If you live long enough, the venerability factor creeps in—you get credit for things you never did, and praise for virtues you never had."

The people listed on page 261 all shared their own unique insight, and I am most grateful for their contributions.

I appreciated the review of the manuscript and the comments provided by *The Indianapolis Star* book reviewer, Rich Gotshall, and Jane Lyle of the Indiana University Press.

Thanks also to Nancy Gaubatz, Frank Basile's secretary, who transcribed every word of the thousand-plus pages of interviews. Tom Blandford did a fine job in the tedious task of compiling names and addresses for distribution of this book.

Brenda Coons coordinated the photographic work at our various projects and worked with the photographer, Harold Miller, and the cover designer, Dick Listenberger. My thanks also to these two gentlemen for their fine professional work.

Nancy Baxter of Guild Press of Indiana did extensive editing of my words to make them more readable, and she also coordinated all the elements of the publication process. Despite my efforts to delay, and perhaps even derail this project, Nancy continued to follow up to ensure that we stayed on track.

A special thanks goes to our company associates, suppliers, and contractors who through the years have made our success possible. Their skills, knowledge, hard work, and loyalty carried us through these last fifty years and I am deeply indebted to all of them. Many have become lifelong friends.

Finally, the person to whom I owe the most, in both my personal and professional life, is my loving wife, Marilyn. As I indicated in the dedication, she has been my closest friend, confidant, and partner during these last five decades, and without her, this work could not have been written.

Chapter 1

Beginnings

The child is the father of the man.
—William Wordsworth

I SUPPOSE I'VE ALWAYS been interested in the way families shape people. How do people get the way they are? I think about that from time to time. But there were two reasons I grew up being aware of my roots. The first reason is that two grandparents lived right in our home when I was a child—and you couldn't miss the connection with family history.

We lived at 36th and Salem—a street that runs between Meridian and Illinois only between 34th and 38th in that part of Indianapolis' Northside. After they were married in 1910, my parents had moved into a home built by my mother's parents. At the time Mr. and Mrs. Reuben Glick came home as newlyweds to Salem Street, there was farmland across the street, with cows grazing in a field on the north side of 36th. I was born there in 1921; my brother Arthur came two years later.

My father's mother, Rachel Faust Glick, later came to live with us in that two-story house, sleeping in the middle bedroom. And my mother's father, Adolph Biccard, who adored and spoiled my mother even when she was a grown woman, slept right in the bedroom with my brother and me.

Adolph Biccard spent his youth in Rochester, Indiana, then was married and held public office there in Fulton County. About 1902, when my mother was sixteen, they moved to Indianapolis and he took a job as manager of the Indianapolis Brewing Company. Eventually he became manager of the Knights of Pythias Building, and we would visit him there.

His influence on me was strong, though I was only a youngster when he died. I can see him now—rotund, loving, reminding me of Norman Rockwell's painting, "Grandpa," with children dancing around him and putting their hands in his pockets for change. He and I used to go downtown together to Keith's vaudeville theatre and watch the stand-up comics. Our tastes were similar—or maybe it was that he indulged me almost as much as he had indulged my mother. He died when I was six, suffering a fatal heart attack as my dad and he walked the streets of New York City.

Rachel Faust Glick was born in 1858 in Lafayette, Indiana. They moved to Indianapolis when she was a young girl. At the age of twenty-four she met Elias Glick, and they married on February 24, 1880.

Born about 1849 in Hungary, Eli, as my grandfather was called, came to the U.S. while still a young man. Rachel's family initially disapproved of the marriage. For one thing, Eli Glick was twelve years older than his bride. For another, the Fausts were very "proper" German Jews who tended to look down on Jews from Hungary and other parts of Eastern Europe.

We've all been entrepreneurial. My dad was a paper boy in the 1890s—James Whitcomb Riley was one of his customers. Dad would take the paper to Riley's office and there would be a note telling him to deliver the paper to McGillicuddy's bar on the Circle. Finally Dad quit going to the office and just brought the paper to the bar.

He also watched the Soldiers and Sailors Monument being built. One day as he was passing by, one of the plumbers said, "Kid, we're going to turn the fountains on. Do you want to be the first one to have a drink?" I suppose they did that more than once and there were a lot of kids who thought they'd had the first drink.

My father, Reuben Frank "Ruby" Glick, had his own automobile supply business and also sold new and used cars for one of the first Ford agencies on the north side. Governor Samuel Ralston was one of his customers in an odd arrangement. Ralston used to stop by and say, "Ruby, we get home from speaking tours late. What will you charge us to have your van come pick us up at the Interurban station and bring us to the governor's mansion?" (At that time the mansion was located near Fall Creek and Meridian, just north of the Marott Hotel.)

Ralston was a huge man—three hundred pounds or so—so when Dad thought about what he should charge, he took that into consideration, and also that the driver would have to wait, so he said "How about a dollar, Governor?"

The governor thought a minute and said, "Ruby, make it fifty cents and you've got a deal." My dad was honored to have somebody pick up the governor. I'm sure that at best he broke even, but he believed you can sometimes take business for other reasons than making a dollar.

Indianapolis in the twenties was a thriving distribution and railroad center for much of the Midwest. The population of the city was approaching 315,000, and the foreign-born population of 17,000 was the largest of any community in the state. African Americans in the city numbered nearly 35,000, also the largest concentration in Indiana.

The city, which had celebrated its centennial the year before my birth, rapidly was becoming a manufacturing center, particularly for the emerging automobile industry. The city's newest factory in 1921 was that of the Duesenberg Automobile and Motors Co. Inc., located on West Washington at Harding Street. My dad's choice of the automobile business for a career seemed well-matched to what was going on in Indianapolis at the time.

Later on my dad was a partner and head of sales for a wholesale auto parts dealership at 527 N. Capitol. Dad taught the salesmen to sell auto parts around the area—to automobile dealers and garages.

This company also made trunks—before trunks were a part of cars—and installed one of the first automobile heaters, the Hades Heater, in cars.

I remember when I was seven or eight years old, and the Hades Heater first came out, the attractive secretary from the company put on a devil's suit and paraded around to attract customers during the auto show at the fairgrounds. Times don't change much in the auto world.

Dad was a real mechanic. He could put a race car together or build an automobile engine. He was often out at the Indianapolis Motor Speedway and knew Barney Oldfield. Most of all, though, he was a great salesman. He would assemble and install these Hades Heaters, and then go looking for customers, insisting on the coldest days that customers "just come out to the car for a minute." They wouldn't want to do it, but after a few minutes of conversation in the front seat the customer would say, "What's going on here? It's getting hot!" Dad would tell them they couldn't afford not to have this wonderful device, a car heater, and he couldn't write the orders fast enough.

Dad's partner, Jay Emerson Fettig, was a big, tall, handsome man who was also very funny. He had the gout (which isn't so funny) and when I'd go to visit when I was a boy, he'd have his foot up on a stool and he'd say, "Glick, I don't want you to even look at my foot. The waves from your eyes hurt my toe." I've always appreciated humor in the business world.

Dad, this supersalesman, couldn't stop selling, even when he was retired, working well into his seventies and eighties. He worked for us, selling homes and renting apartments in Indianapolis. I still run into people who say, "How's your dad?" His influence is never far from my mind; whenever I enter my office his cheerful portrait greets me from the wall, and I remember how hard he worked, sacrificing for us when taking care of a family wasn't easy.

I SAID THAT there were two logical reasons for me to be interested in "roots." The first was that the grandparents were with us. But the second is that they—we—were Jewish.

My mother's family were Reform Jews, at least in my time. Grandfather Biccard was one of the old-time members of the Indianapolis Hebrew Congregation. He had come relatively young from Alsace-Lorraine, from a little village called Geillgen, across the Rhine from Schaffhausen, Switzerland. Not too long ago I took the family over to Germany and we found the little ancestral village my daughter Arlene had researched. We looked for Biccard gravestones in the cemetery and found some, with the name spelled different ways, including "Biccart." I stood in the cemetery on a hill overlooking the Rhine Valley, and thought, "I'm here where my ancestors walked all the way back in the seventeenth century."

I can't read Hebrew, so I couldn't decipher the inscriptions of the ancestors, but apparently a lot of visitors to the cemetery were like me, because someone had marked the graves in English too.

My mother's family had come to America when my grandfather was young, ending up in Rochester, Indiana. There they were in the cornfields, with few fellow Jews around them. When they came to Indianapolis it was different, and the family became very active in the Reform Jewish movement. Adolph Biccard was the progressive-thinking president of the Indianapolis Hebrew Congregation from 1916 to 1920.

When I was a boy, and my mother insisted, we went to temple at 10th and Delaware. Dad went grumbling one or two times a year—High Holy Days only. I would yell and scream about going to Sunday school, and Dad would intervene—but not on my behalf. He made me go, but he did so reluctantly, I believe. Like nearly all the boys in my class, I was "confirmed," rather than bar mitzvahed. Now all our grandchildren go through the authentic experience.

There weren't many Jews in our neighborhood, but from time to time I was reminded that I was different. Another kid named Eugene used to torment me sometimes. He'd call me "Christ killer," and push me around. The rumor was that he was abused, beaten up by an alcoholic father. He had to have been four years older than everybody else at school because he always flunked, year after year. He wore tattered clothing and shoes.

One day he was bullying me, and I was yelling for help, when a fellow came by, about the age of the bully. This fellow knew me, and he grabbed the bully by the collar and said, "You son of a bitch—you pick on this kid again and I'm going to murder you." The bully was scared by that and backed off, pretty much for good.

On a day not too long after that my dad and I saw him walk by the house. "That's the guy who calls me 'Christ killer,' " I said. My dad called the boy over. The kid was scared, but my father said, "Do

My mother, Faye Biccard Glick, and her mother, Minnie Allman Biccard, in 1891.

My paternal grandfather, Adolph Biccard. He was an official in the Knights of Pythias, and the manager of the K of P building. I think he was also the president of Indianapolis Brewery for a while. That's probably where I developed my taste for beer.

My parents in 1910, around the time they were married.

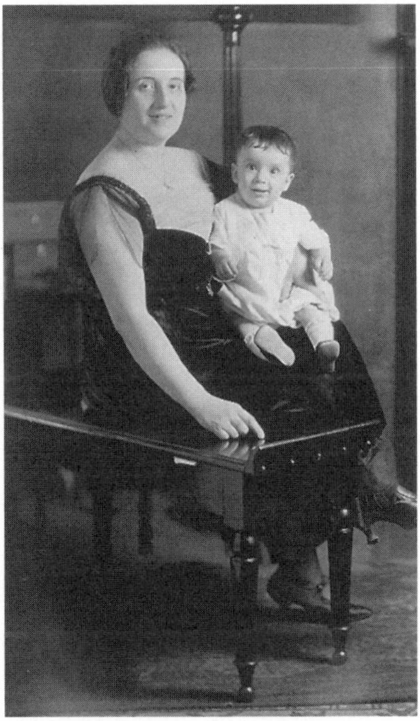

My mom and I, 1922.

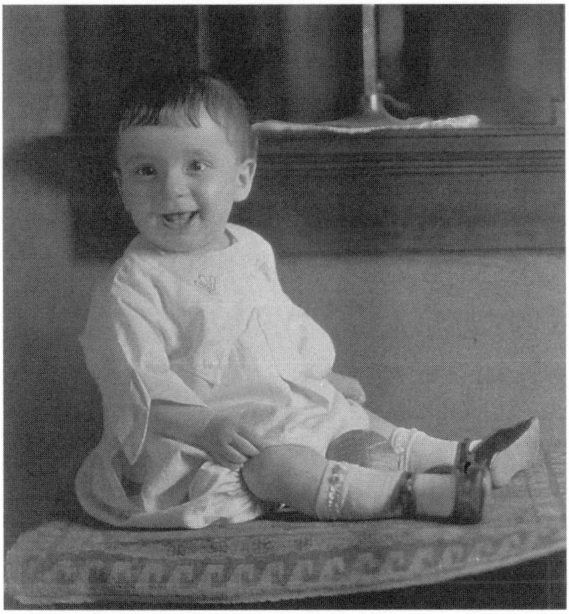

This baby Eugene is smiling. The thought just crossed his mind that he'd go into the building business, which makes him very happy!

you know this boy's name?" The kid said he knew it was Eugene.

"From now on, when you talk to him, call him Eugene. Do you understand?" The boy said he did, and that was the end of my troubles with him.

Unfortunately, it wasn't the end of *his* trouble with antisocial behavior. When I was overseas in the Army, my mother sent me a clipping saying that he'd been executed in the electric chair after murdering someone in Washington, D.C. It certainly supports my view about the role that poverty plays in filling the death rows in American prisons.

Of course, there were many other things that shaped us. The neighborhood was one of them, and there were all sorts of social groups there, from the poor kids like that other Eugene who lived above a store, to wealthy types in fancy mansions. You could learn a lot there. I used to watch the neighborhood kids carefully, as if I were trying to decide what kind of kid, or maybe adult, I wanted to be. A kid named George Kingsley had been well schooled in politeness, came to the house, and I introduced him to my mother. "Mrs. Glick," he said, showing his polite smile, "it's a pleasure to know you. I certainly do enjoy being with your Eugene. We share a lot in common, you know. You surely have done a good job with him."

"Well, there's a boy with a great upbringing," Mother said after he left. "You would do well to learn to speak as he does when you meet people." I listened to her, as I usually did, and so, when I met Mrs. Smith or Mrs. Jones, I'd begin the "How very pleased I am to know you" routine, and I found I liked it. And so I discovered a lifelong trait of mine—I enjoy people and I like to show them I appreciate them with courteous conversation—to show respect.

About this time the muse awakened my interest in the romance of music. Or perhaps it was just the music appreciation program in the public schools in those days, which offered welcome relief from math and spelling. I can still hear the thickly German-accented voice of conductor Walter Damrosch, who eventually became the director of the NBC studio orchestra, piped into School 60: "Now children, we are going to identify the various instruments. First I will have the musician play the instrument and then I will tell you what it is, and you remember the sound. Then when you hear a symphony you will know what is making the music." So someone far away in the New York studio would squeak away on the strings and he'd say "viola"—or cello, bass, kettle drums, and so forth. The teacher would later ask us to identify the instruments heard. Then Walter Damrosch would say, "Now, teacher, hold up the picture of the viola," and sure enough, she'd do it and we'd learn. Television takes care of all that now.

I had ambition to improve myself. I decided I had to—really *must*—have piano lessons. My mother played a little piano, and she taught me to pick out a few things. I seemed to have some talent at it. A half-hour lesson at Arthur Jordan Conservatory of Music was two dollars, big money in the middle of the Depression, but my father found a way to pay for the lessons. Then baseball season hit. I'd come in on piano lesson day and say to my teacher, "I just don't think I'll take my lesson today. I've got other things to do, so here's the two dollars anyway." Then I'd rush off to play baseball. When my father found out, he was about as mad as he could get. I don't blame him—he had to work hard for that two dollars.

So the musical interlude in my life ended. I joke that Indianapolis was deprived of another Van Cliburn, but what I really regret is that I didn't stay with it enough so that I could play popular songs and semiclassical selections just to entertain myself—and keep my fingers limber.

Art was another talent I aspired to. In this case, my yearning was hopeless—I had absolutely no ability in drawing or painting. But I think it's important that I yearned so for it even at that age, loved art, thought it magical that someone could create images from nothing on a blank piece of paper or blackboard. The school system would have artists come around two or three times a year to draw Santa Clauses or turkeys or Easter scenes on the blackboard, and I begged to stay after school to watch them work. I had to get special written permission to stay—I couldn't imagine why everyone didn't want to stay and watch the magic.

Artistic talent in others intrigued me. A girl in the neighborhood could draw like an angel! I used to ask my mother if I could have her come over to visit, or I'd go to her house just to watch her draw. I'd sit entranced as something would appear from nothing on the blackboard or drawing pad—wonderful! She went on to a professional career.

Maybe, just maybe, I thought, this could be taught. I convinced my parents that I needed art lessons. John Herron Art Institute was located at 16th and Pennsylvania; I could reach it by streetcar.

Times were hard for everybody; I remember those art teachers sitting with my parents after a while, encouraging them to continue the lessons (and payments) because "we've seen what he does and he has talent." My mother wanted to believe it, and maybe I did too; when you get older you learn about tricks of the trade.

Anyway, my masterpiece in the Herron classes was an elephant. Everybody could choose an animal and model it, with the teachers giving just a little help to the work in progress, and then enamel and sandpaper the animal. I got a "superior" on my elephant, and I took it home, where it stayed until after I grew up. I guess it got lost in the shuffle after my father moved into an apartment.

I don't know why people kept trying to convince me I had talent, but they did. Mrs. Mize, the sweet soul who taught art at School 60, saw that I couldn't make a likeness of anything. Hopeless. I'd work hard at drawing a dog or tree and it looked like nothing recognizable. So I'd make geometric designs, easy to do. Mrs. Mize would come around and look at them and say, "Eugene, you have a talent in abstract art. You don't need to make likenesses." She gave me an A-plus in abstract art. By this time I was scornful of all this praise for nothing. I knew the truth and told my mother that Mrs. Mize was "just saying that." Why would she say you had talent if you didn't? Mother wanted to know. Finally money and energy ran out and I exited my artistic phase.

Of course, grade school was in full swing by then and I kept finding out about life there, as everyone does I guess. School 60 was a well-established and respected school when I started first grade in 1927. School work in those days was always basic and well organized, often demanding, and sometimes very interesting. The teachers encouraged everyone in the class to be the best he or she could be, and we didn't want to disappoint the teachers—or parents—so we responded to the encouragement.

Mrs. Savage, my grade school math teacher, encouraged me in that way. She made math come to life, and I loved the class. She asked me to stay after class and tried to communicate her love of the subject to me, and told me I had ability in math. I know she must have encouraged many kids this way, but I thought what she said was just for me. I didn't want to disappoint her, so I achieved even more. The last time I saw her I said, "You taught one subject well. I think the old saying is true: if you teach a child to do one thing well, he or she will do everything better." I really do believe that and tell people who work in our youth Pro-100 programs, particularly the coaches, that their job is to get kids to do one thing well.

In addition to school work and the required reading at School 60, I read *Peck's Bad Boy* and a lot of other things, forming strong reading habits which have lasted a lifetime. Now, besides reading, I listen to books on tape too, because I can do that while I dress, shave, eat, and drive to the office.

But school wasn't everything, and I looked forward to the weekends when I could have fun and—I hoped—some adventure. In those days we'd all go to Riverside Park to watch the giant hot-air balloons go up. Huge crowds would gather, and we'd crane our necks to see the men blow the heated air into the balloon, while the roustabouts held onto the ropes as the balloon tugged against the stays. Then the parachutists would yell, "Cut 'er loose!" What daring they had!

I watched Ethel Pritchett, a well-known parachutist, go up in a balloon. It rose steadily against the sky until you could see the chutes open: two white breakaway chutes and finally a chute which was red-white-and-blue! That day she went up, I told my dad to follow the descent in the car. I saw one of the white chutes descending, and I got out of the car and ran after it. When Ethel Pritchett arrived to claim the chute I asked, "Can I help you fold it up?"

"Why sure, sonny," she said, smiling, and then shook my hand. She was almost killed a couple of years later at Riverside when the first chute she tried to open tangled around her body. With the crowd screaming in horror, she fell towards earth until, at the last possible second, another chute opened and she crashed into a roof. She strained some ligaments but came out alive.

I suppose Riverside exists in the psyche of everybody who grew up in Indianapolis, with all its rides forever imprinted with indelible excitement, horror, or fun. I had my favorite kiddie race car ride, where I'd ride an orange sports coupe. They couldn't get me off those cars. As soon as the ride was over, the car pulling into the push-off dock, I'd look at my grandfather with begging eyes and he'd cave in. Off I'd go again, gritting my teeth, rubber pedal to the metal, ready to roar around the track.

It was athletics that captivated me, though, in my youth. I was a good sprinter and I did well in races when I was in grade school. Boys and girls would have their own classes on the field just north of School 60. One season in the seventh grade the boys competed in high-jumping. They kept raising the pole, and everybody fell out. "Why don't you try it, Eugene?" the teacher said. I nodded and jumped over it and the teacher said, "Suppose we try it a little higher?" So they raised it an inch or so and I made that, but on the next jump I knocked it down. "Well, I guess I'd like to try again," I said. I ran and heaved myself into the air; the stick wobbled but stayed up.

One of the girls' fathers who was visiting the school that day had seen it all. He asked about me, and said, "I was watching, and you can really jump, young man. I'd like to shake your hand." I shook his hand but that wasn't all. He turned and said in front of all the school, "Let's give this boy a round of applause." I couldn't wait to get home to tell my folks, who were naturally impressed. Odd how memory works: I can still remember that man, handsome enough to be in the movies (at least as I remember it), and he was kind enough to praise me. What a tremendous incentive.

All of us love to receive compliments, and I think when you have something good to say about someone, say it. There are very few people who don't love an honest compliment—but they know when it's baloney.

More importantly, though, put your compliment in writing.

There's an old saying: "If you want to criticize, do it verbally; if you want to compliment, do it in writing."

Being a traffic boy taught us all responsibility. We were trained by the local policeman to take our job seriously, and then stood at our corner posts, arms outstretched so the children would stay safely on the curb. Such experiences build self-esteem.

But I wasn't the joiner some kids were. I was a Boy Scout, but not for long. I didn't care much for it; it seemed to me—what do the kids today call it?—uncool. They met at Tabernacle Presbyterian Church at 34th and Central. It didn't seem quite sharp to me. My mother wanted me to stay in, so I did something—I told her, "They're prejudiced over at Tabernacle. I get tired of being called a Jew." I was using it as an excuse. They did name-call sometimes, but I wouldn't have let it bother me if I'd liked the Scout program.

I dreamed of baseball success. Maybe I'd grow up to own Perry Stadium, where the Indianapolis Indians played baseball, and have my own baseball team. It was a definite dream of mine. Or, the fast-talking radio announcer would say about me, "It's the last of the ninth and we've each won three games, and we're behind with two outs and three balls and two strikes—and Glick has just hit the ball over the fence!"

The reality was different. I had a pickup team that would play at various lots against other pickup teams. But we never won. John Hart had another team, and his team hit the ball over the fence. Why not us? I finally figured it out. All these other kids were better players. I had my brother Art and all my friends on the team, and that was fine, but it would have been better to have some enemies who could play ball. I gradually figured out that whatever you do, you can't win without the best people who have the talent and desire to do a job right.

One of the kids who came over to play was Bernie Landman, who lived just north of us on Salem Street. He was five or six years younger than most of us on the team, but that didn't stop Bernie. "Let me play," he'd beg, and my brother and the others would laugh, but I was impressed by his guts even then, and I'd tell them, "Let him play for a while."

This kid loved to gamble even when he was six years old. He'd want to toss pennies at the cracks in the sidewalks to see who came closest. I'd play along to humor him and for the fun of it, and we'd bet. Finally his debt to me got to be about two dollars, a princely sum in those days.

"This has gotten out of hand," I finally said to him. "You owe me too much."

"I'm going to pay, no matter what," Bernie would answer earnestly. And he meant it. Little Bernie Landman was true to his word.

"Well, I don't want your money and I'm not going to take it—on the condition that you learn a lesson from this. Don't go beyond what you're prepared to pay, and watch out for gambling." Our paths would cross later—in significant ways.

I liked shop, but I was pretty terrible at woodworking. I recall trying to square one board for the longest time, and during that same time the boy next to me, Eugene Norman Miller, completed a spiffy and well-joined lamp.

The shop teacher gave us advice sometimes. More than once he suggested that all of us boys develop a special field of interest in sports. It sounded like a good idea to me, but since I lacked the inclination to work or practice, I merely let the word get around that I was an accomplished boxer. Riding on that reputation, I challenged a kid about a year older who had the reputation of being tough. I decided he'd been bullying everybody too long anyway, and so I said, "I want you to come over to the house and we'll put on the gloves." I was going to beat the hell out of him.

Then I began to think about what I'd done. This was a big, tough kid. He could harm me. I couldn't back down; a group of the kids had heard me challenge him. So I got my mouth in gear again. I said I hoped I wasn't going to be hurting him too much. That he was going to be meeting a real pro who had taken lots of lessons. Secretly I had made up my mind to charge him, to rush out and take the offensive. I knew nothing at all about boxing other than what I'd seen on the movie screen. Had I made a fatal mistake?

The bully showed up, along with dozens of neighborhood boys

on their bicycles. Where was my mother? I wondered. She should be calling the ambulance in advance! The guys sort of stood around in a circle and we put on the gloves and somebody yelled, "Go to it!" I charged my muscular opponent like a wild man, yelling and shouting. I could see the fear in his face with all that racket, and I started swinging wildly. I hit him, I don't think hard, but he was so scared that when I connected, he fell over backwards onto the ground. "Fight him!" the supporters yelled to the challenger, but the bully mumbled, "Hell, no! You fight him. I'm not going after this bastard. He's had too many lessons!"

Word got around after that: "Don't mess with Glick. He's had lots of boxing lessons and he'll kill you." Nothing could have been further from the truth. I did learn that bullies will back down if it comes to that. Once you face them, they want out.

Interestingly, the same success I earned from feigned ferocity followed me in high school. Some guys said, "We hear you're pretty tough. There's a guy around here who would like to tangle with you." I'm sure this guy also could have killed me, but I didn't have anything to lose by trying the same strategy. I charged out again like a wild man and swung. He fell, too, more out of surprise and fear at what I seemed to be. It was a lesson in perception—they reacted to what they thought I was. I knew nothing at all about prizefighting but they had it in their minds that I had taken lessons and was good. Kid Glick!

Actually there *were* Jewish boxers at the time—Barney Ross and Maxie Rosenbloom. There was an odd aftershock of these incidents. After I got out of the Army and was staying with the folks at the house, the phone rang at about three in the morning. I groggily answered it and a voice said, "Is this Sid Glick, the famous prizefighter?" I said I'd never heard of a Sid Glick the prizefighter. "Well, he used to be pretty well-known around here, and I thought it was you." Other people mentioned a Glick with a famous boxing reputation. I denied any knowledge. I had ended my boxing career after that last title match in high school.

I bet on Joe Louis when his great championship fights came up. I even bet a quarter once. Almost no one in Shortridge at that time thought that a non-white person could achieve much. Still, I bet on Louis. Why? It had to do with my mother, I think.

I can see her now, reading to me as I suffered through the heat and danger of scarlet fever. Talking to me about school at the kitchen table after I walked home for lunch from School 60. Telling me firmly when I was a small schoolboy not to mind if someone called me a son of a bitch—that was just describing the pup of a mother dog. Nothing to fight about. Fighting wasn't a good idea.

My mother was a champion of the disadvantaged and she turned me into one too. She lived what she believed more than anyone else I ever knew.

We lived in a split family politically—my dad was a lifelong Republican and she was a fervent Democrat. She read about Franklin Delano Roosevelt in *The Indianapolis Times* and liked him; he read about him in *The Indianapolis Star* and *The Indianapolis News* and formed the idea that Roosevelt was a dictator, anti-business and too pro-labor. "He kowtows to labor," Dad would complain. Mother would answer, "The working man can't get a fair deal without some help from government." They saw things through different lenses.

She believed, pure and simple, that people are created equal. Everybody deserved respect and everybody deserved to be treated exactly alike—the Golden Rule. We all did have different capabilities. You will be good in some things, not so good in others, so don't be judgmental. You need to stand in another man's moccasins to know what he's experiencing.

The only blacks in our neighborhood were the children of the custodians of the apartment houses on Meridian Street. There were lots of apartments at that time, and so there was a good number of African American children. Mother would look out the window to see black children walking up the street to catch the streetcar to go to Crispus Attucks. They lived by Shortridge High School, and it really infuriated her that they had to take a streetcar and go someplace else when they could have walked to Shortridge the way I did.

One of the children was going over to the black grade school near Attucks. She watched this little boy in the afternoon get off the streetcar and walk toward the apartment where his father was the janitor. He always looked at all of us playing in the yard, then he passed by. So she went out one day and asked him if he wouldn't like to play with us.

Pretty soon she got a call from some woman whose son was also playing in the backyard. "Mrs. Glick, I don't know if you know it or not, but there's a nigger in your backyard playing with the boys." Well, that triggered it. Of course she knew the boy was back there, and how dare the woman refer to this child in a derogatory way! If she didn't like the play situation, she could come and get her child. The woman did come and drag her son away, but pretty soon he sneaked back. The black boy who was playing with us was a good athlete and so was the woman's son. It wasn't long before these two boys and all of us were playing together in that backyard all the time.

Mother would often get on the bus and go downtown to shop. How she loved to shop at L. S. Ayres, Wm. H. Block, H. P. Wasson, the Fair Store—she knew them all. Of course she and my father had limited funds, so she couldn't get much, but it was the atmosphere and the talking she loved. She liked people, really liked them, and she knew the names of all the clerks. During the Depression they wouldn't be too busy, and she'd stop and talk to each clerk about his or her family. "How is your daughter?" she'd ask. "Is your son feeling better? Did he get that job you were talking about?"

Sometimes, if she had a little money, she might take them to lunch. But that would have to be a treat. We didn't have the money to do much. Granted, we never went hungry during those tough times, but I can remember Dad sitting and looking at the bills. They would be marked "This is the third notice," and he'd just be staring at them. I remember on cold winter nights the folks would turn the furnace down to save fuel, and when we'd wake up it would be 40 degrees in the bedroom. Every time my dad got the oil bill, he'd say, "I don't know why your grandfather took out the coal furnace and put in oil. Coal's cheaper."

One day, when times were tough for everybody, I remember being in Taylor's Market and Bakery at 38th and Illinois with my mother. Mr. Taylor had been carrying our family for a long time on his books, and he said, with embarrassment, and wondering if I should hear all this, "Mrs. Glick, you know I'm having trouble paying my bills myself. The wholesalers want their money. Can you give me just something?" And she said she'd try.

My mother's father had his own house three doors from ours, but after his wife died he moved over with our family, and they rented out his house. Some executive from the railroad company leased it, and I can recall that he got behind in his rent in the dark days of the thirties. The poor man had to walk by our house to get to the streetcar, and he'd hurry along so that my mother and dad wouldn't see him, like a beaten dog. He'd get to running before they could call to him and when they did it was as if the dog had been hit or kicked. I felt so sorry for him.

My dad said, "I know you've rented here for twenty years, but I have my taxes." The man said sadly, "I know you do." Soon that family moved, and the house stood vacant for about two years. Finally, I myself found a renter for it—I knew a kid at school who had a big family, and I told him he ought to move into our house. "It's interesting you should mention that. We need a bigger place." So we cooked it up between the two of us.

My mother's heart went out to everybody. How could I ignore the unfortunate with a mother like this? For example, she liked to visit the old folks' home, and the people there touched her.

I remember coming home from school one day and Mother was crying. Two of the three Buchanan children I'd played with all my boyhood years had fallen through the ice into Fall Creek. The older one had gone out and fallen through, and the middle brother had gone to his rescue and gone under too. Only the littlest one was left—he'd gone to get help. My mother made me go with her to comfort these old friends, though I was frightened of confronting the pain. "You're going!" she said emphatically.

In the summertime cars would barrel up and down Salem and east and west across 36th street. There were no stop signs and invariably you'd hear a screeching of brakes, crashing sounds, and shattering glass as they collided. My mother would run out of the house and tend to the wounded, blood all over her hands, yelling at me to call an ambulance. She kept all kinds of bandages and she'd fix the victims up while they waited for the ambulance. Maybe she was remembering one horrible crash we had as a family. We were driving home from a visit to Chicago and Lafayette, when a car with a driver asleep at the wheel crashed into us on State Road 52. It was night, and all I could remember was that my brother and I were suddenly out of the car by the side of the road. My mother and grandmother were in the hospital for quite a while after that collision. Both the driver and passenger in the other car died as a result of that crash.

My mother didn't ask for much entertainment: shopping days downtown, a little fishing in Rochester, an occasional trip to the Smokies, with all of us telling Dad where to go next. We ended up in Atlanta one time. She'd ask to go for a ride in the country on hot summer days. My dad was bone tired when he came home; he'd been in the car all day. But we'd get in the car and let a little air blow through, perhaps stop at Riverside Park and get a drink from the artesian well.

My mother's life was touched by two tragedies. One was the sudden death of her father as he and my dad walked down the street in New York City. She'd been an only child and her dad had doted on her all her life. She was everything to him, and she reciprocated this deep affection. So when he died, I believe she never really got over it.

Perhaps worse, though, she endured something no parent should ever have to experience. My brother Arthur died in 1937 of spinal meningitis. I think Mother could have felt guilty—she'd had her own doctor look after Arthur, but he got worse gradually, with a high fever, until finally he couldn't even walk. I don't think my mother's doctor had ever seen a case of meningitis and he didn't recall the symptoms from his medical training. I was ill too, but fortunately they called the pediatrician who had taken care of us since we were infants. Almost right away he recognized the disease and hospitalized both of us.

My brother and I were taken to St. Vincent's Hospital at Fall Creek Parkway and Illinois Street. In those days the treatment was

Buddies from the beginning—
my younger brother Art and I.

limited—they did a spinal tap on my brother and me to relieve pressure on the brain. It may have helped me; it didn't help Arthur. As he grew worse, my mother could not handle it. My father did the bedside watch. Finally—horrible thing—I heard a strange cough on the other side of the curtain. Then he was wheeled away. He wasn't there on the other side of the curtain any more. "Where'd they take Art? Is he in another room?" I asked my dad, who looked sort of strange. "Why'd they take him out?" I insisted. All he could answer, in his helplessness, was, "Well, he was coughing." Later I got suspicious and demanded to know, and one of the sisters told me my brother had died. For me, they were able to send and get serum, and I eventually got well. So many diseases were fatal then; we can barely recall anymore how it used to be, thank God.

One of the most instructive things we can do to know and appreciate modern medicine is to walk through a country cemetery and see the little tombstones: "Sara, age 3 ½ Died September 10, 1854"—"John, age 5," died the following February—then Louise, died in July. Plagues went right through families. I'm so grateful that in fifty years of business I believe I haven't missed one full day because of sickness.

But it wasn't always so. The sadness of Art's death probably stayed with my parents until they died. Should they have made their decision earlier? Taken stronger action? Probably it wouldn't have made any difference. I'm of the opinion that "Fate is the hunter." It could have been me. If I had been one yard to the left or right in the war I wouldn't be here. My parents lived on with their sadness, talking about it never, at least not to me.

As for me, I had lost my buddy. I don't think anything else in my youth changed me so much, impressed me with the transience of life. I was a year-and-a-half older and we had played together, managed that knockout of a baseball team. We'd wrestle, too, and play basketball, serious basketball. I remember one day we were being our usual highly competitive selves and I was dribbling around looking for an opening and Art said, "I'd kill you for this next point." It was so honest—I knew he wasn't going to kill anybody—

but it was so revealing, so open, it struck me as funny and I burst out laughing at him. I loved him for it.

I sometimes think about the meningitis. I could have gotten it first and then he would have picked it up second and survived. Fate is truly a hunter. My mother and father gave everything they had to their one remaining child. I don't know how many hours my dad had to work to send me to college. They both sacrificed—their greatest desire was to see me graduate from college, as they'd never done. The more I read biographies of people who achieve something the more I'm convinced that behind the Churchills, the Roosevelts, the Eisenhowers, is invariably a mother or a father who set a marvelous example, challenged the child to be the best he or she could be.

And I had not one but two parents like this. And two grandparents behind them. Nobody could have asked for better support.

This one is typical—Art and I both loved to play baseball. He was a better hitter, while my forte was pitching.

My paternal grandfather, with Art (*right*) and me.

My brother (*right*) and I.

My dad's youngest brother, Leonard Glick, was the source of one of the great family mysteries.

Leonard went off to fight in World War I in 1917. He corresponded with his mother during the war, but after the Armistice in 1918 he was not heard from again. This caused my Grandmother Glick much grief and distress.

In 1960 my dad learned that Leonard had died in April of that year from the attorney in charge of Leonard's estate. He had headed the photography department at *The Washington Times-Herald* for years, and had later served as a White House photographer and had been a member of the White House News Photographers Association. He also ran Swann Photo Studio, one of Washington's most prestigious portrait photography studios, for many years.

Leonard Glick is buried at Arlington National Cemetery.

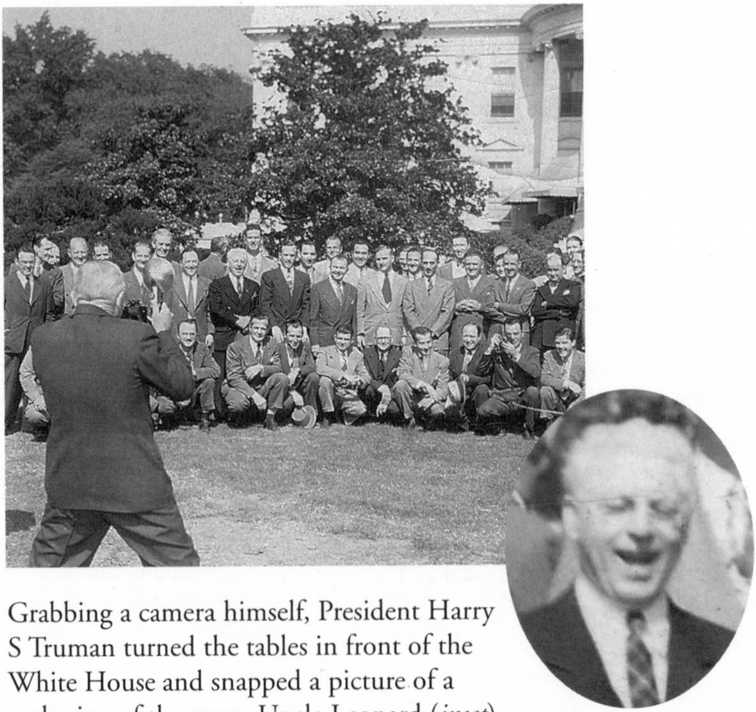

Grabbing a camera himself, President Harry S Truman turned the tables in front of the White House and snapped a picture of a gathering of the press. Uncle Leonard (*inset*) is near the center of the photo, in a dark suit.

Chapter 2
Shortridge and Indiana University

To be without some of the things you want is an indispensible part of happiness.

—Bertrand Russell

I GUESS I WAS BORN with the drive to be an entrepreneur. I suspect most people who become entrepreneurs have the skills to do so innately—they're born with them. I know I instinctively sought out business opportunities when I was a kid. I was considering this a few years back when Indiana University gave me an award for entrepreneurship. After I made an acceptance speech, Professor Mee, a business school teacher, opened the session to questions and I was asked, "Do you think a university can teach entrepreneurship?"

I answered, "I think you can teach the skills required, but I don't think you can create entrepreneurial people. Either you are one or you aren't. The desire to start and spearhead a business through to success is innate." Having your own business demands a certain desire and drive and commitment that isn't just picked up casually. It takes many attributes to succeed, but the most important one is the ability to think, and folks don't do that very easily. Also, the drive to be an entrepreneur must appear early on—in high school or college. When I interview job applicants for the company, I ask them what achievements they are most proud of in high school. If they can't think of any, I suggest they seek employment elsewhere.

Those early business experiences are formative. Sometimes you learn things you don't expect to learn. College kids representing magazine companies would drive up in a jalopy to the baseball fields where we played and convince us that we could sell magazines. All we'd need to do was go up and knock on the doors and sell these poor Depression-ridden souls inside *The Saturday Evening Post*, *Ladies Home Journal*, or *Liberty*.

They'd give us little white belts to throw over our shoulders and the magazines would be held in the slot. We'd go door to door ringing bells and getting doors slammed in our faces.

I could go out three days in a row, and when I was done I would maybe have sold one magazine to my parents and one to a friend. I'd look with frustration at the couple of cents in my pocket. When the boys got back together at the field, they all had the same experience. Sold only a couple, to relatives and friends.

We got wise. "They're using us like slaves," we'd say to each other. "When those sons of bitches come back out here, we're going to kill them." As if it were yesterday, I can see that jalopy pulling up. Those college boys, desperate to sell some of their consignment, got out, carrying those accursed magazines, and we took off after them with baseball bats.

But I did learn this—door-to-door sales is the hardest kind of sales. I acquired the greatest respect for the Fuller Brush men and for today's Mary Kay or Avon salespeople. I always say, "Show me a person who can sell encyclopedias door-to-door and I'll show you a person who can sell *anything*."

I also learned I didn't want to do that. That lesson started a little earlier, I guess, when I was a carrier for *The Indianapolis Times*. I had trouble collecting during these tough times, and sometimes my father had to stand behind me to get the money. "What little profit this kid has today is in your pocket," he'd say. But the worst times came when they were doing subscription drives—sweepstakes, they called them. I'd meet *The Times* people at the paper station and they'd drop me off at 36th and Ruckle. I'd go up and down the street trying to sell subscriptions to *The Times* and I was lucky to sell one in three hours. But I do think it taught me early on how to approach strangers for sales—and how not to take "no" for an answer.

The Times would award a turkey for the most subscriptions turned in during the sweepstakes period. It was easy to see there were a lot of dishonest ways to get the prize. There was a grace period, when the signed-up customers got the paper free. When that time was up, they had to sign up and pay. I never got any turkeys because I was too dense to know that these guys were signing people up who never intended to take the paper. I don't know if I'd have signed up all those fake customers, but I think maybe not. My mother always was so firm in teaching us, "Don't take advantage of anyone."

But I did figure out that I could have an easier and better organized route if I sold on the floors of apartments. I'd be running all over Capitol Avenue, Illinois and Pennsylvania streets, and Kenwood Avenue, and I began to see I had only so many hours after school to deliver papers. If I concentrated my sales where people lived close together, up a few flights of stairs and next to each other, I'd be ahead of the game. They seemed a little easier to sell. Maybe they had a little more cash in their pockets than the people in the homes.

Sometimes they'd ask, "Why should I take *The Times* instead of *The Star*? I already get *The Star*."

"I'll tell you what," I'd answer. "I'll just leave the paper for a week or two and you can see if you like it." I always had a couple of extras. Not everybody would sign up, but a few would, and that free "preview" helped make the difference.

I think what I really loved was the competition. The prizes weren't worth much but the manager was a young man who'd whack you on the back and say, "Good job!" They'd give you a little recognition pin. Recognition—I don't think you're ever too old not to like that. It loses some impact as you get older, sure: you learn that some people say "I love the job you did" just to sell you something. But there's still a lot of room for the sincere compliment.

Still, the manager would nudge me on, and that was good too. " 'So-and-so' is gaining on you, Glick. Better hustle." Eventually I had one of the largest *Times* routes in the city, and he'd point to me in the meetings and say, "Glick is selling papers, lots of them. Why can't you guys do it too?" If they'd had the apartments, maybe they could have had the high sales numbers also.

Still, I really learned how to sell successfully at Shortridge High School. I entered in 1936 already perfectly familiar with the school because I had passed it on the way to School 60 every day for eight years.

You could never really get to know Shortridge, though, until you lived daily in those halls. We were attending high school in a different day and age, and that school was unusual. Everything was designed to educate and inspire young people—famous sayings on a frieze running around the top of the stonework on the facade, classes in Greek and Civics with the best of teachers. A tablet had even been erected by the Class of 1916 to honor a custodian. (I later wrote the inscription down when it appeared in a Shortridge yearbook.)

On the left side of this memorial to the custodian, Mr. James Biddy, was the quote, "Seeth thou a man diligent in his business. He shall stand before kings." Then, on the right side, "He dignified labor, for he knew no master but duty, had no comrade but truth, desired no approval but self respect." We should all have such a thing said about us.

Shortridge was a place which attempted not only to educate but to build character, and there's nothing more important in education than that. I have always admired the quotation of Mrs. Chiang Kai-shek: "In the end we are all the sum total of our actions. Character cannot be counterfeited nor can it be put on and cast off as if it were a garment to meet the whim of the moment. Like the markings on the wood which are ingrained in the very heart of the tree, character requires time and nurture for growth and development. Thus also, day by day, we write our own destiny. For inexorably we become what we do. This I believe is a supreme logic and law of life."

Still, I think the most important lessons that I took away when I graduated from Shortridge were practical ones. Somehow I gravitated to the *Shortridge Daily Echo*, one of the few daily papers being put out by a high school in the nation. It was printed right at the school, with a real linotype operator and headlines set on site. I enjoyed the print shop a lot, and I made friends with Mr. Irby, who ran it. One day he said to me that he was sorry the *Echo* didn't sell more ads. They had plenty of space and potential, but only a few ads were sold. If they could sell more, there would be more money for printshop equipment and the school programs too.

I got interested right away. "How do you get ads?" I asked.

"People just call up from time to time and put them in."

"Well, that's not a very good system. Kind of random, isn't it? You could have students out selling the ads. Yes—and give them a commission on each sale."

He shook his head as if he didn't understand, but I went on. "We could develop team spirit in this thing. Handle it all in a businesslike way. Yes, we could call up the newspapers and find out what they give in the way of a commission for their advertising."

He gave me the go-ahead, and soon lots of Shortridgers were going up and down the streets to stores, working on commission. Ninety-five percent of what they got went to the school, five percent to the individual. We quadrupled the ads in the *Echo* the last year I was there.

I developed a lot of ideas about selling there, and I had a lot of fun doing it. I canvassed the school to find out where the students' relatives worked. These were prime prospects, along with the recent grads of the school, or parents whose kids had just graduated or were soon to come into the school. Most were very happy to have the opportunity. It was relatively inexpensive. And they'd come back next year willingly—the ads produced results. We put a little tag onto the ad which let students purchasing things at advertising stores get a gift for coming in.

Later on I realized that what I was really working on with these stores was called in advertising "the unique selling proposition." Though I hadn't read it at the time, I later found out what was going on by reading a book called *Reality in Advertising*—a really important book to me all my business life. Rosser Reeves' theory is that readers look at (or listen to) ads for just a few seconds. If during that time that reader or listener can't identify what "the unique selling proposition" is—what it is that's unique about this service or product that makes it worthy of his buying it—you've lost him. Through the years I've emphasized that with our people at the company—emphasize why it is the customer should do business with our company and not someone else's.

I was also insistent that the ads bring in business. I was learning that any transaction ought to provide a benefit that is roughly equal for all parties. You want to make friends of your customers.

When I'd go in to sell these ads in neighborhood stores, I was developing a selling style based on what appeals to people. I'd tell them why they should advertise: The *Echo* was an excellent publication, always winning prizes, with great printing and photography. In addition, the ads we designed brought results! Not only would school-age customers notice their goods and services, but they themselves could be proud, show their son or daughter that they were supporting their school. We called those "be proud" customers the "easy sells" and I'd always like to have a couple of them under my belt right at the beginning of my after-school or weekend sales days. I'd build up my confidence that way, pave the way to winning the sale. You had to think success out there on 34th Street. I've always said, "Show me someone who thinks he will lose, and I'll show you someone who *will* lose."

Where the sales were a little harder, I'd make suggestions about what would "sell" me as a high school kid on that store's merchandise or services. It's always been true, I think, especially in the beginning and middle of my business life—that my taste was the taste of the masses. What I liked, what I wanted, I think most people liked and wanted. So all I had to do was think what I liked best and tell the store owner who had some products high schoolers would like.

As I plotted and planned my sales days, I began to realize that there were some really hard sells. These were the people who had no connection with the school and whose products were very unlikely to be boosted by an ad in a high school paper. There weren't very many who fell into that category. But as I pondered it, I realized I wasn't getting anywhere with these people. I could go in, spend twenty minutes to get one nibble, then forty more to get one bite—it took too long for what I got. So I concentrated on the ones who would buy. The little profit I earned went into paying for extracurricular activities and going out with the girls a bit.

I wasn't the top scholar in the school, but I was good enough. I loved literature, reading. And I liked zoology, especially when we

Gehrlein, William
Tennis team '37, '38, '39. Stage hand Junior Vaudeville '39. Enjoyed chemistry. Indiana University.

Genier, Betty Rose
Gym Exhibition '36. Junior Vaudeville usher '38. S. P. Q. R. Club. True Blue Club. Honor Society. Writer. Butler University.

George, Frances
Enjoyed English and history. Freshman volleyball and basketball. Red Cross representative. Gym Exhibition '36. Nutcracker Suite. Big Sister. Secretary.

Gerrard, Stuart A.
Enjoyed science courses. Captain, R. O. T. C. Vice-president, Officers' Club. Favorite sport, swimming. Naval architecture. Michigan University.

Gerringer, Irene
Came from Hayden High School. Basketball. Girls' Sunshine Society. Junior Red Cross. Essay pin. Catholic Youth Organization.

Gill, Norma
Co-tryout editor, Friday's Echo. Press Club. N.S.P.A. convention. Correspondent to Spectator and School Board. Gym Exhibition '36. Journalism. Butler University.

Gilliom, Richard L.
Varsity golf '37, '38, '39. Co-editor of Friday's Echo. President, Stamp Club. Co-sports editor of Christmas Echo '38. Assistant club editor of Annual. Chess Club. Bowling League. Social Committee. Crew Club. Honor Society. Michigan Law School.

O.C.G.

Glick, Eugene
Enjoyed English, German, and history. Hobbies, baseball and boxing. Executive management. University of Southern California.

Glossbrenner, Emily Louise
Fiction Club. History Club. True Blue Club. Club committee of Annual staff. Honor Society serious project committee. 4H Club. Chemistry Club. Senior honor roll. Swarthmore College.

Godbey, Demcie
Annual art staff '38. Enjoyed art classes. Commercial art school.

Goddard, Melvin
Attended Manille High School. In basketball line Campu Jo

When the copy was written for the senior class portraits, my plan was to study executive management at the University of Southern California. My plan changed, though, and I ended up going to Indiana University instead.

went out and did field work in Bacon Swamp, north of 52nd Street near Keystone Avenue.

We'd get up early, grab our binoculars, and catch the streetcar for the swamp. Then we'd study the plants, trees, shrubs, and especially the birds. Our teacher, who could stimulate interest in the most non-bird-loving person, would prepare us with knowledge of the head, tail, legs—we were all primed to see birds nobody at Shortridge had identified. One day, after poring over the bird book, I pointed to a tree and said, "I think I see a rose-breasted grosbeak." Our teacher said, "I don't think so. Those are rare." I showed her where it was and she looked up and said, "By golly, that *is* a rose-breasted grosbeak!" So everybody had a new bird for the list.

I worked hard for superior teachers. One of them was Lester Groth, who taught German. Actually, I ended up taking three years of German, enough to help me understand the language well enough to become a front-line interpreter in the war. Oddly, I have a French teacher to thank for that. After two years of German, I decided I'd take a year of French. The first day of classes in the fall, the French teacher asked me to identify myself and said, "I see you've taken two years of German. If you take two years of German and one of French, you won't speak either language. Better continue your German." I thanked her and went into Mr. Groth's class again, and I got good enough in that last year to sing German songs, read German literature and speak it pretty well—though with an American accent.

Years later I noticed the name "Lester Groth" in a list of officers of the Service Corps of Retired Executives. I sent him a letter, telling him how much his teaching had meant to me, even though he was a tough teacher. We had lunch together. We discussed the decline in academic standards, and I told him again how much that good German teaching had meant to me when I'd been in the war in Germany. He seemed to be in reasonably good health and was as sharp as could be.

I was surprised six months to a year later when his wife called me to say he had died, that he'd been ill when we had lunch. She told me he'd come home buoyed by the luncheon and especially the appreciation letter. He said he wished that other students would write. Then ironically, when he died, many students called and wrote to say what a fine teacher he was. "I just wish they'd told him when he was living," his wife said sadly.

I've heard, and later said myself, "You can never do a kindness too soon, because you never know how soon it will be too late." If you have something nice to say about someone, sit down and write to him or her.

Another German connection occurred during my junior year in high school. As a result of danger to Jews in Germany, the American Jewish community was being asked to take in children fleeing Hitler's early persecution. Hans Steilberger, from the province of Westphalia, came to live with us.

Hans' story was interesting. The rabbi came to my folks and asked if they would be willing to take a boy from Germany. His parents couldn't get out as yet. Mr. Steilberger had thought he would be exempt from persecution; he'd been a much-decorated soldier in World War I. But the Nazis had no such memory or generosity when it came to the Jews. If someone would vouch for these children, and there was money to send them away, they could leave Germany. The ones with the highest IQs were selected to leave. Hans learned English quickly, eventually speaking it flawlessly. I couldn't speak German well enough at that time to practice with him while he was in our home, but I grew close to him. Hans eventually graduated from Butler University as president of his class.

During the time I was in high school I read Dale Carnegie's *How to Win Friends and Influence People*. I underlined parts of it, and when I thought about it I realized that Carnegie's philosophy, at least for me, was wrapped up in putting yourself in other people's shoes and understanding and favorably responding to their interests, ambitions, and motivations.

I didn't particularly excel in science, though it could be interesting at times. I chose as my lab partner for that class a very bright kid named Morris Green. When we were dissecting frogs I made it a point to sit down quickly next to him because I was afraid I'd scrape right through the frog's brain. I was scraping away, and he said, "Go easy, go easy—you're there," and he showed me with a probe where the frog's brain was. Young Morris Green went far beyond frog dissection. He eventually went on to earn a medical degree, and ultimately became the director of Riley Hospital, where he has received many honors for his fine pediatric work.

I learned to play poker during grade school, taught by a friend of my mother's. Almost every Friday night in high school, my friends and I had a large stakes game—for fifty cents (a noteworthy sum in the late thirties). I can still recall the tremendous elation of winning—and the bitter taste of losing. I never played after high school. Other things absorbed my competitive instincts, I guess.

In 1939 my father began to plan seriously for my college education. My father hadn't really gone much past grade school, so sending me to college was a real goal for him. Oddly, I got it in my mind that I had to go to California for college. My aunt lived out there, and she had always written to us of the mild climate, beautiful countryside, and oranges to be picked off trees. My dad would nod and say, "I'll pay for you to go to any school with just as much tuition money as I'd be paying at a state school in Indiana. No more."

In effect, that ruled out California, although I thought I might go there after a couple of years at the state school which seemed to be my destiny.

At Indiana University I was an eagle, ready and able to fly. After all, almost every day of my life so far had been spent in one square mile. I went to grade school and high school a few blocks from my own front yard, and I even ate lunch at home every day, not in the school cafeteria. My lunch would be sitting on the table, put out by Mother or the meagerly paid maid, or my grandmother, and I got grilled along with the food: "When did you go out?—What time did you get in?" I was ready for a change, and I got it.

What didn't change was my mediocre academic performance. There was one difference, though. For a challenge I'd decide to excel in a certain class and prove to myself I could beat them all, no matter what the discipline. I didn't like cost accounting, but I said to myself, "I'm going to get an A-plus in this just for the hell of it." But how to do it? I wasn't particularly interested in cost accounting.

I was aware that there were people in the class who lived and breathed accounting. It turned out they were for hire, as tutorial assistants. But how to get the money to pay their pretty expensive rates, and to buy some of the other things I wanted and needed but couldn't afford? I had an idea about that.

I went into the charter bus service.

I had noticed that when students wanted to go home for the holidays, they complained that the Greyhound bus ride was long and the buses were always full. Somebody told me that there had been students who operated a bus business, hiring charter buses which would take students up to northern Indiana. These entrepreneurial students, when graduation neared, would pass the business they'd developed over their school years on to other young would-be businessmen. It was a franchise. You had to negotiate for it.

I found the senior who had formerly operated the bus business, supposedly owning "an exclusive right" (which he may or may not have really had). He showed me his records, how much business he'd done and how much he wanted for it. I'm never going to make any money on this deal, I thought. I prepared my own cost estimates on what it would take for me to operate a bus business, went back and told him what I was willing to pay, and I got the so-called franchise.

I decided to better him on the operating expense budget, and I went to Greyhound and negotiated a better deal than he'd had for charter buses. I arranged with the Student Union building for my agents to sit there, where everybody passed by, and sell tickets for my buses. I'd considered the normal routine of going around to sororities and fraternities to offer my services and decided against it; that took too much time. Using my old Shortridge ad campaign knowledge, I created an informational ad—and did we ever have the business! In short order, we doubled what the previous franchise owner had done. Soon the Glick buses were running to Whiting, East Chicago, and the end of the line, the Windy City. As far as profit goes, I suspect I made about twenty-five dollars per busload, which was not bad money in those days, and I could take the girls out a little now and then.

I also made enough to hire that accounting tutor, and it paid off with one of the best performances and lessons of my life. I got a little help, I asked questions before the tutorial and before my class, but then I studied, worked myself blue. And after a major test, the teacher, Professor Mikesell, said to the class, "I am holding up a paper of the best test I've ever had—100 percent. I want Eugene Glick to stand up." I had worked, and worked some more, to get to that performance level, and it taught me that above all, hard work wins the prize. That and setting goals—I'd decided to go for the A performance as a clear-cut goal.

Living accommodations were pretty basic at IU. I lived with a bunch of other students in an apartment on Fess Street. It took four to seven of us to make expenses, and we slept on lumpy bunk beds and studied there or at the old library.

It was at this time that business classes and their implications for entrepreneurship were spurring me on, just as I was founding the bus service. I decided to use the bus business to try out a few things I was learning. First, be sure you're going to be able to give the customer a unique service and advertise it as such. Second, be sure you're delivering quality, possibly the best at a competitive price. Finally, be sure you make it easy to acquire your goods or service.

So we sat in the Student Union and people came in clutching their ads from the *Indiana Daily Student* and signed up to be whisked away in comfort (sort of) to their home cities. And I counted my little piles of cash and got involved in some activities.

Another job I had in college was during Christmas vacation in December of '41. I worked in a department store in the toy department. We sold beautiful bikes for twenty-five dollars, but few could afford them. I asked the supervisor, "Can't we sell them on credit? We could sell a lot more." So I showed the bikes, and when families were interested sent them right on up to the credit department. We began to sell a lot and it taught me a lesson: carefully managed credit can be a key to brisk business. It pleased me to see these kids have the pleasure of shiny new bicycles.

I played in pickup games in college, intramural sports instead of organized sports. I did run in a marathon when I was a freshman. It actually was a university requirement. Thoughtfully, they provided ambulances—they called them "meat wagons"—to follow us when we collapsed. I thought I was going to die, but I said to myself, "Why don't you finish and then reward yourself by never being in a marathon again?" So I did finish, and true to my word, I have avoided the historic twenty-six-mile run ever since.

My real track achievement, if you can call it that, occurred in a shorter race, something like 440 meters on the track at IU. Some fast runners were up ahead of me, one in particular from another state, but I surprised myself by gaining on him and the others ahead. I was twentieth, then I was fifteenth, then I was tenth. The out-of-stater ran at the head of the pack.

I thought, This is better than I thought it would be—I'm not going to give up! Some of my friends were yelling, "Go, Glick! You might win!" The out-of-state runner was still ahead, with his friends yelling, and mine were screaming and cheering for me to close on him. Then my legs began to give out, but I gave one last push, with the ultimate ounce of energy I had, and I won!

It was a good example of what an enthusiastic cheering section can do for performance—within limits. And also of good sportsmanship—in this case on the other guy's part. Just after we had passed the wire, the former front-runner turned and clasped me by the shoulders and shook my hand. "I didn't even know anybody was in back of me," he said, "and I didn't dream anyone could pass me at the last second. Congratulations!" And I thought, Hooray for the home court advantage!

Chapter 3
The War Comes

The capacity to care is the thing that gives life its deepest meaning and significance.

—Pablo Casals

ROTC—Reserve Officer Training Corps—loomed on my college horizon rather suddenly; I hadn't worried about the two years of ROTC required for graduation from Indiana University because I was planning to finish school at the University of Southern California. And even my junior year, I didn't worry about the Army training program; I would be far away on the West Coast my senior year. But it became clear by spring of my junior year that I wasn't going to go to California, so ROTC became menacingly near.

Army Captain Barr called me in. "You've got to complete this requirement. And it's not going to be good enough for you to take just one year of ROTC. The two-year requirement stands. You're going to need to double up."

The man who owned the apartment where we bunked taught in the ROTC program. He was a huge man, so large that when he got on the ground to show us how to fire a rifle, three or four of us would have to help him up. He and several others put us through our paces, and I had double doses of everything. It was probably a blessing in disguise, because I got plenty of training quickly, and eventually the apartment owner and others of his ilk were saying to me, "Glick, we've got reports to make up. You know this stuff by now as well as we do. You teach the class." So I taught the late afternoon classes.

Meanwhile, the war in Europe was advancing. I started at IU concurrent with the Nazi invasion of Poland—September 1, 1939, it was. I was there through '39 and '40, the fall of France in the summer of 1941, the German invasion of Russia, and finally Pearl Harbor. The war was hanging over everyone's head. I remember going to the library and reading about the experiences of the men in World War I. It seemed particularly gruesome to read about trench mouth and trench foot, men drinking their own urine because there was no water, mustard gas, and shell shock.

I registered for the draft while at IU, and that was sobering. The more it became apparent that the U.S. was going to be involved in the war, the more I went to the library and read the World War I books. If I wanted to graduate, my arrangement with the Army was that I would enlist, then finish. But they insisted I go to summer school, too, so I could get out in three and a half years. The summer of 1942 was horribly hot, and the upstairs apartment was like a roasting pan. I'd buy a fifty-pound block of ice, put it in a huge tub of water, and let my oscillating fan blow over the tub, providing some cooling and a lot of psychological encouragement.

I kept myself in pretty good shape, and the ROTC training had some physical components. We had to participate in some fitness and sports activities. One of them was wrestling, and we didn't take that very seriously. In fact, all the students agreed we'd just fool around, pretend to wrestle. It was sort of a joke.

The first real match I had was with a tall, skinny guy, about a head taller than I and very serious. They blew the whistle and told everybody to start wrestling. But instead of pretending, he grabbed me, picked me up and spun me around over his head. He tripped, and we both fell to the mat. My forehead landed right on his teeth. I still have the scar from that encounter. I knocked out two of his teeth. He went to the dentist and I went to the infirmary, and from then on, I took baseball for the physical activity.

I graduated in December 1942. We walked across the snow at the winter commencement, looking like penguins on the ice caps. It had been a sacrifice to take all that ROTC training along with my classes in such a short time, but I knew my parents had denied themselves a lot to put me through college. They wanted—needed—to see a diploma. And there they were, smiling and clapping, along with Aunt Alice, my California great-aunt, who had come to live with them by that time, Hans, and Aunt Louise and Uncle Morris.

I had no time to celebrate or even heave a sigh of relief. My friend Sid Jaffe and I had been busy arranging for tests to be Navy pilots, getting recommendations. We went to Purdue University to take both written and physical examinations. The written exam eliminated two-thirds of the applicants, but Sid and I passed. "I'm in," I thought jubilantly. There was only the physical, and I knew I was in great shape. There was, of course, the eye test, but that would be a cinch. I'd always had good vision, except possibly at night.

The eye tester said, "You flunked. Failed the eye test."

"That's ridiculous," I said. "I've always had twenty-twenty vision."

"You need better than twenty-twenty. You flunked." I demanded to see the person in charge, and he finally agreed I should take the eye test again, with him watching. "Sorry, fellow," the supervisor said. "You won't qualify to be a Navy pilot." Sid didn't make it either. His eyes weren't any better than mine.

I was to report to Fort Hayes in Columbus, Ohio, where college graduates from the central part of the country were being processed. As dawn lightened the sky, I said good-bye to my mother, trying to ignore the tears in her eyes, and my dad drove me to Union Station and left me there. Two other Indianapolis fellows, Arnold Marks and Robbie Robinson, were there and joined me on the train ride to Fort Hayes. From there the three of us were sent to Camp Robinson, Arkansas, for basic training.

At that time I also met two people who grew close to me during the war. Bob Firth was an Irish Catholic who had gone to Notre Dame, and Frank Hill had gone to Boston College. A really rigid and demanding colonel was putting us through our paces to see if we could qualify for Officer Candidate School. We were given three times as much as we could accomplish, just to see if we'd break. I recall getting into bed at three o'clock in the morning, all of us just exhausted. Some of the men would say, "How do they expect us to do all of this?" and I'd say, "Forget it. They're just testing us to see who will ask to quit. You know you're capable, so just go to bed. I'm not going to stay up all night over this. Three A.M. is enough for one day. If that isn't good enough, then they can wash me out."

I guess I've always been that way: don't take the problems to bed with you. Get your sleep no matter what. I can remember when we were first building houses, and we'd be up trying to figure out how to make payroll, and about 2 A.M. I'd turn in. My wife, Marilyn, would ask, "How can you sleep with all of these monumental problems?" and I'd say, "I'll be better at figuring them out when I'm fresh in the morning." Of course, that wasn't always possible.

At Fort Hayes I became acquainted with regular Army men for the first time. The regular Army had its share of malcontents and goldbrickers, but they were the exception. During training, they'd seat us raw recruits with a regular for meals. One sergeant who looked like an ape ordered us to "pass the butter." When one man took some off for himself as it went by, the sergeant roared, "Don't you ever do that again, you SOB! That's short-stopping!" Well, of course, it hadn't crossed the recruit's mind that it would have been courteous to have passed the butter on without taking any. Maybe he had never heard that before. Believe me, it crossed his mind after that.

Finally we pressed on to Camp Robinson. Because of all that ROTC, especially the instructing I'd done, I was chosen to instruct at the camps. I'd developed my own teaching style, not based on the typical Army method of either intimidating everybody by calling them stupid SOBs or scaring everybody to death by telling them, "You won't survive at the front for ten minutes unless you listen."

I tried to be a bit compassionate, to see who was really having trouble. It was easy to distinguish the guys in trouble from the malingerers. Those who needed help were pale, anguished-looking. The goldbrick, the fake, wasn't showing real pain.

I helped with rifle instruction, Browning automatic rifles and carbine machine guns, and basic combat—everything except close-order drill, and I tried to give the men incentives to learn fast. "Let's get this over with," I'd say, "and then we can get out of the hot sun and go back to the barracks sooner. You can read or do something else if we learn this correctly and quickly."

When basic training was over, the Army had done what it typically does: overprovide. Too many of us had completed OCS. There was an excess of second lieutenants, and they didn't have places yet for us at Fort Benning, Georgia. While we were waiting to be assigned, we'd be made instructors. So I was made a formal instructor, first at Camp Bowie, Texas, and then at Camp Blanding, Florida, near Jacksonville.

The combat course was considered stressful, and so the Army gave instructors three days off at the end of a session, instead of one and a half. Naturally I liked that amount of free time and opted to teach combat. The men had to be pushed to climb ladders, run up to the second story of a barn and jump into the hay, and crawl under barbed wire while live ammo was firing overhead. We had to teach the troops how to fall from a standing position when they heard enemy fire, to break their falls with the butt of the rifle, their elbows and their knees. My elbows and knees still hurt just thinking about how many times I showed the men how to fall.

On the obstacle course the recruits were expected to jump from the second story of a barn. Some of the instructors pushed reluctant soldiers off, but the Army manual told you not to do that. They could be injured. Some of the men would balk about going under the live fire. You'd have to say, "Come on now, stay with me. You think I want to go under fire? But we can do it."

We simulated detonation—the sound of a real shell landing. I had to stand in the foxholes holding wires that led to dynamite charges, wearing earplugs and earmuffs to block the sound. It was all so easy the first time, until you heard the shattering noise and felt that concussion. It was painful. After that first time my body resisted. The initial message was clear: if you join those wires, there will be intense pain. My hands shook awfully but I did it.

Map-reading, patrolling, pitching a tent, surviving in the forest or the jungle, digging a slit trench, moving around at night—those were our subjects. I had realized by now that I really did have poor eyesight at night, so I wasn't too good at stealthy movement in the dark, but I did the best I could.

I'm the world's slowest eater, and I was even then. I would get up early to give myself a little extra time in the mess hall for breakfast, and I'd be the last person to leave after dinner, but sometimes I couldn't finish lunch. The whistle would blow, and I'd still be eating.

Still, I tried to do things the right way—as I saw it, that is. After the training was over, men would come up to me and say, "It's obvious you aren't a regular Army man. There wasn't any of that barking and screaming and swearing that the old regulars do."

An interesting sidelight came out of this period. Years later, when we were building a housing project at 42nd and Post Road, a young minister named Carver McGriff called project engineer Jim Bisesi and asked him about a five-acre plot the Methodist Church wanted to buy out there. He was the pastor, and in the process of securing the land, Reverend McGriff mentioned to Jim that he had had an instructor in the war named Gene Glick, and he wondered if there was any connection. They discovered he'd been in basic when I was instructing in Florida.

McGriff and I had lunch together. "Do you recall Sergeant Schick, one of the instructors?" he asked me. I told him I did. Sergeant Schick was a man I admired, with an IQ of 154. Then he named another sergeant, whose first name was Ray, and who was insensitive and mean-spirited as well as stupid. I said I had remembered him very well; I'd often said to Ray, "You're doing things to those guys that you shouldn't be doing, and I want you to stop it. You're going to end up killing more GIs than Germans."

"Do you want me to tell you how we referred to the three of you—the three instructors?" McGriff asked. "We called you Glick, Schick, and Prick." Remember now—McGriff was a soldier back then, not a Methodist minister!

When I heard this I said, "Carver, maybe we are under the same star." He told me I was luckier than he, because after basic training he was sent to the front and was quickly captured at Omaha Beach. I guess the training of "Glick, Schick and Prick" wasn't all that good. "Is it too late to apologize?" I asked him, smiling that day at lunch.

McGriff later was named minister of St. Luke's United Methodist Church on 82nd Street and he built it into one of the largest

This picture was taken shortly after I finished basic training at Camp Robinson, outside Little Rock, Arkansas.

Methodist congregations in the nation. When he retired, the church wasn't large enough to accommodate all his well wishers, so the church had the final good-bye at Clowes Hall.

I WAS AN INSTRUCTOR from March of '43 until June of '44. They never did need more second lieutenants for combat units. But that didn't mean I was off the hook, not at all.

The Allies undertook the invasion of France—D-Day. They were needing every man they could get from the States to execute those momentous landings which would change the course of the war, and for the mile-by-mile fighting which would follow them.

I had been in the Army fourteen months and still hadn't had a furlough. We were scheduled to be shipped out in June, and when I asked again for a furlough, I was told it was impossible. I couldn't take that for an answer. I wrote to Eleanor Roosevelt. As if by magic the Army brass called me in and said, "Of course you may have a furlough. What's the furor? All you needed to do was ask." But I knew better than that. I went home to talk about my heroism in the Army—which had consisted so far of training exercises, squiring girls around, and eating king-sized steaks. Then it was back to grim reality.

In June of '44 we were sent overseas—Frank Hill, Bob Firth, and I—on a troop ship. We were ordered to bunk in the "Stygian caves," the area several decks down in the bow of the ship. "There are nine million guys down here," I told Frank. "This is ridiculous—let's go up and pitch our tent and sleep on deck." We found a remote corner where the winds blew through—did they ever!—but at least we were outside, away from the confinement and the smell of hundreds of dirty feet. MPs generally didn't find our corner, but the few times they did, this was the conversation:

MP: What the hell are you guys doing up here?

GLICK: Colonel McBride told us we could stay here.

MP: Who the hell is he?

GLICK: You ought to know him. I'm surprised you're on this ship and you don't know Colonel McBride.

We'd never see him again. These MPs were officious bastards who loved the job because they could spend the war riding back and forth on a ship, never seeing a day of combat. They looked like Bulldog Drummond, or maybe a dumb version of Dick Tracy. Hill was a little nervous that they might check, but I said, "What are they going to do with us? Send us to the front? Hell, we're already *going* to the front."

IT TOOK TEN OR ELEVEN DAYS to get to Italy, our destination, zigzagging as we did to avoid Nazi submarines. Naturally, we were operating under Navy routine: Lines for everything, breakfast, lunch, and dinner. The lines were so long that everybody would run out of things to say while we waited for chow. We'd just stand there, dully waiting. Hurry up and wait, hurry up and stand in line. I grew to dislike that intensely, so today I always make a restaurant reservation, even if it's a Bob Evans we're heading for, and I don't go to places where they say, "There's a half-hour wait."

There were shrill whistles and endless orders: "Now hear this: You can do this! You can't do that! Chapel is at this hour." Sick call. Meetings. Housecleaning issues. We had books, thank God, and we read them there in our little tent on the deck of the ship.

We docked at Naples, but our destination was the replacement depot nearby. We were being warehoused as spare parts for units cut down in the invasions of France. As we disembarked, Italian kids would run beside us, and pulling out their knives they'd slit the packs of soldiers carrying a lot of gear, scoop up the gear, and be gone. And as they scampered about, they called up to the tall GIs:

"Hey, Joe, you know where you go?"

"No—to Rome maybe?"

"No, you goin' to Caserta."

In Caserta, a short distance outside of Naples, the replacement depot was located on the estate of Count Ciano, Mussolini's son-in-law. It was a huge tent city in the midst of surrounding hills, beautiful by night as lights twinkled on the hills. Come morning it was a different scene, filthy, with the light of day revealing debris and trash in the bay, trash on the hillsides.

We built little tents with mosquito netting around our bunks to keep out the malarial insects. In the mornings, 4:30 or 5 A.M. the bugler's crisp notes sounded reveille and we got out of nice warm beds into freezing air.

We went through regular drill during the day, waiting for the Army to evaluate our qualifications. Frank Hill received a call one day from the priest. He was a good Catholic and the priest drafted him to serve as his assistant. He knew the liturgy backwards and forwards and also could play the piano and organ. Frank ended up spending the whole war as the priest's assistant.

He said to me, "Why don't you get a job as a rabbi's assistant?" I told him I wasn't very knowledgeable about religious practices and couldn't speak Hebrew. But soon an Orthodox rabbi sent for me anyway, whether at the instigation of Frank or not I never knew. I let myself be talked into helping this rabbi for a while. My job was limited to writing letters to families telling how convalescent soldiers were progressing or thanking people for gifts. I spent my time in this sort of activity, and in attending the morale-boosting shows that came. During these productions, we sat on our helmets in a huge amphitheater, our posteriors going to sleep, as we watched comedians tell jokes and pretty girls sing romantic songs for us.

Shortly after Rosh Hashanah, the Jewish New Year, an announcement came: Get your stuff ready—you're going to the front in Italy. I knew that was a static front, and immediately the books I'd read on World War I came to mind. Trenches, trench foot, trench mouth, boredom.

"Hell, if I go to the front, I've at least got to go where it's mobile. I've got to get to France," I told myself. I located the person who was working with the list, and I said, "Look, I don't want to get stuck in Italy. You must have something going to France in the next day or two. Shift me over there." He snapped that he didn't have the authority to do that. Only Colonel So-and-So had that authority, he said, and he was in his tent. It was midnight. "You can find out where his tent is by going to regimental headquarters, but I sure as hell wouldn't bother him if I were you."

I did it anyway. What did I have to lose? In three more hours they were going to send me to Trench Mouth City. I got regimental headquarters to find the colonel for me amidst a million tents. He was across the camp, sleeping in the ranks of the other big brass. Carrying my torch, I made my way through that camp and, miracle of miracles, found the right tent, where I stood, literally shaking, outside the door flap. I summoned courage.

"Sir?" I said, standing next to his tent.

"What?" demanded a sleep-heavy voice.

"Sir, I want to go to the front in France, and if you sign this paper they said that they can send me to the front in France, so, sir, it would be a very big favor to me, sir!"

The voice growled from the bed, "Give me the blasted paper!"

"I'll be damned!" said the man with the list when I returned the paper to him.

Two days later I was on the boat for Marseilles. Once on land, we loaded onto "40-and-8s"—the old French box cars that carried men to the front. (Each boxcar had originally carried forty men and eight horses, hence the nickname.) As we rode up the Rhône River Valley, the French villagers threw fruit to us and shouted encouraging words.

The Germans were still putting tremendous pressure on the Allied armies which had landed at Normandy on the west coast of France. The Seventh Army's job was to help take the pressure off by joining with the French First Army to fight the Nazis in the southern part of France. The United States First Army and the British were in the north with General George Patton, and the Third Army in the middle in central France.

We were dumped, finally, in Épinal, and I finally had a moment to realize that I was in France, in the middle of one of the most intense battle campaigns in history.

IN THE SUMMER OF 1995 I took my family to England and then to France, to visit scenes of my war experiences, scenes I'd never really told them about.

As I stood at the Épinal American Cemetery and Memorial, in an expanse of green grass studded with thousands of simple crosses and stars of David, I was overwhelmed by the number of men from our outfit, the 179th Regiment of the 45th Infantry Division, who had been killed during the winter of 1944. I called my grandchildren over, saying I wanted to take their pictures with the markers to remind them and their children, and those who would come after them, of the tragedy of men not learning to live together in peace.

I told them how fortunate I had been to have escaped with my life and to have enjoyed the love and companionship of a wonderful wife, children, and grandchildren—things that had been denied to those young boys who had been my comrades some fifty years ago. I remember how the poet Archibald MacLeish had described the thoughts of our astronauts when they first landed on the moon and saw our fragile Planet Earth:

> *To see the earth as it truly is, small and blue and beautiful in that eternal silence where it floats, is to see ourselves as riders on the earth together, brothers on that bright loveliness in the eternal cold—brothers who know now they are truly brothers.*

I suppose if children study World War II in school they learn about Normandy, D-Day. I wasn't there for that; we were replacements, part of an advancing force which was ordered to bludgeon its way through to the very heart of Hitler's Germany. I hope, as they grow older, my grandchildren will remember my place in the war and recognize the significance what they saw at that cemetery in France, and remember my words on that memorable day when the vista was so tranquil, yet symbolic of the folly and horror of war.

I had brought a guidebook that had been prepared for me by Lu Palma, our former marketing director who now performs special assignments for me. Lu had worked closely with a retired Army captain who does research into the Army archives to identify for former GIs where they may have fought during World War II, and my book had an almost day-by-day recap of where I was and what I did while I was in Europe.

As I said, we had been dumped at Épinal—that was the jumping-off place. The book said that the Second Battalion arrived at the assembly area at Hadol, receiving orders to move into position to cross the Moselle River at St. Laurent. One line in one of the reports read: "F Company, composed mostly of replacements who had never been in combat before, was to be kept in reserve and was to follow G Company." F Company—that was mine.

In effect this meant that the Seventh Army's mission was primarily to relieve pressure on the main thrust on the west coast, the landing at Normandy, and to divide the efforts of the enemy. The report of October 22, 1944, told the real story:

> *At 0545 F Company started crossing the Moselle River in assault boats under enemy fire. Some boats capsized but the men continued wading through the water holding their guns overhead. The company was successful in crossing the river and at 0640 had reached its objective—seizing and holding the high ground northwest of Arches. After this objective was taken the battalion was in constant contact with the enemy until relieved near Baccarat on November 6, 1944.*

The struggle really was for Alsace-Lorraine—the ground the Germans had lost to their humiliation in World War I and then pounced on in 1941 at the beginning of the invasion of France. I can recall the words of Nicole, our guide during the family's sentimental journey to the old fighting grounds: "This is a district which is located northeast of Épinal. There are several small villages where Mr. Glick was, like Azerailles, Fontenoi, Xerméménil, Vioménil, Grandvillers." They all sound foreign today, but she was right. There were many small villages—but they had to be taken yard by yard in some of the fiercest fighting in World War II.

We had been in Épinal about a week. It had recently been recaptured from the Germans, and we were to be housed in a huge warehouse. Officers took us down to a big parking lot, showed us some straw and told us to fill mattress ticking with straw. We put the straw mattresses on wooden slats and these rude bunks served as our beds. You could hear gunfire—the front was nearby. The realization struck me that I could be killed out there just a few miles beyond us. It wouldn't be long until somebody took us sixty raw recruits up the road in trucks, dropped us off and said, "Get out and march. Take the safeties off your rifles."

When it happened, we all stood there waiting with our rifles at the ready. Then a tall officer came up and shouted, "Any of you speak German?" I raised my hand, disobeying that universal army rule never to volunteer. He spoke to me in German for about two minutes, then turned away and said, "You'll do for front-line interrogation with the scouts." My German wasn't good enough for in-depth questioning, but I could do some preliminary questioning should the scouts capture any Germans.

The scouts were "Fearless Fosdicks"—like the detective in the Dick Tracy comic strip—keen of eye, confident, able to read the moss on the trees. They thought as the enemy would think. It was good they had keen eyesight because I didn't. After dark, I was afraid I'd run into a tree, or fall into a pit, so believe me I followed them closely.

The job of the scouts was to find evidence of the Germans. "I see footprints," they'd mutter and I'd say, "Where?" But they knew. And soon, sure enough, Germans would come through the underbrush with their hands up. Then I'd have to talk to them.

I noticed that most of these Germans were a lot younger or a lot older than the average GI. Typically, they seemed to be sixteen, maybe seventeen, or in their late thirties or forties. The Russian campaign had taken a real toll—the Germans were spread so thin on both fronts that they were just about to snap in two.

Clearly, these men weren't in their prime. They couldn't do what a strapping, nineteen- or twenty-year-old could. The older Germans were worn down. They weren't severely shell shocked, but their nerves were frayed. By this time in the war they were desperately afraid that they'd be killed or—worse yet—captured by the Russians. So capture by the Americans was a sort of golden parachute. They had heard that Americans treated prisoners fairly and that the food was good.

I'd ask in my high-school German what their plans were: "Are you retreating? What is your plan of attack? What is your strength?"

Many of them answered, but some gave only name, rank and serial number. I remember one German-born American officer who was interrogating a twenty-five- or thirty-year-old prisoner. This American talked so fast to the German that I couldn't understand him, but the German soldier just kept on repeating his name and rank. He was scared out of his mind, but he wouldn't talk. "Take off your clothes," the American officer ordered and took out his belt to whip him. "I'm going to ask you one more time." The prisoner did what he was told; he was standing there, stripped and shivering, and I finally said, "I don't want you to hit him. Don't do it." Finally the American officer gave up in disgust.

The prisoners seemed happy when I came up and talked to them instead of shooting them. They were almost gleeful. It was an honorable way to get out of the bombing and killing.

I wasn't out on patrol with the scouts all of the time. Mostly I was just a dog-face, trying to do my duty and avoid death. I guess I was cautious. I'd often see foolhardy things, as if people were in love with dying. Just before we got to the front, we were told to sleep near our artillery. One night we were all in a barn, trying to sleep, though we were scared to death. The guns fired all night, and when I finally dropped off, I heard a metallic sound. The guy next to me—a blond, blue-eyed nineteen-year-old as good-looking as a movie star—was cleaning his rifle. "I can't wait for tomorrow to kill me some Germans," he said. It was as if he were John Wayne in some war movie. I looked at him askance.

Just a couple of weeks later we were out, with shells landing all around, trying to remember the "primary instruction" which was: "Don't bunch up. Spread out." I saw a swale and dove into it; some of the other guys dove into slit trenches (emergency shelter ditches two feet deep, three feet wide, and six feet long) and foxholes the Germans had already dug.

Most of the guys were caught, though, because just at that minute a German half-track pulled up. An officer raised the lid and said in a thick German accent, "You fellows are surrounded. Give yourselves up." The GIs got their hands above their heads and began walking toward the half-track. All this time I was lying in the swale thinking, *Maybe they won't see me*. At this moment the John Wayne kid shot at the officer. The Germans started spraying machine gun fire around, killing the men who were trying to give up and some of the ones in the slit trenches. Thank God John Wayne didn't hit the officer; if he had, they would have systematically killed us all.

The graves registration team later asked if any of us knew the dead men killed near the half-track. I looked and saw the young soldier who couldn't wait to kill Germans. He had a bullet hole right between the eyes. And his bravado had been responsible for getting a number of American soldiers killed.

Oddly, none of us in that unit got to know each other well. Sixty of us, and I can't recall many of their names because I knew few of them even then. You'd meet them on the way to the front, then they'd be gone—from pneumonia, trench foot (it was inescapable even on the move), all of the afflictions known to man. The Army tells me that sixteen of the sixty were killed. I know that only four of the sixty were still around when the war ended.

WAR WAS COMPLETELY MOBILE for us, which made me glad. If I was going to be at the front, I wanted to be on the move instead of stalemated in some bank of trenches. Heroes? There were some. I remember a soldier named Sabasinaky, from Hamtramck, Michigan. He said he was going to walk or crawl towards the Germans, and told us to shoot mortar fire over his head. He'd string a telephone line and take it with him, and give us the range as he advanced. That was dangerous as hell. If you lost the range, a mortar would drop right on you. He walked, then crawled, whispering the range into the phone and asking, "Can you hear me?" Mortars sailed over his head—two hundred or three hundred yards—and we heard him say, "We got a direct hit that time!" Ahead, on the phone you could hear the Germans screaming. He crawled back to safety; we reported his heroism to headquarters and he was later awarded one of the Army's most distinguished medals, the Silver Star.

One October night we were on a night patrol when we saw a German contingent approaching with a white flag. The spokesman of the group said in German that one of their group was seriously injured, and if we would take their friend to treatment, they would all surrender. We didn't know if it was a trap of some sort, but in ten or fifteen minutes a group of soldiers came out carrying the wounded fellow. We marched them back to the first aid station where we left the wounded soldier and turned over the others to the military police.

I can still hear, and feel, the percussion of the incoming shells. In the movies, shells simply land with a "boom" and the dirt flies. It's nothing like that. At first you can't tell the difference between shells coming in and shells going out. The veterans would laugh at us because we'd dive for cover at everything. But soon we learned to discern the differences in sound: when a shell lands near you get to know that sound like nothing you'll ever know again. Anyone who says he wasn't scared out of his gourd when shells came in is either out of his gourd or lying. You're deaf as a post for two hours when a shell hits nearby. The concrete shakes, the earth shakes—the word hell doesn't cover it. You're just shattered. Worse, you know that you wouldn't even be around if the shell had hit just two feet closer.

There was one awful day—November 11, 1944, the old Armistice Day—the worst, and to this day I consider it a low point, or better, a guiding star. The shells were coming in thick and fast, and I saw a slit trench nearby, two feet deep. It had ice on it, about two or three inches thick, I figured. A shell came in and I dove in. But the ice was only a half-inch thick, and I plunged through it into three or four inches of water. I lay there, flat belly, face down in the freezing water. Shells rained down and I was terrified that the shrapnel hitting in the trees would fall and kill or maim me. It seemed to last that way for four hours, but I suppose it was only ten or fifteen minutes. When the shelling began to die down I looked at my watch. Ten minutes to eleven, November 11, 1944. I remember thinking: "Wouldn't it be wonderful if World War II could end as World War I did, November 11 at 11 A.M.?"

Of course it didn't happen. And I said to myself, "How much

worse can it be? If I survive, I'm not going to forget this day. Any time I think I've got it tough or things aren't going well, I'm going to say to myself, 'Glick, how does this compare with November 11, 1944?' " That day has become the guiding star to me, the point of comparison for my life.

Believe me, nothing does compare. Any problem or frustration I might have today is nothing when looked at in light of that day.

WE PRESSED ON, and the German resistance faltered. Finally, as spring came, we began our push into the German heartland. Nuremburg was severely damaged by British and American bombs. It took a week, I guess, to get from Nuremburg to Munich. The fighting was almost a cakewalk—the Germans were really disengaging after extremely brutal battles to save Alsace-Lorraine. By this time, citizens in each city were flying white flags to preserve their homes from destruction by bombing. I recall that one of the towns we marched into was in flames, burning like Hell itself.

We arrived in the town after dark, but the fires made the night seem as if it were day. So many German soldiers were surrendering that we didn't know what to do with them. We started them marching several abreast towards the rear, and sent instructions to the MPs (wherever they were back there) to intercept the prisoners and set up compounds. As we walked or rode along, we saw bloated dead cattle lying in the fields amidst the ruins of blown-up tanks. Weapons lay abandoned all along the roadside. I was shaken by the horrific unreality of it all. It was as if I were in a surrealistic painting or movie. I remember thinking, This is a dream—soon I'll wake up and find myself in my bunk. But I knew I wasn't in a dream when the MPs later asked us, "Where in the hell did you get all them Krauts?"

Soon we were ordered to return to a little town named Kaiserslautern, which we'd taken earlier. I was sent back three or four hours ahead of the rest to locate quarters, which I'd then allocate as the men came into the burg. The homeowners had a standard argument about why the Americans couldn't use their homes: "We don't have room—we are full with refugee relatives." I would calmly explain that they had two choices: They could accept the soldiers, do their laundry, and give them food, or they could be tossed out. You never saw such a transformation, such bustling about to heat up the laundry tubs and find whatever poor food they had. (We usually gave them food for their services, anyway.)

I was stationed in Kaiserslautern in a home with two brothers and a couple of sisters, one of whom was very attractive. I couldn't find any shaving gear, and I didn't know the German word for shaving. I mimicked the action, pulling an imaginary razor over my cheek. I can still see her pretty face today, trying to understand, then saying proudly, "*Ach! Rasieren!*" As it was, her brothers didn't have a razor, but it was an entertaining exchange anyway. I was with the family for only a day or two, but while there, I asked them to speak German with me so I could improve my language skills.

I remember the struggle to stay clean. On Christmas Day, 1944, I took my helmet to a creek, filled it with icy water and shaved and took a sponge bath. I felt like a human being again.

We had met very stubborn resistance through the fall of '44 and the winter of '45. But by mid-April of '45, German resistance almost ceased. We marched on, cheering our P-47s, P-38s, and P-40s in the air above and knowing that the beating we had endured was finally going to end. We knew the Russians were advancing the other way to meet us and were aiding in our offensive, and we knew their generals' names—Zhukov, Konev, Rokossovsky, and the rest.

What amazed me was the ironclad control the Nazis seemed to have over their soldiers. Most wanted desperately to surrender, and they wanted to surrender to us, the Americans—not the English, and particularly not the Russians. But the Nazis were adamant: Fight on for the Fatherland. We'd see soldiers who had tried to surrender or desert hanging from trees.

And then finally, the end of April in 1945, we liberated Dachau, the huge concentration camp outside of Munich. When we got there, the German guards had all fled, and the Russian soldiers hadn't yet arrived.

I had known in general how cruel the Nazis were to certain segments of the human race, to Jews in particular, and I certainly didn't want to be captured by them. But almost no one in that advancing force knew what we, the first group to liberate Dachau, would find there. Russian prisoners were in the camp, and they tried to tell us about the mass murders there.

I saw the ovens, the crematoria. I saw the gas chambers, where Nazi guards herded masses of people into make-believe showers and then gassed them. Russian prisoners took me to a huge pit, and in sign language and charades showed me how their captors shot prisoners at the pit's edge and pushed them in. Worst of all were the railroad coal cars, still on the tracks. They were filled, not with coal, but with human bodies, overlapping, limbs sticking out, heads hanging out over the top.

The next day, when the jeeps came up with the soldiers' backpacks, I grabbed mine, removed my camera, and returned to photograph what I had seen the day before. I resolved to have the unspeakable scene recorded—for myself and for the outside world. When I took the film, lots of it, to a Munich shop to be developed, a pretty German girl was behind the counter. She was very upset with the pictures. "Why did you take such terrible pictures?" she asked. They would show the German people in a bad light, and she wanted to destroy them rather than returning them to me. I was just short of threatening her when she finally gave them to me.

I sent the photos home to my parents. Twenty-two years later, in 1977, the United States Memorial Holocaust Commission, the United States Information Agency, and Emory University all wrote to me, saying that they had found my name in the Army archives as a liberator of the concentration camp, and wondered if I had pictures of Dachau. I sent the photos to Emory, and to the Holocaust Commission, but received no response from either.

Years later, Marilyn and I were on a trip to Palm Springs, where we planned to meet our youngest daughter. I was alone, watching a World War II documentary on late-night TV, when a story came on about the liberation of the concentration camps. There were pictures of Dachau. "My God," I said, "those are my pictures!" My name was listed in the credits, but seeing them on the screen was still a surprise.

Some of my Army buddies and I when we were stationed in Munich, Germany, after the war. There I am, kneeling, on the right.

Frank Hill (*left*) and I went through basic training together, got sent overseas together, and were stationed in a replacement depot together. He remained in replacement depots throughout the war, while I went to the front. We still get together almost every year.

Bob Wolfe (*right*), a Chicago native whom I knew before the war, and I in Innsbruck, Austria, in May 1945. I thought at the time the scenery around Innsbruck was some of the most beautiful I had ever seen. When I went back with my family fifty years later, it was just as beautiful as I remembered.

Dachau inmates cheer the 7th U.S. Army liberators, 1945. The Nazis had slated many of these prisoners to be exterminated that same week we marched into the camp and freed them.

In later years I sometimes wondered if the horrors at Dachau had all been a dream, if such horrible scenes could actually have occurred, if such misery could have been perpetrated by man against man. But I had my pictures to show that I had been there, that I had seen it.

That was, truly, the end of the war for me, in more ways than one.

But it wasn't the end of the war for everybody. A fine noncommissioned officer, Sergeant Al Stricklicks, was killed, so senselessly. He had survived the terrible offensive we'd been through, and now we were driving along on wet pavement. The driver of our transport truck—after a long visit to the local bar, I'm sure—was driving like a madman. We pounded on the roof to try to get him to slow down. He made a sharp left turn at an intersection and threw the guys on one side of the truck over the side and into the street. On our side of the truck we were thrown to the opposite side, where I clung to a railing, just in time to see Al Stricklicks crushed between our truck and another truck that was driving in the opposite lane.

One of the men in the truck had a badly bruised and cut face, and I can still see the young women near the apothecary shop where we landed rush out to help. But Al, a true gentleman with a family awaiting him back home, was beyond help. I hope when the notifier went to the home of this fine man, he didn't mention the cause of death. "Friendly fire" seems almost too great a burden to bear for the families of Americans who gave their all for their country.

ANOTHER STORY EMERGED at from this time, brought to my attention only recently by a fellow veteran of the Forty-fifth. Don McDonald wrote to me to advise that his book, *Uncle Sam Was My Travel Agent*, contains the following anecdote about me:

At this time, it was the Army's policy to place all captured towns under the command of the ranking officer, which in our case was a colonel. To him and the other officers, presumably, this was just another unwanted assignment to add to an already-heavy load.

The standard procedure was to gather a group of townspeople and assign governing duties to them. I learned that the displaced persons were furiously opposed to this practice, and claimed that it was in fact Nazis who were getting these governing positions and were laughing themselves sick at the "stupid Americans."

One evening, after mess, I got Don and Dave Crotty together and told them if they wanted a little excitement to grab their rifles and come with me. We headed for the apartment of the acting chief of police (a Nazi) where, according to my informants, the chief was hiding a German soldier.

Don tells the story this way:

> *Gene knocked on the chief's door and, when he appeared, spoke sharply to him in German. The chief shook his head, saying, "Nein, nein!" But his extreme nervousness told us differently.*
>
> *Gene was not to be put off and, assuming the voice and mannerisms of the Gestapo (as seen in many Hollywood films), pointed his pistol at the trembling man's throat and demanded that he produce the hidden soldier.*
>
> *Meanwhile, I was asking myself, "What the hell have I gotten myself into?" But then the German went back into the apartment and returned shortly with not one, but two German soldiers who, hearing the commotion, had hastily donned their uniforms. We took them prisoner.*

IN MAY OF 1945 TREMENDOUS RELIEF flooded over me like a tidal wave. I was still alive and there was more ahead of me in life. I felt exactly as I had at Indiana University when we'd taken our last final and I had reason to believe I'd done fairly well—all the blood, sweat, tears, and toil were over, and the next semester had begun.

In this case, we knew what the "next semester" would bring. As trained combat infantrymen, we knew we were scheduled to head for the Pacific. We spent the month in Munich rehearsing to invade Japan. It was a rehash of basic training—climbing walls, running around—valuable for getting us in shape. We also were given plenty of physical work like deck-swabbing and cleaning. All of this was designed to keep us busy and out of trouble. Get 'em up early, work 'em hard all day so all they'll want to do is go to bed at night. It worked only so far.

We were all young, and the guys in the barracks just couldn't obey the rule not to fraternize. That was like telling them not to be human. Since I was the only one who spoke German, they'd come to me and ask me to talk to girls for them. "Will you go out to lunch with me? How about dinner?" I'd teach them a few words to say, none of which probably did any good except maybe "*Ich liebe du*—I love you."

That's one they seemed to want to use a lot, because everybody was falling in love the minute he saw a girl. I felt the same way; we'd been deprived of female companionship for so long. I remember one night I was walking down the street and I saw a girl on a balcony just above street level, looking like the Lorelei. Our eyes met and in German I said, "Good evening." That seemed to amaze her, and we spoke for a while and I asked her to go to a beer hall. We began to see each other; she was a slender, attractive ballerina. I couldn't develop an intellectual relationship, unfortunately, because my German wasn't good enough. Sometimes we'd go to the Dante Schwimplatz, a place in Munich like Broad Ripple Park. Here the Isar River, which flowed through the Alps, meandered by a lovely green area where they had placed a swimming pool. The ballerina and I would swim there, then go for a stroll.

I was determined to find this place of my youth again when I took the family on the trip to Europe. I thought it would have been long since torn down, replaced by a modern office park, but no—the guide took us there and it still existed. They'd expanded it into a regional park, spreading out at the foot of gently sloping hills. There were jogging trails, sledding hills, sunbathing areas, and four beautiful pools. And suddenly I was in the past again, strolling with my lithe, young German date. Reality intruded though—my teenaged grandsons and I saw a bare-breasted blond walking towards us. Sunbathing standards have changed. I said to my grandsons, "Why don't you go up and say hello to her? Tell her your grandfather, a

World War II vet, thinks she may be the granddaughter of the ballerina he dated years ago." I couldn't convince them to do that: their eyeballs were stuck in the ready position.

Immediately after the war, we'd go to the boisterous beer halls and look at people, sometimes searching their eyes to read the sentiment there. It was difficult to tell if the looks they gave were of hatred or relief. Probably something in between. I guess they were glad the Americans were occupying Munich instead of the Russians. When I'd go in with a buddy, there was really no conversation with the Germans. We'd speak English and drink our beer, and nobody would speak to us. But if they found out I spoke German, it was amazing how many people would want to say one thing to us: "We didn't want the war. It was forced on us. We were victims." Maybe some of that is true. Probably a good many of them just wanted to get on with their lives and see Germany prosper again, and so hadn't looked too deeply at Hitler's evil potential and deeds.

Though we were working hard preparing to invade Japan, we could have some time off. A buddy and I took a trip to Innsbruck. The trees were budding, the month was May, and the foothills of the Alps were just beginning to awaken to spring. Even after fifty years, the beauty of that mountainside scenery is fresh in my mind. The streams were crystal clear as we passed them in the jeep, the snow-capped mountains majestic. Sometimes trips taken in the distant past take on a romantic hue, painted in more vibrant beauty than reality justifies. Not so the trip from Munich to Innsbruck. Fifty years later when I retraced it with my family, it was every bit as lovely as I remembered it.

Soon we were at LeHavre, waiting to board the ship to take us home for a leave before we went to the Pacific. I lay on the ground on a grassy knoll one balmy June day, and I watched the American flag wafting in the perfect blue sky above me and thanked God I was going home alive. I was in one piece while so many others were not. There was also the feeling that all of us had done a damn good job of fighting and surviving. We were proud that we had played a part in ridding the world of one of the cruelest and most mindless regimes in history. I felt that all was right with the world.

CHAPTER 4

CIVILIAN LIFE

The three grand essentials to happiness in this life are something to do, something to love, and something to hope for.

—Joseph Addison

IT TOOK ONLY ABOUT A WEEK to journey home. Of course, on the way over, we'd been in convoy, zigzagging to avoid the enemy. The Navy whistles blew again: "Now hear this—lunch mess is at so-and-so." I again read books and thought about what home was going to be like. We passed the Statue of Liberty and landed in New York. We were scheduled to embark by train and head for Texas to "re-hearse" for our next assignment in the South Pacific, but first we were given about a week's furlough to enable us to visit our homes, which we hadn't seen in over a year. August came while I was on furlough, though, and then the United States dropped The Bomb.

We now know as a result of the opening of the Stalin files that Stalin was well aware of the development of the atom bomb, through his tightly controlled spy network. Truman and Churchill had decided they should tell Stalin about the bomb in advance, and they were both surprised to see him show no interest. What they didn't realize was that he already knew.

I am infuriated at these revisionists who say the Japanese were ready to surrender anyway and it was inhumane to drop that bomb. It was obvious that the Japanese were not at all ready to surrender; they had fought tooth and toenail to defend the outer islands. What would it have been like if we had invaded their homeland? There would have been more loss of life—American and Japanese—than we can imagine. Truman did what he had to do, and I'll never be convinced that what he did wasn't 100-percent correct. And what a relief to those of us ready to go to Japan. I knew what real fighting was about, and knowing the Japanese were even more fanatical about fighting than the fanatical Germans I'd encountered, I dreaded going to another theater of war. So it was paradise, pure paradise, to learn the war was over.

There in the Dallas camp, waiting to be discharged, we had a lot of time on our hands. They put us through some drill during the day, but nobody was really serious about it. And at night we were on our own. I had met a pretty WAC and I'd take her out dancing or to get a drink. I wasn't really serious about her, but evidently she thought I was, because sometimes she'd tell me to "go home and take a cold shower."

That seemed an odd thing to say because I wasn't really heated up. Why'd she say that? Another fellow told me that she had brothers, and they'd warned her about soldiers, saying, "If they even start to look amorous, tell them to go home and take a cold shower." She was tall, good-looking, but not very interesting. I think it was all over for me when one night I wanted to go dancing and she said, "No, my feet hurt." And that turned me off. (My wonderful wife of fifty years has often mentioned that on many occasions when I suggested we go dancing, she wouldn't say a word about her aching feet!) The WAC introduced me about that time to a small, not quite so pretty girl she knew who was a dance instructor at Arthur Murray's dance studio. Her name wasn't Ginger, but she seemed pretty gingery—vivacious and fun, not at all like the cold-shower WAC.

She suggested that instead of picking her up at home, I come down into the heart of Dallas and wait for her at Arthur Murray's. Here were all these beautiful girls teaching men how to dance. Ginger was always busy, the last one to finish. She was popular, able to tell all of her partners that they were swell dancers, really learning fast. Then, while I was waiting, the other girls who weren't busy would give me a few free lessons, teaching me the latest tangos and rumbas I'd missed out on while I was in the Army.

When I'd pick her up I'd say, "You know, you give more lessons than all these other girls combined. The guys ask for you." She replied, "I think it's because I love to teach, and I've had good practice at it." But I also thought it was because she praised her pupils so much, and that gave them good incentive. Instead of criticizing, she taught with praise. It was a good lesson for me.

So finally the time came. All the months I'd served were tabulated and I was discharged. I was ready to get on a plane, take the bus—unfortunately I couldn't do either. I had spent all my money. Now, I must have received more than three hundred dollars in discharge money, but I'd spent it all on girls and good times. After all those months of privation and Spam, I'd been starved for steaks and the smiles and dance steps of the pretty girls. I had enjoyed the modest pleasures of many wonderful Dallas-area steakhouses, and now I had to pay for that by hitchhiking.

It was easy and safe to hitchhike in those days. Just put out your thumb and someone would take you down the road, fifty or a hundred miles. Finally we came to Indiana, and I caught a ride with a man who had another man and a couple of women in the car. We had a flat tire, and I remember all of us getting out to try to help. It began to pour rain and when we finally arrived in downtown Indianapolis, I was weary, drenched, and eager to be out on Salem Street. I began walking past the familiar sights I hadn't seen in three years, up Meridian Street, and I came to my front porch at 3 A.M. I woke my mother and dad to let me in, the returned warrior, looking and feeling like a wet chicken.

There was a problem, though, and I knew I was going to have to face it one way or another in the morning. I hadn't told them I'd been in the battle for Germany, fought among hedgerows and all that. I hadn't told them I'd been at the front at all. I've already said that my mother was very sensitive, that she had been crushed by her father's death and the loss of my brother, Art. I knew it would have been too much for her if she'd had to worry about losing me to a German bullet every day I was gone. So I didn't write that I was at the front. I found a way to break it to them gently. And after all, I was home now in the U.S., a survivor.

I decided to concentrate on what I would be doing for a living.

I'd had almost all of the money I'd made in the Army—three thousand dollars—sent home. I was discharged in November of '45, but it was time to go to work. When I visited Innsbruck, just before we left France, I'd gone to see the son of one of my mother's friends. He had made a success in business in Chicago, a sort of fast-food place specializing in top-quality food. He'd been at the house a number of times before the war, and then he'd become a mess sergeant in the Army. When we were at Innsbruck, I'd said to him, "Maybe we could work something out when we get out of the Army." I was thinking of a joint enterprise: He'd do the cooking, and I'd do the marketing and management.

I think it would have been something like the Toddle House, long before the concept of Burger Chef or McDonald's. When we returned from the war, I kept after him, wanting to pin it down. I needed to get started. After I'd been on the case for a while, my dad finally told me that the man had called to say I was pressuring him too much.

That's the last time he'll hear from me, I thought, and it was. He never did anything with the idea, but I sometimes wonder what would have happened if we had become partners. I know if I'd had the opportunity to operate one of those early McDonald's, I'd have wanted the food served up excellently and fast. I'd have seen that those burgers and fries were the best.

So it became obvious that my future wasn't going to be in hamburgers. I sat around home, scanning the paper for work opportunities, and one day I saw that Peoples Bank downtown was looking for a mortgage loan officer. I rushed right down for an interview. The bank officers asked if I knew anything about mortgages. "Well, I can spell mortgage," I said lamely.

The bank officer told me they needed someone with experience. "However," he went on, "we do have an opening for a teller."

I said to him, "Sir, my father has worked hard all his life to send me to college. No offense, but I don't think he'd be happy to know that he and my mother had deprived themselves for so long so I could be a bank teller. I hope you understand; I'm going to pass on that opportunity."

Still, I didn't give up. Two weeks later I went back and asked the bank officer if he was still considering me. He told me, "We have not filled the position, young man, but we are still searching for someone who has had experience." I told him I still wished to be considered—definitely.

I went back another time, and got the same answer. Three, four times—perseverance pays. I really believe that strongly.

Finally, the bank officer said to me, "Young man, you just keep coming back. I don't see how you're going to be our man without knowing a thing about mortgages. Still, I admire your spirit."

"I may have an idea, sir," I answered. "You go on looking for someone to run your mortgage loan department. I can understand how you want someone who knows the details of the field. But while you're doing that, let me do something that can make the bank money. I can open a GI loan department. There are thousands of young men like myself out there. They're just out of the Army and they're looking for a home. Some are married, some not, but all of them would like to start housekeeping. Now, sir, the government has set up the GI loan program to show the country's appreciation for what the GIs did. I am proposing that this bank show the GIs that same kind of appreciation."

"Peoples Bank shows its appreciation by a GI loan department?" he wanted to know.

"Yes, sir, and there's more," I went on. "Not only will I start this department, but you don't have to pay me. At the end of six months, if I haven't made enough money for the bank to more than pay my salary, you don't have to pay me anything. Not a cent."

He called me back a short while later and said that my idea about the GI loan program had merit. Still, they couldn't hire me without paying me something—but it wouldn't be much. He'd found out that along with the GI Bill for educating there was also the GI training program. He told me to check with the Veterans Administration; perhaps it would fund my training in the bank mortgage loan department. Thus my salary would approximate a living wage.

So I did it. The VA agreed to pay me, and with the addition of some bank money I made about a hundred and fifty dollars a week.

I was there about three years, beginning in November of '45, at the office on Market Street between Pennsylvania and Delaware. During those years I learned everything there was to learn about banking in general and the mortgage loan business in particular. I was especially interested in how the banks make decisions on loans to customers. I made Peoples Bank's GI loan program the most successful one in the city. Peoples was relatively small at that time and could have only so many mortgage loans in its portfolio, so I sold the loans beyond what the bank could legally hold to other Indiana banks and to the Reconstruction Finance Corporation. I sold 4 percent loans at a 2 percent premium, which means the loan was four percent to start with, and these other banks were paying us two percent to get the loan. Obviously that's not possible today. We serviced the loan and got that advantage, so, like most successful arrangements, everybody benefited.

I REMEMBER ONE YOUNG MAN came in with a picture of the house he'd selected and wished to get a loan on, and he had his pregnant wife with him. They were so happy; it was their dream house and they would be in it, arranging their baby's room before her time came. I began to review their financial picture, and this is the conversation that followed:

GLICK: I'm sorry, but you aren't making enough money to qualify for the loan. Your salary just isn't large enough.

YOUNG FATHER-TO-BE: Oh, no. That can't be. I promised my wife—with the baby coming and all. We have to have this house. Mr. Glick, isn't there anything you can do?

GLICK: Well, you can get a co-signer. Perhaps your father would co-sign the loan for you.

YOUNG FATHER-TO-BE: My father doesn't have any money. He couldn't possibly do it.

GLICK: Is there another relative you could approach?

YOUNG FATHER-TO-BE: Well, my uncle is sort of wealthy, but I've never thought of asking him for anything.

GLICK: I'm sorry, but that is the only way you are going to be able to qualify for this loan.

He did ask his uncle and—miracle of miracles—the uncle said yes! We all got together at the bank for the signing. The young man said, "Uncle Joe, I'll never forget what you've done for us. You've made it possible for us to have our own home. I hope someday to be able to do for someone else what you've done for me."

The uncle answered something that I've never forgotten: "Bill," he said, "I want to tell you something. Amassing a sum of money is relatively easy. Spending it wisely or giving it away intelligently is complicated and difficult."

I thought about that after they left. It didn't make much sense to me. I decided to talk it over with someone who was fast becoming pretty important to me—a girl named Marilyn Koffman, whom I'd started dating. Neither of us quite understood what the man was talking about—*easy to amass a sum of money, difficult to give it away intelligently*. We were missing the key word—*intelligently*.

IT'S TIME NOW to speak of my meeting with that most beautiful girl in the world and most wonderful partner of some fifty years. One chilly November day after I came back from the war, a friend and I went to Willowbrook Golf Course at 46th and Allisonville Road. I'd returned from this chilly golf game and was in the shower trying to warm up a bit when my mother began yelling through the door.

MOTHER: Marilyn Koffman is on the phone.

GLICK (through the door with shower water running): Who?

MOTHER: Marilyn—you remember, the girl who moved to town when you were a senior in high school. The one who came over with her mother when you were on furlough.

GLICK: Hmm. Well?

MOTHER: Listen, she wants you to come over tonight and play some bridge with some other young people.

GLICK: Wait a minute—let me turn off this shower. Bridge, you say? I wouldn't want to mislead anyone. Tell her I don't play bridge.

MOTHER: That's not polite. Tell her . . . tell her that you could come if they were going to have a table to play something else.

GLICK: Yes, I could go if they were going to play something else but bridge. I don't care for bridge.

So I went over. She lived in an apartment a stone's throw from our house. She now tells the story that she was intrigued by me—maybe puzzled is a better word. We had first met in 1939, shortly before I went off to college at IU. Marilyn's aunt lived in an apartment on Meridian Street and was a good friend of my mother's. One day when she and her mother were visiting the aunt my mother and I were out for a walk. The aunt asked us to stop and visit for a moment, and she introduced us to her niece.

She'd thought I might call later; we were at the age when a lot of dating was going on and she was used to getting calls from the young men she met. But shortly after we met I went to IU and then off to war, so I saw little of Indianapolis for the next six years or so.

But now I was back and Marilyn was inviting me; there was a lot of talking, not much bridge playing, and there were "serious" couples there, people who later got married. She served soft drinks and pretzels and snacks, and when the evening was over everybody left like someone had yelled "plague"! I offered to help with the dishes; after all, I was used to it. In those days, when men sat and read the paper while the women fixed supper and cleaned up, my mother ran an egalitarian household—well, at least as far as I was concerned. I helped. My dad sat and read.

Marilyn thought it was thoughtful of me to see all those messy dishes and want to help. We had a good conversation, the first of thousands that are still going on. I asked her to go downtown to the Sapphire Room of the Washington Hotel for dinner and dancing, and it was then that she learned that I could be a practical joker. "I don't know how to dance," I fibbed mournfully to her. "Maybe you'd be good enough to come over to the house and show me a few steps before we go down to the Sapphire Room." So she came over with some records, prepared to teach the poor klutz how to dance. I acted as if I had two left feet and stumbled around and had a great time pretending to have her teach me the fox trot. Later she was chagrined to find I could whirl her around the dance floor like a semi-pro, thanks in part to those Arthur Murray dance lessons.

Soon we were dating a lot and it didn't take long for me to decide that she was the person I wanted to spend the rest of my life with. She said she felt the same. So, while I was working at the bank, it was normal that I would talk to her about almost everything that came up. It was the beginning of a working partnership which eventually saw her become absolutely indispensable to me in a business as well as a personal sense.

As we loaned money for homes, word got around that Peoples Bank was a good place for those wanting new construction loans. Builders and developers began to bring their customers in to get financing. Then the builders themselves came to get financing for their own spec homes and developments. Many of the bigger builders in town, those who had been around for years, began to tell each other that we had a quality mortgage loan department, one where the customer could get efficient service and a quick answer—very important in that business. The answer might be no, but you didn't have to go through a committee and a string of letters and interviews to get it. I was interested in volume and the ability to realize a profit, and we could make money on builders when we made a construction loan, then sold the loan, then serviced it.

In the spring of 1946 Peoples' president, Felix McWhirter, told me he wanted me to visit construction sites. Since we were doing so much construction loan business, he wanted me to meet at the sites with the FHA appraisers, bank appraisers, and VA appraisers so I could learn what constituted good-quality construction, poor-quality construction, and property values in general. Following Mr. McWhirter's advice, I met at various sites with the bank inspectors and the government inspectors, and they were all very helpful.

I've never had people turn me down when I sincerely asked for information. Far from it. When I asked what made sound construction, these people would just pour out information. On one of the visits to these sites, the carpenter foreman I encountered was Gene Miller, an old grade school friend. I've recounted how poor I was in

Marilyn when she was a little girl.

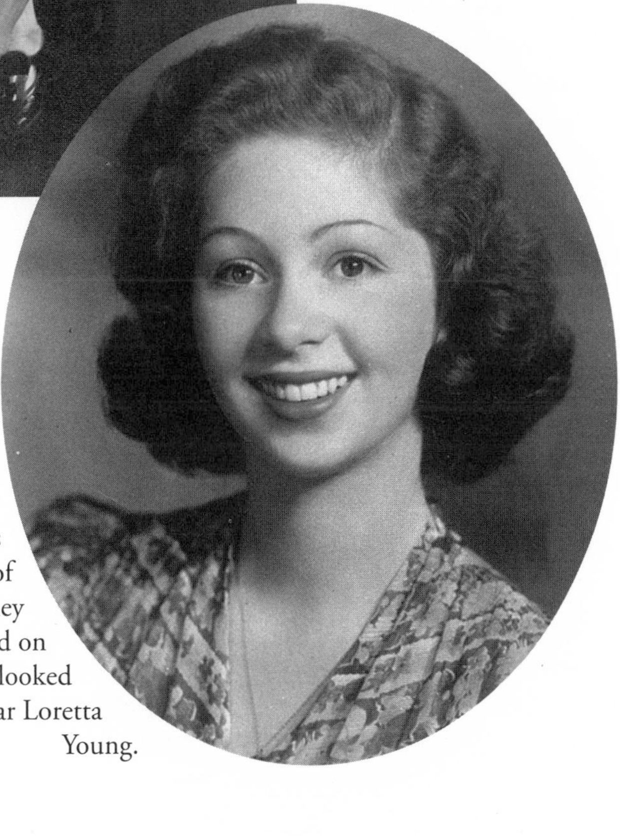

My parents loved this portrait of Marilyn. They often remarked on how much she looked like movie star Loretta Young.

shop, that the boy next to me was creating a masterpiece while I was still fumbling to get one piece of wood planed. That boy was Gene Miller, now a master craftsman.

It was a day in spring and I had been walking around the site, watching the progress of the home. The earth was freshly turned, a beautiful, wholesome scent to me. Lumber was there, freshly sawn, in big piles. It looked so neat and so new and so . . . promising.

"Whose house is this going to be?" I asked Gene. The earth-moving equipment was pushing that brown earth around.

"It's a GI," Gene told me, spreading out his plans on a little makeshift stand. "I know him. He keeps coming over, watching everything, telling me that it's his dream house."

I went over to look at the blueprints. There they were, the rooms—the living room, the dining room where they'd be eating Thanksgiving dinner, the kitchen where his wife would cook meals—where he could forget about the war he'd just been through and live happily with his family. And the bedrooms, where they'd sleep peacefully, knowing they had home ownership for themselves and their children for the rest of their lives.

I walked away, realizing then and there that I wanted to spend the rest of my own working days with these things—with the moving of earth and the sawing of lumber and the reading of prints that really weren't paper plans but the realization of people's best dreams. This is what I wanted to do with my life.

Marilyn and I were engaged by this time, and when I saw her that night I said to her, "I know how I want to spend the rest of my life. I want to build homes for families with children and grandchildren. Something fine will be created from nothing." She understood. More than that, she said she would always help me.

I knew I had much to learn, and I knew where to get the knowledge I needed. I had been helping many of the state's biggest builders get fast, efficient service on the loans they needed in the midst of construction. "We've got to make payroll and we need a loan here to see us through," they'd say. "No guarantees, but let us help you process the paperwork," I'd answer. And we went out of our way to do it. Marilyn was working all day as head of the reinsurance department as well as being the secretary for Walter Huehl, vice president of Indianapolis Life Insurance Company. She and I would work at night, typing these builders' loan applications.

They would be very grateful if and when the loan came through, of course, and one day I said to one of them, "You can help me if you will. You can help me understand the construction industry. Tell me about the costs, who the good, high-quality builders are and what makes them quality builders. And most of all, what mistakes and pitfalls there are in this business." They were very generous in explaining the business to me, and when the time came, let me see their plans so I could get a feel for what makes a fine quality home.

Marilyn and I would look at the plans to see what the houses' best features were. Then we'd get in the car after work and drive around to the sites, looking to see how the features on the blueprints were actually working out in the homes themselves—the breakfast bars and nooks, the picture windows and fireplaces.

At the same time we were involved in another aspect of the home business: real estate sales. Marilyn and I became a little real estate agency as an outgrowth of the work at the bank. People would come in and want to know if we could recommend anybody to sell their homes—I guess they had great confidence in anybody who worked in a bank. Across the street was a big real estate firm, Jack Carr and his Forty Gentlemen of Sales. But some people wanted a more personal touch. It occurred to me that I could sell houses for them and give them the same individual and personal service I tried to give each loan customer. Why not?

Since I was an unknown, I felt I had to offer something special to gain their trust. "I know I'm just out of the Army and unproven in real estate sales, but that doesn't matter. I am so positive I can sell your house for you that if I don't sell your house in thirty (or sometimes sixty) days, I'll give you a hundred dollars."

That was my unique selling proposition: catch their attention, show I could compete in the real estate business—even with Jack Carr and his Forty Gentlemen. Just promise to sell, and if you don't, pay the hundred dollars—big money in those days. I guess I did have a lot of confidence in myself and Marilyn.

We were married in January of 1947. Although we had hoped to be married in the fall of '46, there was a decision to be made, and we had to subordinate our wishes to the strong needs of the moment. For one thing, we were doing a tremendous volume of mortgage loan business at the bank and I didn't think it would be in the bank's best interest for me to take ten days to two weeks off during the busiest season. Secondly, we needed the nest egg that selling homes after work could provide. So we planned the wedding around the time when builders, and therefore the mortgage loan business, would slow down. And it was a right decision: Shakespeare said in *Julius Caesar*,

There is a tide in the affairs of men
Which, when taken at the flood, leads on to fortune.
Omitted, all the voyage of their life
Is bound in shallows and in miseries.

It was a modest but memorable wedding at the Marott Hotel. The women of Marilyn's family, as usual, looked absolutely elegant. Marilyn's father had died of a heart attack right in the midst of the Depression, leaving her mother with very little. They were used to living on a tight budget, dressing with style while shopping the sales. Rabbi Maurice Goldblatt of IHC married us, and we followed the ceremony with a brunch at the Marott. Then we took the train to Cincinnati to begin our honeymoon, Marilyn proudly wearing her orchid wedding corsage and I sleeping the whole way because I was exhausted. I slept a lot on that train ride. I was so tired because of all the work we'd been doing. I'd been madly arranging loans, rushing about the state to sell mortgage loans to banks, and managing our little real estate business with its hundred-dollar "without-fail sale" promise.

We went on to Palm Beach, usually staying in modest accommodations because of our pocketbook crunch. (We did enjoy a visit with some people in the posh Breakers Hotel, even though at that time Jewish people weren't welcome there.)

After the brief interlude of our honeymoon, we ran an ad in the paper, promising our spectacular monetary promise and its surefire results. We began to get a lot of listings, and the big fish in the real estate pond began to take notice. So did the Better Business Bureau. They called Marilyn while I was at work, saying they'd had complaints and that we'd need to take the ads out because they misrepresented what we did. Marilyn was upset; she didn't know what to think. So I got on the phone.

"Please give me the head of your organization," I said to the Better Business Bureau. When he came on I told him, "You have called my wife and complained of misrepresentation. I suppose you have some evidence of someone who has found we misrepresented our business promise." The director said no, he knew of no one who had found we misrepresented our situation. Still, he said that we couldn't continue to make that offer. "I'll tell you what," I said, getting angry. "Not only are we doing it, but we are going to continue to do it. And if you or any of your friends or relatives has a house to sell, you send them to the bank and I personally will give them a hundred dollars to keep if I do not sell their house in the promised time. This is a frivolous call—do not call me again. Do you have any questions? I know you have received a complaint, not from a customer, but from a competitor. My wife and I are thoroughly annoyed at your call; still, I invite you to come around and take us up on our offer."

We always managed to sell the houses listed with us and never had to pay the hundred dollars. We came close, though, on one property at 40th and Washington Boulevard. The woman selling the house had insisted we promise to give her five hundred dollars instead of a hundred, so when sixty days had passed and we hadn't closed, I was beginning to sweat. But sure enough, we closed, just before the deadline, and I got the money back—fortunately for us.

One secret to our success as real estate people was that we didn't promise the moon. We'd tell customers that the bank appraiser would appraise the house and we'd base the selling price on that fair appraisal. Sometimes we'd explain our method and the person on the other end of the line would say, "Oh, that's too low. I can't work with that," and hang up. Often, months later, these same people would call back and want to take us up on the offer. We often agreed, but strictly on our terms. It had to be that way.

Finally though, the construction bug that had bitten me that day on the job site got too persistent to ignore. I wanted to build a home. Realistically, I knew we couldn't put up a new home for anyone yet, but I thought we might be able to sell a remodeled one.

Marilyn had three thousand dollars saved from her work at the life insurance company, and I had three thousand from my Army savings. We had agreed—actually, before we were married—to pool our savings, purchase a couple of houses inexpensively and remodel them. The first house we put our hand to was out near Kingan's on the west side, fortunately on the upwind side of the slaughterhouse. We remodeled that house, put it on the market for about five thousand dollars and showed it at night, after I got off work. Marilyn would take the calls during the daytime, and we'd both show the house, praying we didn't get an unusual east wind which would smell up our business deal.

In those days one didn't need a real estate license and, of course, there was a lot of negotiating if we had to work with another broker. The contractors I'd talked to gave me the names of subcontractors who could do the remodeling work; it was certain I couldn't do it. Still, most of the people the big contractors knew wouldn't be interested in one little remodeling job. We didn't know who to approach, so Marilyn just looked in the Yellow Pages. The name Boykin was listed, near the top of the list, of course. She called him, he seemed sensible, so we asked for references and hired him.

He turned out to be very capable, but there was a problem. One of the plumbing subcontractors who was going to work with him for us called and said to Marilyn, "Boykin is a good contractor and an honest man, but he doesn't pay his bills on time. You need to make checks payable to both Boykin and the subcontractors." So I did just that. Later, when this Boykin went bankrupt, I was glad we'd done that; otherwise I might have had to pay twice.

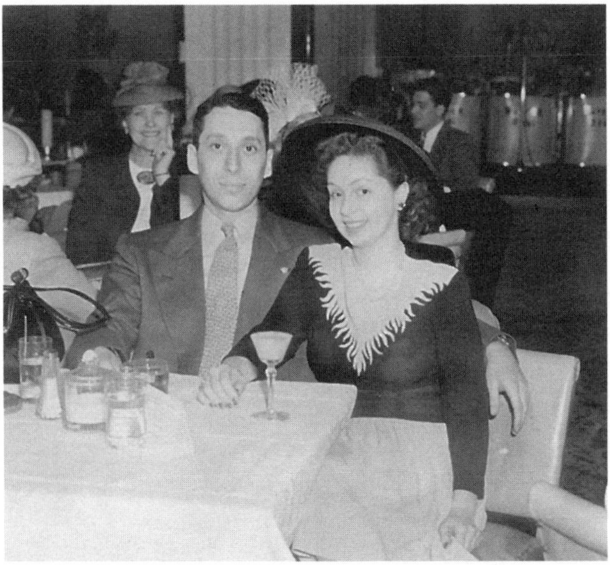

Marilyn and I dined and danced at the Sapphire Room in the Washington Hotel in 1946 when we were dating. They had great food, drinks, and dancing, and we enjoyed going there for many years. (*Below*) Our wedding day.

Chapter 5

Starting the Company

Nothing in the world can take
The place of persistence.
Talent will not; nothing is more common
Than unsuccessful men with talent.
Genius will not; unrewarded genius is almost a proverb.
Education alone will not; the world
Is full of educated derelicts;
Persistence and determination alone
Are omnipotent.

—Unknown

WE TOOK THE PLUNGE with that first house in 1947, but it wasn't enough for me to simply remodel somebody else's house. I wanted to build from the ground up, and soon I had the opportunity. A friend of mine from Shortridge came into the bank to arrange a loan for a house. He was ready to go with a large construction firm operated by a man named Cunningham who was building a hundred houses a year. I got hold of my friend later and told him that I could build him a home on a lot we had at 4701 Ralston for the same price as the larger contractor.

He agreed, and we commenced! Early every morning I would visit the job site with Marilyn. I'd dictate instructions which she'd write out in shorthand—what subcontractors to contact and which materials to order. Then she'd drive me to the bank and return home or to the site to contact all the suppliers and subcontractors.

What a hole I might have dug for myself with that house at 47th and Ralston! Prices were rising all the time. I'd go out at night to the site when I got off work and after I'd dropped Marilyn off (she had to pick me up from work—we had only one car in those days). I'd jump in and do a lot of the work myself, including helping the workers lay the hardwood floor. I rented the sander, sanded the floors and applied the varnish and filler so I could save money on that house. Spring of 1948 came, and, amazingly, the house was nearing completion. Marilyn and I went out and bought shrubs and put the plants in. I even graded the yard myself.

A recent review of the abstract of that house shows that it sold for $6,990 in 1948. The current owner says he bought it in the seventies for $19,000 and that today comparable houses in the neighborhood sell for $50,000 and up. So the housing industry goes.

There was a lot of anxiety connected with that first house, but also a good deal of firm faith that we were doing the job we were cut out to do. You need that hope and faith along with the anxiety. Samuel Johnson said, "Life affords no higher pleasure than that of surmounting difficulties passing from one step of success to another, forming new wishes and seeing them gratified. He that labors in any great or laudable undertaking has his fatigue first supported by hope and afterwards rewarded by joy." Well, I don't know if 4701 Ralston, with its hopeful-looking little windows and its bargain-basement shrubs along the front, was a "great or laudable undertaking," but we certainly entered upon it with great earnestness.

Marilyn and I stood, finally, in the front yard of this first house we built: 720 square feet, two bedrooms. We collected our $6,990. The price included a small garage, the lot, sidewalks, completely finished exterior and interior, seeded yard, shrubbery, hardwood floors, kitchen with nice cabinets, even storm windows. Even with all the special touches, we broke even somehow.

More importantly, the homeowner and his wife were very happy with their lovely little product born of the Glicks' sweat, tears, and—at least on Marilyn's part—sleepless nights.

They told others, and we eventually received good referral business, building homes for the buyers' friends and relatives. We continued to look in the papers, and to go to the courthouse to see who owned lots in the Ralston-Indianola area. We bid on several of them, and during 1947 to 1948 we built four houses. The next year we doubled that.

Locating the lots was time-consuming. Marilyn would call someone offering a lot in the paper and ask him or her the price, and then I'd send the bank appraiser to appraise the lot. He'd come in at about a third of what was being asked, so I instructed her to call and offer them the appraised figure. She balked at first. "That will be embarrassing," she insisted. "What do we have to lose?" I'd ask. She'd call, tell them we'd had an appraisal and offer that amount, and at first they'd say, "Absolutely not! We're going to get our price!" After it had been on the market for a while, they'd call back and say: "Are you still in the market for that lot?"

We continued doing our apprentice-builder homework, visiting luxury builders' sites, trying to see what was being put in fancy new homes, what little touches we could use to add a little luxury to our little homes. I think we were the first to put in wood-burning fireplaces as a standard feature. We'd add a little touch of marble in our bathrooms, a little ceramic tile, and instead of just a tub we'd have glass doors around a shower. We'd see them putting in breezeways and automatic washers and dryers in houses in Crows Nest, or out on Ditch Road, and we'd do it in our own small way, too.

When I wasn't working at the bank or working at a building site myself, I was begging suppliers to furnish us with lumber and tile and paint. Of course they had all the business they could handle in that postwar period, and they didn't know us—we had no credit and no reputation. But Marilyn and I would say, "Look, we know we're a risk. But someday we're going to be building a hundred homes at once, maybe two hundred, and if you do us a favor we're going to be loyal to you. If you stay competitive, we'll be loyal to you down the road when it can really do you some good." And we were!

I'd get up early in the morning, drive Marilyn to the site in our one car, leave her with a list of people to call, and check on her during the day. She'd stay on the phone until she got what we needed: delivery of that piece of plumbing, promise of the drywall we needed. Then we'd drag back home to work on another spec house we were building at night.

One of the suppliers was the Spickelmier Company at 52nd and

Richard Day

We took the plunge into the construction business with our first house at 4701 Ralston.

When I ran the GI loan department at Peoples Bank, we made more GI loans than all the other banks in the city combined. This was typical of the type of ad we'd put in the paper, encouraging vets to come to Peoples to finance their dream homes.

BY EX-SERGEANT SANSONE, CREATOR OF THE FAMOUS G. I. CARTOON, "THE WOLF"
Sansone
"DARLING! NOW WE CAN HAVE A REAL HOME. I JUST GOT A G. I. LOAN AT THE BANK!"
ATTENTION, VETERANS! Make us your headquarters for information about the financial features of the G. I. Act (and the new amendments). Also turn to us for a home loan under the Act if you decide to borrow. We'll be glad to give you the benefits of our experience in the real-estate mortgage field.

Carvel Avenue. Their drywall shipping head was a man they called Rocklathe Whitey. Drywall was in such short supply that every time a truck would arrive at Spickelmier's, builders would follow Whitey around to see where the trucks went. Finally the poor man had a nervous breakdown from the pressure. When he returned from his time off, he told Marilyn that she was one of the chief reasons he'd had to take off to recuperate. But I'm sure she wasn't the only one desperate for building materials.

Soon, however, we had bought up about all of the affordable lots that were readily available in the Ralston-Indianola area (and in Forest Manor, where we also were looking) and were frustrated with trying to locate owners who lived out-of-state. We decided to seek an area with a lot of open space and lots still available. That area was on the east side of Indianapolis, east of Emerson and north of 10th Street. The first lots we bought there in 1949 were along Ritter Avenue, between 10th and 16th streets.

I could now devote myself full-time to the building business. To that end, I had left the bank in the summer of 1948. The routine of dropping Marilyn off at the job site, going to work and calling some of the subs from work and worrying about the rest just got old. In addition, of course, I was swamped trying to do two jobs. So the day came when I went in to see Mr. McWhirter and said, "I'm going to start up my own building business." I assured him I would stay on half-time to train the two very talented young women who were my assistants and continue to work with them until they became professional loan officers. And so I came in early in the mornings, met the new customers, and passed them on in large part to these two executive-caliber women.

I received half pay from the bank for about nine months, then left. But I left with a sense of gratitude; Peoples had been good to me. It was probably the smallest bank in Indianapolis then, and I had been involved in all aspects of the mortgage banking business, something that wouldn't have been possible if it had been a bigger bank. Also, Peoples was very conservative, and that conservatism I took from there has served me well as my business has grown through the years.

I suppose I was like a hunter in a primitive society, but instead of dragging home a carcass, I was supposed to drag home enough money every week to provide for my family—with no guarantee of success, no security from a steady income. Every entrepreneur does that. I suppose that shows he has confidence in his product. If you're entrepreneurial, you believe there is a public out there that is ready and eager to receive the product you've conceived. You trust that they will find it good enough so that your family's future, their very existence, will be secure because of your idea.

But entrepreneurship is second nature to me; I'd loved it as a paper boy, as a high school ad salesman, and as a bus travel agent and a bicycle salesman. I knew that whatever I did, I was going to give it all I had, and I was destined to love it, or whatever I went into, and never to consider it work. I think all successful people are like that: in those days I'd sometimes work until I saw the sun coming up. Though I really liked to be in bed by the middle of the night, if I needed to I'd go home at 5 A.M. and never think that it was anything onerous. No, it was living to me, and the thrill of it has never ceased.

There's no doubt that I was an idealist; many in my generation were and are. The contribution I wanted to make to society was part of the everlasting thrill. I still believe sincerely that the contributions my children and soon my grandchildren will make to society are the greatest success of my lifetime. And my own ability to help some of my fellow travelers on Planet Earth to achieve better lives has rewarded me greatly. Still, I don't want to discount the wisdom of comedian Joe E. Lewis, who would look out at the audience and say seriously, "Folks, I've been poor and I've been rich, and I want to tell you that rich is better." I think very few would disagree with that, so the monetary incentive was important to me too.

About 1947 we set up as Indianapolis Homes, Inc. The organizational details of setting up the corporation were formidable, and since budget was always a consideration in the first two years, I got a lawyer's manual and had Marilyn type all the papers according to its instructions. When we went to file the papers of incorporation, we were told we had to have an attorney take care of the filing. I wondered, *Wasn't there a way to handle this without a lot of expense?* I went to a friend and told him we'd followed all the legal precedents, and prepared the documents according to the book. He said he'd look them over and file for us.

When a bill came for twenty-five dollars, we were horrified. We couldn't imagine what he could have done for twenty-five dollars—a princely sum in those days and a real dip into our capital.

Setting up according to the Secretary of State's office and obtaining the necessary business permits was only part of the paperwork. We were responsible for helping our buyers get loans for construction, and there were several steps to getting the loans, based on FHA guarantees. Of course, we'd had experience and that was in our favor, but the actual payout of the loans still took management.

Each month was a cliff-hanger. You would agree with the mortgage lender that you would get certain construction draws depending on the percentage of construction that was completed. The draws would be paid only after the basement was actually completed, or the house framed up. The process was very specific: when the drywall was in, another draw; when interior trim was completed, another. Ten thousand dollars, an amount the first draw might represent, wasn't very much in that cash economy we were working in. We used it to pay for all supplies and construction expenses, and we were also living on it, so it wasn't long before we were desperately trying to get one phase done on the house and collect before we ran out of cash to even start another. Contractors had to pick their paychecks up because they had to pay carpenters and plumbers who were putting food on the table—and let's face it, liquor in their glasses—with the sweat of their brows. We were living under real pressure, the type golfer Lee Trevino spoke of when an announcer asked him if he was under tremendous pressure putting for a fifty-thousand-dollar prize. "No," said Trevino, "Real pressure was being a poor barefoot kid in Texas, and picking up golfballs to pay for food, and getting into an after-hours putting match with tough kids where everybody pays the winner five dollars each—and you don't have the five dollars and fear what they'll do to you—that's pressure." And for me that was real pressure, to keep these people paid on Friday. Hans Steilberger, our former "roomer" and my foster brother, assisted me in that early period, and he has this memory of those rush-around, try-to-make-ends-meet days:

> *Indianapolis Homes, which was also at one time called "Doc and Doll Sales Company," was unable to countenance interruptions in the construction flow plan or last-minute cancellations of scheduled deliveries. Glick did everything within his power to avoid such occurrences. For example, a load of concrete for pouring pilasters had been scheduled for delivery one morning. It had rained hard the previous day, whereupon the temperature dropped below freezing. Fearful that the pilaster supports would be covered with ice and thus unable to form a solid bond with the concrete, Glick donned a set of old army fatigues and a pair of hip boots, borrowed a pickax and around 10* P.M. *set out for the construction site. There he jumped into the "basement" and while I aimed a flashlight, chopped the thick ice from around each of the three supports. The concrete work went without a hitch the following morning.*

The reason the sales part of the early operation had been briefly called "Doc and Doll Company" was that Marilyn's nickname for me was Doc. I, in turn, called her Lady Marilyn. The people at the bank must have been gullible. Word got around that I was engaged, then married, to a titled Englishwoman. And someone stopped me in the parking lot and asked me to diagnose a child's ailment. "Why are you asking me?" I wondered. "They call you Doc, don't they?" Indianapolis Homes was really a better name.

As we built more houses, the pressure to meet payroll grew. When we were building in the Ralston-Indianola area, and then in the earliest days on the east side, 1947 to 1949, we were juggling several financial balls. It was like getting a slug in the solar plexus when someone who had made a deposit on a house called and said, "Well, we've changed our minds. We want the deposit back." Sometimes we'd started the house, so we'd have to turn around and re-sell. As we had more than one house being built, sometimes we'd have one or two on spec. But to suddenly find we had three or four—it made me feel sick.

Sometimes I'd get tired of worrying and being optimistic, and I'd just call Marilyn and I'd use one of my false voices and invent a fake customer—just for the hell of it. In those days Marilyn didn't know my fake voices, so I'd start asking about the amenities of the house. She was so eager, so desperate really, to sell the house, that she'd really wax eloquent about the wonderful features. Behind all this was the fact that in 1949 we were completing a house that was due to sell for more than thirteen thousand dollars, and we were kicking ourselves for having ever gone into such a luxury venture we might never be able to sell. We'd often find someone who loved the house, couldn't do without it, but didn't have the money to really buy it. So, in talking with this "customer," Marilyn was trying to scope the situation out, to find out if the "fake" me had money. Would I need to take the bus out? No, I said in my funny voice, I had a very nice Cadillac, thank you. You could hear the excitement build in her voice. Then, she hung up. I called her plenty fast as the real me, demanding to know why she'd been on the phone for so long. "You've been talking to your mother, I bet," I said, barely able to contain my amusement.

Irate, she told me she had been talking to the world's most promising customer for the expensive home. When I told her I was the one who had held her on the phone for that long . . . well, she was not amused.

I remember I carried this fake voice ploy to extremes later one day at Broadmoor Country Club, on an evening when conditions were favorable for projecting your voice. She'd hit a ball into a neighboring yard, and I yelled, "Better not go over there; there's a big ferocious dog in that yard. It's only a golf ball; let it lie." She climbed the fence anyway, and since it was dusk and she couldn't see me I projected my voice. "Whoof! Whoof!" I barked and she came flying back over that fence, white as a sheet. Since then she's come to know my "whoof" and all the rest of my practical joke voices.

In any case, this fairly ritzy house was definitely sitting on the market, and we had put many of our special touches into it, including a customized basement and a leatherette dining nook made specially by King's, the billiard table company in Indianapolis. It could seat six to eight people in its colored leatherette seats and was a beautiful family innovation. We chewed our fingernails waiting for someone to buy this expensive spec house. One day a man came over to the site and stretched out his hand. "I'm Shiloh S. Shambaugh," he said, smiling. I took him and his wife all around and they admired everything.

"The view is wonderful here," he said. "And with that dining nook the kids can eat with us in a lovely place in the kitchen without having to go into the dining room. How much is this house?"

I thought I was going to collapse. In a voice completely devoid of confidence I murmured, "It's $13,290." Then I waited for the rejection. It never came. Instead, Shambaugh said, "Reasonably priced. We'll take it." They'd take it! I was ready to lie down and roll on the floor in joy. They signed the contract. We got the home in move-in condition for them, and soon they began eating their Wheaties on that classy leatherette in the nook.

Since our marriage, Marilyn and I had been living in one side of a double house across from the Butler Fieldhouse. Then in 1948 we built our own first home, in the 3600 block of North DeQuincy, not too far from the Shambaugh home. It became the model for the rest of the homes we built in that area west of Emerson, south of 38th, east of Sherman Drive. Streets like Arlington, Riley, DeQuincy, and Wallace were included in the area. We furnished our home attractively and told prospective buyers that the home we'd build them would look like this one.

We lived on DeQuincy for about one year. But the house had only two bedrooms so when we discovered that Marilyn was pregnant (with Marianne, as it turned out), we decided to build a three-bedroom home at 3725 Wallace Street. The baby was born in November of 1949, and Marilyn had a room decorated and ready for her when we brought her home.

The middle bedroom, paneled in knotty pine, served as the office for the company. The contractors would come in to be paid on Friday, and we'd have Marianne's playpen out in the living room where they'd pass. One day a burly, 250-pound gentleman came into the office-bedroom where I was and he said, "I scared your little girl out there. I'm so big and ugly I made her scream."

"No," I told him, "she's just hurt because you didn't pay any attention to her. She's used to having the workers pick her up and play with her a little. You've insulted her." I had to plead with him to go pick her up, but he finally did, and she settled down.

We lived in that twelve-hundred-square-foot house for ten years and brought all of our children home to it: Arlene in 1952, Alice in '53, and Lynda in '59. That house had a full basement—very labor-intensive to build. Today's earth moving equipment moves tons of dirt with the touch of a small lever. But not back then. Still, building a basement in those early days wasn't prohibitively expensive, so we decided to have a basement in each of the homes we built as one of our low-cost but special features. I got very interested in what could be done with a basement. After all, it was a very usable area and—for us—cost effective to put in, as opposed to building up for space. So we got fancy and innovative with what we came to call the "lower level." Laundry rooms, finished recreation rooms, simulated windows with lights above them—these basements were nicely finished and everybody loved them.

It was about this time that, with the birth of each child, Marilyn's direct involvement with the company had to diminish progressively. Although she had thoroughly enjoyed herself and been a significant partner to me and influence on the business, she needed to now devote herself to that most influential role in the world: that of mother. She continued to be active in the business for some time, but her hours were limited.

As we began to expand, we took to the newspapers to advertise our product. Early in 1950 *The Indianapolis Star* announced that we were putting up a fifteen-home project along Ritter Avenue, between 10th and 16th streets. In June of 1950 we announced that we would also be putting up a subdivision of fifteen homes "in scenic Forest Manor, along Riley Avenue, between 36th and 38th streets." Things were going strong!

Of course we were playing into a huge building boom, the

strongest in fifty years. In 1900, only three and a half million people had owned their own homes. By 1950 the United States Savings and Loan League estimated that sixteen million non-farm residents were homeowners. Home ownership had grown more affordable. Half of those sixteen million people made less than twenty-five hundred dollars a year!

The tradition of owning a nice frame, brick, or stone home as the center of family life had developed in the 1880s and '90s. In the last years of the previous century, many middle-class people and working folk proudly built their own homes, often using the "pattern" house plans easily ordered from Sears and Roebuck or other firms. The white pine forests of Michigan and Wisconsin, cut between 1870 and 1900, provided wood for comfortable homes erected on roomy lots along recently bricked and macadamized roads. Improvements from 1870 to 1900 in the production of cement, the mass production of nails, the development of electrical wiring in homes, and the organization of city and town water, gas, and sewage systems encouraged home building.

In the first two decades of the twentieth century, with the depletion of the northwoods lumber forests and changes in the economy, home building slowed. After World War I there was a rejuvenation, however, and the ratio of home ownership to total families rose to approximately 46 percent by 1930.

World War II, of course, closed down the industry. By the time the war was over, there was an unprecedented pent-up desire for housing. I had seen this firsthand. The year most of us GIs returned there was nothing to rent, let alone the opportunity for new housing. In 1945 and '46, the morning papers would arrive and desperate families would phone—sometimes scores of them—trying to rent whatever overpriced and pitifully inadequate housing was offered in the want ads. There were races across town to put rent deposits down; there were arguments at landlords' doorsteps. Returned veterans and their families were living in basements, in shacks with old-fashioned potbellied stoves, in mouse-infested attics. They desperately wanted homes.

So we were on the threshold of a huge building boom. By 1951 the head of the Savings and Loan League, Henry Bubb of Topeka, Kansas, could say, "Of all the tremendous developments which have come out of the last fifty years, none has more enduring and far-reaching importance than the drive for home ownership."

A few statistics from 1950—the year we advertised those "two major home development projects"—are instructive. During the month of July alone more than 2.6 billion building permits were issued in this country. In that year mortgages set records: 3,540,000 families were on the rolls nationally as having borrowed to obtain home ownership. Building permits valued at more than $30 million were issued in Marion County in the first six months of 1950 alone.

Clearly, we were entering a bonanza market in 1950 as we went into full swing in Forest Manor. We had great expectations! More importantly, we knew we would be contributing something substantial to our community by providing quality homes for postwar families.

THINGS PROGRESSED RAPIDLY in those heady days, with buyers eager and all of our energies poured into our projects (and survival). By now we were calling our building efforts "home developments"—groups of similar houses in blocks.

Having been interested in quality from the first little home we built, we were determined to offer the most home we could for the buyer's dollar. *The Indianapolis Star* announced in its real estate section in June of 1950 that the Forest Manor development would have "two- and three-bedroom homes with kitchen, dining room, living room, bath, and full basement." Ranch-type, Cape Cod, and modern American architecture would be featured. The details were important, and we made sure that *The Star* got them right: automatic oil heat, tile bath with shower over tub, front porch or breezeway, aluminum windows, double laundry trays, breakfast bars of knotty pine, and garage with overhead door. The prices of these homes varied from $11,200 to $18,350. Down payments were $2,500 and monthly payments were a minimum of $55.

We got to know so many fine people personally during that building period beginning in 1950 and lasting through the mid-fifties. We'd help them design their houses, listen to their needs, re-design. One man and his wife sat looking at the plans, discussing and discussing the bedroom size. "Your mother won't be with us forever," the husband kept telling his wife. "We don't need such a big bedroom—she won't be here forever." We worked with them and got the bedroom big enough to suit her (and her mother), yet small enough to suit him.

Some time later, when I was teaching Marianne to ride a bike out in the driveway one day, a car rolled by with two women in it, crying. It was the woman and her mother. They stopped, and I asked them what the matter was. "Remember when you were building the house for us, John always said, 'Mother won't be here forever?' Well, John died of a heart attack last week." You can never tell what you will live to enjoy, so you'd better enjoy it now, I thought.

I remember another family who began a house, put down the thousand-dollar deposit and then called to say they were unable to continue. Something had happened. I later found out they had relatives who were loaning them the money, and they'd had an argument with the relatives. But all I knew then was that they were sticking us with a house that was going to be difficult to sell, because it was all customized for them. I felt cheated.

"We've put in special things for you, things that not everybody would want. It will be very difficult to re-sell your home. I think that thousand dollars should belong to us for the work we've done."

But in a month or so the couple called back, ready to start up the house again. The relative who had told them to go to hell had patched it up with them. Soon they moved in with their little girl, a much-worshipped only child, and the child's grandmother. So it turned out well after all. That little girl rode her bike around as queen of the neighborhood for quite a while.

Another time an engineer for General Electric came to Indianapolis from Pittsburgh and was searching for a home for his family while his wife remained in Pittsburgh. He came to see the model and was delighted. "I see you have a home under way," he said. "Can I put five hundred dollars down and then firm up the deal after my wife comes over to see it?"

"Certainly," I said, uncertainly. The wife was due in about the time the basement block was laid and framing begun. Just before she came there was a torrential rain, and the basement filled with about six feet of water. Though there wasn't anything down there that would be hurt, I looked at it with dismay. I should have had the backfill done with sand, but we couldn't afford it, and it would have been fine if the rain hadn't come so hard. "Look at that basement!" the man said. "I know my wife would love this house and okay my decision, but once she sees this water in the basement, she's going to nix it."

"Never mind," I told him. "I'll take care of it." She was to arrive in two days, so I rented a portable sump pump and raced over to the basement and held the hose until the son-of-a-gun was dry. I called the grading people, who should have done a lot better job in the first place, and told them I'd pay time-and-a-half to fix the drainage. They arrived and pushed the dirt around so it drained the right way. Then I left the sump pump in the basement for insurance. All of this took a full day; Marilyn was at home worrying that she was going to be a widow, with me working in water with electrical equipment!

But it stayed dry, and the wife came and approved the house, and I had the pleasure of seeing them move in. That engineer was a wonderful man who was proud of his home and took pleasure in working in his yard and growing vegetables. One day I picked up the paper and saw that he had been killed in one of the large plane crashes of the fifties. Fate truly is the hunter. But it pleased us to think he'd had some good years there with his home and tomatoes.

By this time I had good help in the business—"a few good men." I hired James Craig, as I needed a little part-time help. Then Jack Kline came, also for temporary help because I kept looking at the payroll outgo. (Temporary in Jack's case became thirty-five years of employment with the Gene B. Glick Company.) Jack took over my routine, calling the subcontractors, checking to see if they'd begun or completed work. And, along with Hans, Jack baby-sat Marianne. Because I was gone all the time getting new business and Marilyn needed to be away checking on house A or B, we finally had to hire a full-time household helper. But sometimes the housekeeper was busy too, so Jack ended up with a bouncing, curly headed toddler on his lap. He also helped at the rip-roaring real estate open houses we had. Some of them became the talk of the neighborhood, certainly of our family for years to come.

Jack describes the kind of construction we were doing then:

We were working out of a little two-room office north of 10th and Ritter. The staff consisted of Gene, a painter named Harrison Howard, a laborer named James Craig, and myself doing everything from selling houses to dealing with subcontractors. Those were the days that basements were built of concrete block, and had to be waterproofed on the outside with a black tar substance. This was Craig's job. Harrison Howard, in addition to painting, was an all-round handyman. To pick up a few extra dollars, I did the landscaping with the help of James Craig.

I was also the complaint department. FHA regulations called for planting two trees out in front of each house. I recall one incident when a lady called to tell me that a tree planted in her front yard was crooked. The tree had a slight notch in the trunk, but to this lady it was a catastrophe. In another incident a customer had picked out a certain color for the trim on his house. Gene liked it, so we used it on another house on the street. The man got mad at Gene for using "his color."

I recall the first house we built with the garage under the house. We had concrete block retaining walls leading into the garage. One night we had a very bad storm. The next morning we found that the owner had parked his car in the drive and the block walls had caved in on top of the car. I let Gene handle that one.

One of the most frustrating problems we ever had was on a

house we built in Forest Manor. We built the house about ten feet too close to the front lot line. We had to move the basement back and poured a large slab in front, which gives this house the dubious honor of having one of the largest front porches on the block.

It wasn't exactly because we were "hot news" that *The Indianapolis Star* was printing good, illustrated articles about us in their Sunday real estate section. We had consciously decided to seek newspaper advertising and we were willing to commit our meager resources to pay for it. *The Star* and *The Indianapolis Times* would send reporters and photographers out if you bought what they called an "advertorial," in which they would do a feature on your real estate venture on the front page of one of the sections. It worked well for us.

One of the largest of these ads appeared in 1951, on Sunday, June 10. The paper trumpeted that Gene Glick was undertaking "a project of thirty new homes with total value of the development starting at $500,000." A model home would show what the splendid new houses would look like, the article added. Behind the hyperbole was this: we had an option on a tract on Ritter not far from the first Ritter section we'd built, and a good deal of hope was involved—along with our new faith in the power of advertising. Most importantly, we had faith in the quality of our product. As secretary-treasurer of the company I announced in print that "the company is one of the few to give a certificate of guaranty to purchasers with unqualified guarantee of materials and workmanship." I promised newspaper readers that these houses would be among the very best values of the year in central Indiana. Three large pictures of our already-standing Ritter homes accompanied the article. We prepared our own home to hold as an open house, to show as the model home of this new, rather large (for us) development.

But this was not our first open house. The first one had been the year before, also holding our own home open as the model, and had indeed been an affair to remember. When an advertisement appeared, we were inundated with customers. It was a happy quandary, but we went berserk that afternoon. Cars spilled down both sides of the street, and people poured into our little house. We called everybody we knew to come and help show people through, pass out sample contracts, and take them to the lot sites. Marilyn would duck off into one of the closets to nurse the little one, and then run out to serve the customers. A middle-aged couple came up and whispered in my ear, "Do you know that man walking through your rooms shaking his head and looking concerned? It's Walter Justus, the home developer." Sure enough it was! We were becoming important enough for the competition to care about. We could have sold ten times the number of lots that we had that day, but I'd been conservative in what I'd take on, having been trained at ultraconservative Peoples Bank. It was just as well that I developed that policy, because we never got overextended.

So we knew open houses worked. In the next three years we built everything we'd optioned for on Ritter. Then we moved into a section called Eastridge. We bought property to construct twenty-six homes—almost every home on Ritter, Leslie, and Layman streets between 10th and 13th. Eventually we took almost all of Mr. Wayne Harriman's property for our building projects. He had owned acre after acre of land in that neighborhood. In the early fifties he died of a heart attack, and the board of Community Hospital came to his widow and offered to buy the land for the new east side hospital. Since we had an option on part of the piece they wanted, we worked out a trade with Mrs. Harriman and the board. The board got our land along Ritter north from 13th to 16th for the hospital. We got their land between 10th and 13th along Layman and Leslie. It wasn't long before they built that fine facility which has served the city so well.

We built 85 to 90 percent of the homes in the Leslie and Layman (Eastridge) section, though a few people bought the lots and hired their own builders. We used the mortgage banking services of Savill and Mahaffey. They would act as a mortgage broker, placing our loans with various lenders or the government. Not wishing to gamble with interest rates we tried—needed, really—to get advance commitments on mortgage loans. It was necessary for us to get a guaranteed rate for a specified amount of financing, so that if rising interest rates priced our prospective home buyers out of the market, we could get them affordable financing.

We didn't do any tricky financing in the Ritter developments, in Forest Manor, or in Eastridge. We didn't want to gamble with money. We played it safe, buying fixed-rate mortgages so we could build our profitability around a fixed rate and know what our interest would be. We wanted to sell a home and make a profit—a reasonable profit—on it, and we used commitments to do that, passing the interest rate on to the buyer. There never was any real gouging in our industry, because there was always competition.

The homes we built continued to be custom-designed for customers who were by this time growing ever more sophisticated. The homes in Eastridge, completed in 1953, were advertised as having "one section of the basement clear for a social room, ceramic- or glass-tile bath, birch kitchen cabinets, picture windows, marble sills, and yards graded and seeded." By this time we were known for specializing in these unique lower levels, all paneled and tiled, which made the homes look spacious and useful for children and for entertaining.

In those days Marilyn, Jack, and I worked for hours with the buyers, getting to know them, their children, and special interests, and trying through all of this to deliver marvelous service. The newspaper article said, "The firm prefers to sell its homes from blueprints and permit the purchasers to personalize their homes by selecting everything themselves." Thus, we set the company up in a way which would never change, so that the customer would always be satisfied.

We insisted on an inspection with the buyer once the home was built, and we went through it with him or her with a checklist of things to be corrected. Once the family moved in, we provided an additional "fix-up" service: a hundred dollars' worth of ten-dollar coupons which they could use to call us and get little things adjusted during the one-year warranty period. At the end of that period we'd have them turn in unused coupons and receive their cash value. This gave them incentive to watch the calls they were making, helped us monitor their needs, and allowed us to train them about thermostats and circuit breakers and so forth. It also minimized the wear and tear on my employees. I remember our men yelling, "That dumbass! He's plugged in fourteen cords and tripped the circuit breaker again. That's the second time he's done that in a week. We'll have to educate him!" And that we indeed tried to do.

Many of the people who bought our houses were in their fifties, finally experiencing the home of their dreams after their children were away at college or married. Actually, we had generational business: the married children would come to us, and eventually some bought lots in Florida from us when we branched out there. One family group bought five of our homes overall.

My mother was pleased with my success, and I was proud that she could see it. She didn't drive, but I'd have lunch with her and show her some of the new places and then put her on the trolley for home. Sometimes she'd go downtown with me and have lunch, and I'd hope she'd invite my Aunt Alice, of whom I was very fond, and who lived with my mother and dad for some eighteen years after I was gone. "Please, no," Mother would say. "I see her every day and this is my special time."

THE QUALITY HOMES we were determined to deliver depended on excellent workmanship and supervision. Louis Papparazzo came to us to supervise our conventional home building, but soon went into business for himself. Then John Kleinops came to supervise the carpentry. Good workers were at a premium, and John found them in the community of Latvian immigrants who came to this country after the war.

We were putting in city utilities, paved streets, and sidewalks in those east side developments, and we had to learn to deal with the complexities of subcontracting. One example stands out in my mind, and it shows how business was largely done on a handshake, or at least with mutual trust. A gentleman named Raleigh Burke had bid on the infrastructure of one of our roads on the east side of Indianapolis, and I called him in and told him he was the low bidder. Then, on further review, I noticed he had deleted something which would have raised his price fifteen hundred dollars. I called him in and said, sadly, "Well, Raleigh, I told you you had the contract and I'm not going to change it. Through no fault of yours, I did not see the deletion which makes you higher than the lowest bid by fifteen hundred dollars. That's a lot of money, but I'm going to stand by what I told you."

Raleigh said, "You know, Glick, I've made mistakes like that. I've had to eat my bad contract reading. But I'll tell you what: because you've been straight about this, I'm going to take the fifteen hundred off the contract."

Meanwhile, as I've said earlier, the Glick family was thriving in that little home on Wallace. Here, as the fifties moved along, Marianne, Arlene, Alice, and eventually Lynda were growing up, each adding a unique element to the family. Our office was no longer in our home. We had mini-offices scattered about, wherever the construction was going on.

I was determined to be home with the family when I could. My hours have always been odd, so I didn't make it every night for dinner, but when I did get home I'd play with them. Weekends were for them. Marianne remembers I taught her to ride a bike by putting a lawnmower handle on the back of the bike, running along behind her and then pulling the handle off while she went sailing. I think she was happy in that little neighborhood on Wallace Street, playing with the neighborhood children. We had a little awards ceremony when she learned to ride the bike and all the kids applauded for her. I couldn't find a silver cup to present, so I gave her Marilyn's silver soy sauce pitcher. I tried to encourage the girls in sports. They all have individual ability in different sports. Beyond that, I think they have a strong sense of sportsmanship, which is more important than skill. We don't all have to be "Kid Glick." That's one of the lessons I learned as I got older.

It was in the mid-fifties when I myself took up golf as a regular pastime. I had played golf off and on since I was a kid, but had never taken lessons. So I developed a lot of bad habits. Golf became my game as the years went by, and I tried, definitely I tried. One time in Florida I remember I was hitting a bucket of balls on the driving range, and a man came up and stood behind me, watching. I could feel his presence as I whacked them out there all of a hundred yards. Finally, the man, who I later found out was the pro, said, "Hey, fellow, that's a nice pair of shoes you've got on!" George Valuck was his name, and he had recently completed a Dale Carnegie course on how to win friends and influence people by paying sincere compliments. I guess that was the most sincere compliment he felt he could give me then.

We took lessons from George there in Florida and brought him up at least once a summer for lessons for the whole family. But his shoe comment became a family joke; if one of the kids performed below average, another one was sure to say, "Wow! Like your shoes!"

I enjoyed the game. If I broke ninety, to me that was true happiness. I also like to give myself a challenge, to make the game more interesting. If I can't break ninety—and nowadays that's most of the time—I give myself "points." Through eighteen holes I get one point for a par and two for a birdie. Therefore I can say I have two opportunities to find happiness on the golf course: one if I break ninety, and two if I earn six points!

Arlene was the most sports-inclined, and George approved of her smooth swing. "Why can't you all play like Arlene?" he once asked the rest of us. I called the man aside, and told him, "George, you can ask that question of my wife or me, but don't say it in front of her sisters. It spoils the game for them."

Our firstborn, Marianne, December 1949.

Marilyn and Lynda.

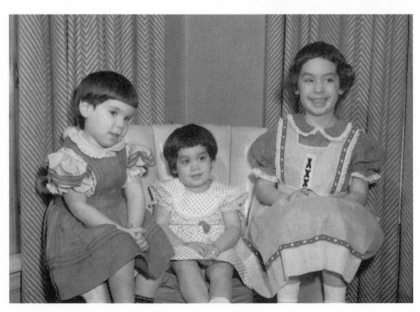

(*Left to right*) Arlene, Alice, and Marianne. Lynda hadn't arrived yet.

CHAPTER 6

BUILDING NATIONAL HOMES

The first mark of good business is the ability to deliver—to deliver its product or service on time and in the condition in which the client was led to expect. This dedication to provision and quality gives rise to corporate reliability. It makes friends and, in the end, is the reason why solvent companies remain solvent.

—Michael J. T. Ferguson

THOUGH WE WERE QUITE BUSY in the present in those early years, my sights were also on the horizon. Bob Whipple, a longtime friend, was a key salesman in the company's early period and the husband of Helen, my secretary then. He once said that as an accountant he'd had clients who always wanted him to "change yesterday." He could never find out how to do that, he said, but at our company he saw we always tried to look out for the next day, next month, next year.

By the mid-fifties we were beginning to do that. It wasn't that we tired of building single-family, residential homes; it was just that we set our sights always on the next idea, wanted to consolidate our energies, build more homes more efficiently, and get a greater return for our work. We turned towards something a little different, and that something was National Homes.

As I've said, there was at this time a tremendous pent-up and continuing desire for home ownership. The economy continued to heat up as the fifties rolled along. Returned servicemen and workers who were being paid to man America's peacetime machines continued to want homes of their own. Single-family custom home builders like me could never answer the need for all those houses, especially in the low-cost market. I began to read in the trade publications that a new concept of mass-market building was being tested successfully. It involved prefabricating of house walls and assembly line production of small homes. These homes could be put up in a few days if necessary, with standardization of the plans and services as the key. It sounded interesting.

I went with my future next-door neighbor Fred Falender to a seminar on some of the new building techniques at Purdue University. The first day of this two-day seminar was boring, but during one of the breaks I talked to the representative of National Homes, which I knew produced manufactured homes. "I'd like to see your product," I said, and he invited me to come to the plant. What I saw was really revolutionary. It was an assembly line of prefab house production, with various phases of framing being prepackaged right under the roof and in the yard there.

George and James Price of Lafayette had actually started National Homes in 1940. They had paid a dollar for a factory site and borrowed $12,500 from friends to begin producing prefabricated homes. The first National Home had been built on south 29th Street in Lafayette the summer of 1940, and the Prices sold it for $1,398.24 to a developer, who in turn sold the home for $3,250.

Ten years later the Price brothers' National Homes was the largest U.S. manufacturer of prefabricated homes. By early 1955, when I was beginning to be interested in them, they'd already built eighty-four thousand prefabricated homes through more than six hundred franchised builder-dealers in forty-one states.

There was a method for how this revolutionary building concept worked in practical application. Almost without exception, National Homes were built on concrete slabs. The underground plumbing, heating, wiring, and so forth were placed in the slab prior to the time the concrete was poured, and was ready so the final work could be quickly done. Then the prefabricated segments of the home were brought in and quickly "plugged in." Over a period of time a rig was developed to lift the heavy panels to the construction site, where carpenters could assemble them. Framing took a day, possibly two. It was entirely under roof in another day or two. Then subcontractors came in to whisk up the drywall and slot in plumbing and kitchen fixtures. In our heyday we were able to complete four homes a day. From the time the home was delivered until it could be occupied fully completed was routinely about three weeks. We did an experiment and were able to put a completed home up in one long day.

Naturally these sophisticated prefabrication and building organizational methods saved large amounts of money. I came home and told Marilyn, "This National Homes is coming out with a very inexpensive home, and I think I'd be interested in becoming a builder for them." Even poor people could afford their spiffy little Cadet model, so that's what we chose to build. Again, the concept of "how much can we give 'em for the money and still make a profit?" was driving me along.

Preserving quality within the modest price structure was an intriguing challenge to us. We took great pride in the fact that most people could not identify the homes we built as prefabricated homes. We traveled around the country picking up new ideas from the brightest and the best in the building industry and incorporated these into the National Homes. The homes had either two, three, or four bedrooms, often with a family room, full kitchen, some with two baths, some bi-level or tri-level. All of the developments were on fully paved streets with all utilities provided, including curbs, sidewalks, storm and sanitary sewers, gas, water, and electricity.

I had sensed that the National Homes concept was a revolutionary one, and I was right. The idea of quick, expertly prefabricated homes for the masses really extended far beyond individual National Homes franchise owners and house purchasers. In the first place, having thousands of new homeowners stimulated the economy wherever the developments sprang up. New shopping centers were built; services had to be provided within reach of the developments. Schools and libraries and hospitals were built and staffed. Everybody benefited.

Suburbs popped up like colonies of mushrooms. With the concept of prefabricated homes, America could very quickly come of age as a nation of home owners, and National Homes led the way. The concept of prefabrication in the building industry caught on quickly. Soon prefab units became available through some of the larger lumber yards in the area, and Burnet Binford and Southport Lumber learned the techniques of assembly-line prefabrication and began to compete with National Homes. Eventually assembly-line, highly organized, and intensive focus building to meet cost-time limits became the standard in the housing industry everywhere.

In 1954 we became a franchised dealer for National Homes' Cadet model and began plans for a subdivision just west of Emerson, near 30th Street. First, though, we had to straighten out how the financing would work for the individual home buyer. Financing is always the number one consideration in home building. We submitted the Cadet plans and the basis for our ability to put up a home in one day to FHA and VA. FHA stated that these plans did not fit their standards and they had no way to waive them without a lengthy procedure in Washington. VA, on the other hand, provided a means to financing, in part because local directors had more discretion as to whether or not they could waive standards in plans. The local director, a farsighted man named Paul Burkholder, realized that veterans would best be served by getting them into homes of their own. "Glick," he said, "I think what you and National Homes are proposing makes sense, and you have such slight variations from VA standards that I'm going to waive them." And he did.

In 1954 we completed a small model of the Cadet in the new subdivision. The homes were to sell for about five thousand dollars, really phenomenal when you think of it. Truly, it was a social revolution and a gift to home-starved American workers, with two bedrooms, a living room, dining room, full kitchen, and bath, built on a paved street with curbs and sidewalks and all utilities in place.

We advertised, had the model home nicely furnished, and pitched a tent next to it, because we knew we'd have plenty of people. But even we weren't prepared for the turnout. Again, we were overwhelmed. It was like a gourmet food shop; people had to take a number and wait in line to discuss the home with us. They were actually fighting with each other in those lines! Marilyn and some friends of ours had typewriters there (we were prepared this time) and they typed the contracts. By the end of the day all seventy-seven Cadets were sold.

Of course, some buyers didn't qualify and we had to re-sell a few homes, but that wasn't a problem this time. When the weekend was over we had sold all of them.

The next year we built a slightly larger National Homes model at 32nd and DeQuincy, and we had a harried time with our open house this time. The weather at that time—the end of March—was terrible; we tried to pull the ad from the paper because we didn't think we could handle all that traffic in bad weather. The ad appeared anyway on Saturday, and things got worse from there. Two of the children had chicken pox; Marilyn had an infection in her leg, which hurt terribly and to which she had to apply hot compresses; and the live-in housekeeper was away for Easter week. Still, the people came, and still, we had to find ways to sign them up.

We built 150 homes on DeQuincy in that second phase of the National Homes development, and it was only one part of the building we'd soon be doing.

ZONING HAD NOT BEEN A PROBLEM for us in the years we'd been in business, and I was accustomed to going to the planning commission routinely. But at one meeting there in 1956 we received a surprise. The planning commission turned us down, without really saying why. "Somebody's objecting," said the attorney, "but I really can't get a handle on it. It's peculiar." They rescheduled the hearing, and in circumstances that seemed strangely fishy, the commission turned us down again. We'd have to return all the money, an awful prospect for anyone, but particularly for us in those cash-poor days.

I went to the driving range. I bought a bucket of balls and, steaming with ire, began to hit them. I teed up a ball. "This is for Commissioner So-and-So!" I fumed and then hit the stuffing out of the ball. "And this for ——," and another sizzling ball. I whacked all of them off into kingdom come with great satisfaction and then left, the bucket empty and my anger relieved. It was one of the few times when thinking of November 11, 1944, didn't help. After that, going out to the driving range became therapy for future frustrating situations.

Why had we been turned down? Political heat was evidently being turned up on the commissioners from an unknown source about the traffic problems our development would create. Apparently not everyone thought National Homes developments were perfect for an area. Politicians don't like to hear that voters will be irritated by traffic problems. But we never really knew.

In the mid-fifties several developers were building National Homes on the west side of Indianapolis: Bill Jennings and John Lookabill; DeCamp Realty with Harry Tousley, Bob Park, Bob Welch, and Herb Lewis (who was inducted into the International Hockey Hall of Fame); and Roy VanArsdale and John Hart. The Paul Cripe Company, which included Cripe, Jim and Bill Dankert, and later, Al Oak, was involved in the building of National Homes for individuals who owned their own lots.

The lots and houses sold quickly, and thus by the mid-fifties we were looking for more land. In 1956 we began the Sycamore Heights project, a 148-home National Homes development along East 42nd between Emerson and Arlington avenues. As I've said, some of the time business in those heady days was done by handshake and trust—and sometimes it wasn't. The year before, 1955, I had run into a rather important deal that wasn't.

As we planned to build in the area south of 42nd between Emerson and Arlington, we had to secure the land we needed. A big-time operator from New Orleans had bought a large tract of land in the area. A portion of that land had been bought by a first-class character I'll call "Porky the Pig," because he looked like that cartoon character. We were trying to buy that part of the New Orleans man's tract but couldn't, because Porky was holding up our man, knowing we wanted to make a deal. Porky hadn't paid for the land, and the New Orleans businessman was threatening to foreclose, but Porky held him up as if at gunpoint; he knew Indiana law and knew that foreclosure was slow and difficult. "You can forget selling to Glick or anybody," Porky told him. "I'll declare bank-

This home in Forest Manor is an example of typical construction of the early 1950s.

The grand opening of Sycamore Heights, a National Homes project, was a tremendous success.

ruptcy and you'll never get the land. It'll be held up in court proceedings forever. You better make me a deal." Finally the man did manage to make a deal with the Porker, after offering a cash consideration to him beyond the actual land price.

The final settlement was expedited by my old neighborhood friend Bernie Landman, the former six-year-old who loved to play ball with the bigger kids and who had also developed an early penchant for gambling.

Other developers were involved with us in trying to develop this tract between Emerson and Arlington. Al Lieberman and Joe Goldsmith, the father of Indianapolis Mayor Steve Goldsmith, were planning to build conventional homes in an area west of us. Stan Herman would be to the east of us. We were involved in having to solve the land problem together.

Bernie, one of the attorneys representing Stan Herman, distinguished himself as a superior lawyer in the proceedings. In the final negotiations, when both sides bogged down amidst the complex contract details. Porky the Pig finally threw a fit and stormed out, muttering, "You guys can all go to hell! I'm going home!" I followed him out and tried to calm him down. I knew he wanted to sell the land, and he knew I wanted to buy it. Surely the two of us could reach an agreement.

We did so and went back in the room and announced that we had worked things out but we needed the contract right away. My attorney said he couldn't get to it for two weeks, and Goldsmith and Lieberman's attorney said it would be a month before he could work on it. At that point Bernie said, "Give me the papers." The two of us went off into another room. I spelled out the details and in less than an hour Bernie had drafted a final, crystal-clear document that Porky and the other developers signed. Thus the matter was settled, and Bernie became our attorney.

During this period we built him a National Home at 42nd and Ritter. He and his new wife, who was expecting their first child, were living in an apartment development named The Meadows. They wanted a home in time for the birth, so the speed of the National Homes concept was attractive to him, along with what he called "the world's best financing." He and his family lived in the home we built them for many years.

Sycamore Heights was a success, and we quickly followed it with East Sycamore Heights, announced January 27, 1957. Two hundred and nineteen homes were planned for an eighty-acre plot between 16th Street and 21st Street, a fourth of a mile east of Shadeland. Another section known as Bel-Air was soon under way.

Most of the homes in the Sycamore Heights divisions were in the Shiloh H. Shambaugh price range—from thirteen thousand to eighteen thousand dollars. These roomy National Homes were on lots which averaged 75 feet by 150, had a utility half bath, separate dining room, and usually a basement. The home itself was 28 feet 9 inches by 40 feet 8 inches.

In 1957 Indianapolis Homes celebrated its tenth anniversary with several events. First was a giant springtime party on 21st Street in Sycamore Heights. Friends and our homeowners crowded around a six-foot-tall birthday cake. An antique steam calliope belonging to one Harry Shell of St. Louis (one of two similar models in the nation) blasted out circus tunes you could literally hear for two miles. A little curly haired girl named Marianne handed out birthday cake, and my mother and father were there to add to the celebration. He was now working as a part-time salesman.

My father had been retired for six months in 1957, about the time we were selling houses in Sycamore Heights and the other similar area named Bel-Air, and he asked me to give him something to do. He began selling homes for us, and he did so beautifully. He was a handsome man, with a head of thick snow-white hair. Later, when we were selling apartment units, women would come in to look at them and he would flatter them a little, saying, "I don't know if this will work for you. You have to be over fifty-five years of age to qualify for these units." These women were obviously in their seventies. Often they'd talk to him a while and sign up on the spot.

My dad also got involved in selling lots at Port Charlotte, a large development in Florida which had caught my interest about the time the National Homes were booming for us in Indianapolis. I had read in one of the building publications about the Mackle

Company, which had bought thousands of acres on the east and west coasts of Florida and was building and developing an enormous community. In 1955 I had called the Mackle Company and in my typical fashion asked them if they would share advice on how they had assembled such large tracts of land.

The president agreed to answer my specific questions by mail, but then he said, "What we're doing is selling lots in a major development, something that was done back in the twenties and hasn't been tried since. The lot buyers will put ten dollars down and pay on contract—ten dollars a month. You're from . . . where? . . . Indianapolis? We could use a representative for our company up there. We're having a meeting at Key Biscayne in September. Would you like to come down and talk to us?"

We both agreed to check each other out, and we did become a representative for Port Charlotte for two or three years, with my dad as one of the main representatives. Many people tell me my father sold them lots in Port Charlotte, or that they rented apartments or bought homes from him, and they recall their contacts with him with sincere pleasure.

WE CONTINUED TO HAVE SUCCESS building both conventional and National Homes until about 1958. Then events—and the market—seemed to turn against us for a while. First of all, the summer of 1958 was exceptionally rainy. We had had another of those very successful open houses just before this, and we were committed to building the infrastructure. The earth-moving equipment couldn't make any progress, and the workmen from Indianapolis Power and Light Company, Citizens Gas Company, and the Indianapolis Water Company would get all bogged down and couldn't function.

We were getting desperate. People were calling us saying, "Why isn't our house going up? When are we going to get in?" And all we could do is say, "We don't have any control over this. You'll have to talk to The Man Upstairs." I believe it rained each day until the middle of August, then suddenly, it cleared. It seemed to have wrung the cloth dry, rained itself out, because the rest of the year

Jim Price, CEO of National Homes, presented me with an award in 1955 for building and selling in excess of one hundred homes that year.

was beautiful. The sun dried up the mud and finally we began to work and made up in that late summer and fall the time we'd lost in the spring and summer.

I was proud of myself for what we'd done here in this development and I took my mother out to see the homes. She didn't usually criticize the homes we had built, but she looked at the National Homes and said, "You ought to be ashamed of yourself. All these houses look alike. People are going to go to the wrong door." I told her, "There are different style fronts, Mom. Some are brick and some are stone. Some will have shutters and some won't." She nodded, but like thousands of other Americans, she thought the National Homes concept odd. Many other people were saying, "These things will fall down in ten years." But, interestingly enough, they haven't. Many of these homes have been added to, kept up, and the little maple trees we planted have grown tall and the people who bought them have grown old with the houses, and in many cases just as gracefully, I'm sure. In fact, several of these homes have sold recently for as much as eighty-five thousand dollars. The concept worked.

My mother grew increasingly inactive by 1959 and 1960, uninterested in, or unable to travel extensively, as my father wanted to do. I don't think I ever took her out to see the brick and stone fronts, the little shrubs and porches and fireplace chimneys that made the homes on the street look different. And I really don't think anybody ever went into the wrong house.

As I said, our sales lagged a bit about this time, 1959 and '60. I began to worry that our competition would get ahead of us. It seems odd to think so, because by all standards we were very successful. We had 12 percent of the Marion County building market and were building about two houses a day and up to five hundred houses a year. Excellent, really, for a company which had started only ten years before with one husband and wife team frantically trying to cover Friday paychecks on their first spec house.

But we weren't Number One, and the competitors were clever. We'd check their sales as best we could, even to the point of stationing monitors in their parking lots to see how much customer traffic they had. I hired one employee with a motor bike to zip around to their openings and see how many cars were lined up.

We wanted to be more than good—we wanted to be Number One, to let the rest see our taillights. In 1960 I read an article in the National Association of Home Builders magazine about marketing homes. I called the author, Kelly Snow, and asked him to come evaluate our business, our town, and our competition as he could see it. Out he came to Indianapolis and took a look at our operation. He asked to see our ads, visited our sites, and went to those of our competitors. He had a lot of good advice.

Among the suggestions he made was improving our advertising. "You've done well with advertising, but you need to look for a good personalized, small advertising agency to customize what you do," he said. Scouting around himself, he came up with Jack Dickhaus' agency, Venus Arts, and Jack came to work for what was known by now as the Gene B. Glick Company, around 1960 or '61.

Jack Dickhaus was well known for his creative, innovative ads, and he came up with a campaign advertising our seven model homes as "seven plum pretty models." The ad showed seven attractive young lady models dressed in plum-colored dresses. *Plum pretty*—it was a catchy phrase that capitalized not only on a popular and appealing color but on the concept of the plumb line as a symbol of exact and excellent building skill. The good ads he designed caught on not only with Indiana people, but with people as far away as Arizona.

Jack recalls those times himself with quite a bit more color than I can. Let him tell the story:

I came to admire Glick's homes before I even knew him. You could drive down the streets and see all these neat little homes in a row, with nicely growing maple trees in the yards. Some had well-maintained driveways. They just looked good. His consultant Kelly Snow came to see me and liked what I did. The first subdivision we developed a campaign for was Bel-Air at 42nd and Arlington. I designed an ad with a huge arrow that trumpeted forth the values of "Grand Opening" special. Then later we put up a huge sign to give DeCamp Realty and Bob Welch a hard time. The hugest sign you could build was put up on Post Road, with lights on it. It was day-glo red. Right across the street was the R. V. Welch parking lot. I think half the traffic going to Welch's would end up at Glick's.

We used the home and garden section of the newspapers to attract home buyers, and we also had men in clown suits posted along Post Road. They had big cut-out thumbs pointing people to the Glick models there. Eventually we hired Roger Ward and Eddie Sachs, the 500 Mile Race drivers. Later, Debbie Drake, the exercise queen, would go up in a helicopter and shout out that our south side development was just below her.

Any promotion that would get them in to buy—we had a "penny down for a home" promotion, and a "work equity"—put in your own yard and paint the inside yourself.

More than anything was Gene's ability to handle customers with aplomb—to insist that the managers take their "turtle cards" recording their upkeep problems and see that they got done. He listens patiently to people and he tries to help them. I recall once in Florida—later, this was—when we had all been brought down to Palm Beach and we were going into a restaurant called the Petite Marmite, which didn't have our table ready as Gene had expected. Marilyn began to be justifiably upset about the wait and I could see Gene listening to her, nodding patiently, explaining about the restaurant trying to get a table. He was so understanding. She left and a man came up to Gene. "Maître d', can you get us in any earlier?" he asked Gene. "Why do you think I work here?" Gene asked, surprised. "Well, you handled that other customer so diplomatically a minute ago, and she went away so happy, I thought you were in charge!"

Or maybe I just looked like I should be showing people to tables!

Those "turtle cards" had an interesting history. Years ago I'd bought a car from the Pontiac dealer. When I took the car in for its first checkup, they gave me a little green card with a turtle on it, on its back, yelling "Help!" The dealership was supposed to be like a flipped turtle, I guess; it needed the customer to rate the service, to tell the company how its people were performing. I thought that was a great idea. As we were building, many people had great ideas for improving our service, and as we went into apartment management, I wanted them to rate our service each month. What did we need to do? Where were we strong? How could we improve? The turtle cards we passed out then, and still pass out, really serve to give good feedback to our employees. Ninety-five percent of the cards are favorable. It's important that we know about the unfavorable, too. Today these turtle missives are self-addressed stamped postcards mailed to the home office.

One of the best things we ever did was to hire Jack Dickhaus. With his promotion, our own growing expertise, and the huge market for homes during the late fifties and sixties, sales just burgeoned. It gives me pause even today: from 1961 to 1962 the Gene B. Glick Company built 1,111 dwellings, most of them National Homes at three subdivisions on the east side of Indianapolis: Towne East, Young America, and Bel-Air. The 1,111 homes was an all-time record for any Indiana construction company, and in 1962 our company accounted for twelve percent of Marion County's new housing market.

In 1961, on Easter weekend, the Gene B. Glick Company closed seventy-seven sales at Young America, totaling more than $1 million. In the early- and mid-1960s we sold more than 2,500 homes in Indianapolis for National Homes. In 1965 the company sold $5.4 million worth of National Homes units (co-op apartments), and the next year $4.54 million worth.

One thing about those statistics is crystal-clear to me: they are a direct result of the work of many exceptional people. The success we had then, and the success we've had for the past three decades, is directly related to the outstanding associates who came into the company during this period.

I've already spoken of Jack Kline—how he used to help with the sales in the tent, tend Marianne, race about trying to finish projects. He was Jack-of-all-trades, with Glick at least.

Lu—Lumir—Palma came in January of 1962 to become the marketing director, an important position for us now that we had so many sales and subdivisions going at once. He tells a story which illustrates how much pressure we all lived under during those National Homes days, and how good the people in the organization were from top to bottom:

During those days we had a building superintendent named Kelso Lightle, a tremendous, wiry man, extremely competent. The remarkable thing about him was that he understood the relationship of marketing, my department, and building, his. If he couldn't perform building houses I wouldn't have anything to sell, and if I didn't sell, he wouldn't have anything to work on.

He could work under all kinds of pressure. When I'd come to him with a customer who was desperate for a house and needed it within a month in order to close the deal, Kelly would swear at me and say, "You SOB, I'll have it for you in the month." And he would. On a Friday morning I would give Kelly a punch list of things which needed to be done in the model homes—carpet cleaned, walls painted, shrubs watered, or whatever—and by Saturday morning when the weekend traffic was due, it would all be done.

Out on the east side where many developers were fighting tooth and toenail for the business, Perrine began advertising a subdivision he was calling "Brickshire"—right in the heart of Glick territory. Large ads appeared one Sunday, saying "Don't buy a home until you see Brickshire, an all-brick development." These ads appeared two weeks before the purported opening.

The next day, Monday, Gene and I and Kelly were driving to Lafayette, where the Price brothers were to give Gene an award for being one of the premier builders of National Homes, and Gene said to me, "Lu, what are we going to do about Brickshire?"

"Nothing that I can think of," I replied, "because to counter that ad I'd have to have an all-brick home we could picture in an ad for our subdivision by next Sunday. And this is Monday. Kelly

8330 Woodfield Crossing—the current home of the Gene B. Glick Company.

Golf, the beloved pastime.

(*Above*) Fairington of Lafayette. (*Below*) Attractive landscaping, including shade trees and ponds, provide an enjoyable pastoral setting for the residents of the Woodlake Apartments in Indianapolis.

(*Above*) Winter at the Woods of Eagle Creek on Indianapolis' west side. (*Left*) The clubhouse at Chelsea Village on the north side of Indianapolis.

A special anniversary garden is being constructed at each apartment complex to honor the fiftieth anniversary of the company. The trees in the gardens were planted in honor of the company's forty-fifth anniversary in 1992.

One of the most successful newspaper and television campaigns we ever ran was the one in the sixties featuring local celebrity and exercise guru Debbie Drake. We made a practice of asking how people heard about the particular development they were visiting, and they would often tell us they heard about it from Debbie Drake—even several years after she was no longer promoting us!

Air-Conditioned Model Shown By Glick Company

AIR-CONDITIONED HOME SHOWN AT YOUNG AMERICA HOMES
Price Of $11,660 Includes Air Conditioning And Lot.

A fully air-conditioned three-bedroom ranch home priced at $11,660, including a landscaped lot, is being shown today by the Gene B. Glick Company at Young America Homes, East 30th Street and Post Road.

The home is cooled by a three-ton central air conditioning system manufactured by the Bryant Heating and Cooling Company.

NAMED THE Sycamore, this model, in addition to three large bedrooms, contains a formal living room, full bath, kitchen-dining area and storage area. The exterior is of maintenance-free aluminum.

The Bryant heating system which is used in all Glick homes is constructed in such a manner that air-conditioning can be added easily and economically at a later date by those persons not including air conditioning with the origional purchase of their Glick home.

Gene B. Glick, president of the building and development firm, said that more and more persons are buying homes with central air conditioning, not only because of comfort, but also for the cleanliness and healthful living conditions provided by air conditioning.

The air-conditioned Sycamore can be purchased with monthly payments of $73 including principal, interest, taxes and insurance.

Buyers can earn their down payment for this home by completing their interior painting and light yard work through Glick's "paint and plant" program.

Because of extra insulation in the sidewalls and ceilings of all Glick homes, air conditioning operates efficiently and economically in these homes.

IF THE air-conditioning system is added at a later date, the simple installation does not require the removal of any walls, heating ducts or wiring.

All models at Young America are fully air conditioned.

The development is inside the Indianapolis city limits and includes all city services and utilities. Schools, shopping centers and professional offices are within easy walking distance.

Newspaper advertorials like this one for Young America brought 'em in by the hundreds.

INDIANAPOLIS, INDIANA—APRIL 1st, 2nd

$1,000,000

IN HOME SALES ON EASTER SUNDAY FOR NATIONAL HOMES DEALER

71 SALES IN 2 DAYS FOR BUILDER GENE B. GLICK

Featuring these big Nationals—priced from only $9,990 —including lot & maintenance free VIKING aluminum exterior!

MODEL 1433

A spacious three bedroom budget home which sells in Indianapolis for $9,990, including the lot. It contains 912 square feet of living space, including living room, kitchen with dining area, bath and a large inside storage room.

21 SALES

MODEL 1631

Another economy plan, with 989 square feet of living area. It has three bedrooms with floor-to-ceiling closets, bath, living room, kitchen, dining area and storage room. Price with lot in Indianapolis is $10,790.

29 SALES

MODEL 1885

An "L-shaped" home with attached garage and more than 1200 square feet of living area. The house, which sells in Indianapolis for $12,890 with lot, has three bedrooms, 1 ½ baths, living room, kitchen, dining area, and family room.

13 SALES

MODEL 1533

A big 2-level split-foyer home priced with lot at $12,990 in Indianapolis. It has 1377 square feet of living area. The upper level features three bedrooms, bath, living room, dining room and kitchen. The lower level has a 18 by 24 foot area for recreation room, and another 18 by 24 foot area which can be finished for 2 additional bedrooms plus bath, a hobby room, workshop, or various other uses.

8 SALES

Let National analyze your subdivision and provide the house that will sell!

There's a National or subsidiary plant nearby to give you immediate personal service.

An ad featuring our success in selling National Homes appeared in the April 7, 1961, *Wall Street Journal.* Jim Price, National Homes CEO, presented me with the copper printing plate from that ad. It hangs on the wall of our home office.

can't do that . . ." A voice spoke up from the back seat. "You SOB. Don't tell me what I can and can't do."

Gene had a hundred questions. Where would we put it? There were no open lots in the model-home sales area of Young America, the logical subdivision. He wanted to know if there was a less-popular house we could do something with, anything to meet the competition. "Well, we'd have to do a complete remodel. That always takes longer than building one from scratch. But maybe . . ."

To make a long story short, by the time we left the awards banquet, Jim Price, the CEO of National Homes, was saying to Kelly, "Okay—by 4 o'clock Wednesday morning these trusses and panels will go out of here for you." On Tuesday I called our advertising agency and told them we'd need a full-page ad in color in the next Sunday's paper touting, "Here's the brick home you've been waiting for." We had nothing on which to base the ad, but I went on to commit to TV and radio advertising too.

Everything had to happen at once, as it usually did anyway, but particularly in this case. On Wednesday our ad agency lady called complaining. "I'm trying to shoot pictures like you wanted of the interior of the house next door for the ad, and there are thirty guys over there working and making so much noise remodeling that house that I can't shoot. Kelly won't make them stop."

I came over. "Kelly, we've got a problem. We need to shoot . . ."

"You've got a problem. I don't have a problem. I have to have a house built by Saturday. You want a house by Saturday, and I am gonna give you a house by Saturday. Now get out of the way." We worked it out, of course, and by Sunday there it was: big as life, paint still a little wet, but fully furnished and shining, "the brick house you've always wanted"—with sod growing nicely in the front yard. This was a week before Brickshire opened its model.

When our scout went around on the motor bike the next week, there were no cars in Brickshire's parking lot. We were mobbed. And the following Sunday, for their grand opening,

Brickshire had maybe six or seven cars, but our lot was full once again.

There was a lot of strenuous competition among all the National Homes builders. We'd offer low-low down payments, ranging from five hundred dollars down to a penny! I remember the company's controller at the time, John Eckwart (who was funny enough to be a stand-up comedian) told us one of his friends had asked about an ad which said, "One dollar moves you in."

"What's the one dollar for?" the friend wanted to know. John answered with a straight face: "To keep out the riffraff."

John was one of several excellent people who came to the company during the sixties.

I've said it several times in this account: Get good people and give them free rein. And let the competitors see your taillights.

Good people—there are several more that need to be spoken of right about now. But that's the material of a new phase of the Gene B. Glick Company, one that would mean phenomenal growth and a final closing out of our association with the company which had brought us such success—National Homes.

CHAPTER 7
INTO MULTIFAMILY HOUSING

The more people who own little businesses of their own, the safer our country will be and the better off its cities and towns; for the people who have a stake in their country and their community are the best citizens.

—John Hancock

BY THE 1960S MAJOR CHANGES were under way in the building business. Though we'd had tremendous success with National Homes, the Indiana market for these homes had been changing in the last few years. First of all, the original building partnerships had shifted. Harry Tousley of DeCamp Realty, who had been in competition with us on the east side, had gotten out of the single-family building business. Various other partnerships in the National Homes business formed and dissolved. But the National presence was just about complete on the west side, and it was impressive: Eagledale, a project developed by several builders, was the talk of the town. Eagledale became a city unto itself, with shopping centers and its own library and public schools built just to cover the major influx of people into that National Homes community. "They throw 'em up in one day. It'll all fall down in thirty years," conservative people sniffed as they drove along 30th Street. Wrong: like the other National Homes communities (and depending on the upkeep of individuals who live there), Eagledale is still a viable community of attractive homes, with the "mature plantings" real estate people love to talk about these days.

In the early- and mid-sixties Bob Welch was building on the east side of town, south of 38th; we built north. About this time, it should be said, Welch joined forces with developer Leo Lipman. The houses themselves were growing more sophisticated. The public demanded more spacious houses—twelve hundred square feet, with family rooms, and more elegant exteriors and interior planning. Central air conditioning and gas-fired furnaces had come in, a great improvement for modest homes, because some homeowners couldn't afford to keep their buried oil tanks full, and during a heavy rain they'd pop out of the ground.

We looked for amenities, and even within the National Homes parameters, we were able to do some customizing. We had a pretty snazzy model, and the customer could add space on either side in four-foot increments. When Bernie Landman bought his house in 1956, after the Porky the Pig incident, the salesmen returned to us to ask, "Is this right—LaMarque plus four plus four on the left and four plus four on the right?" Bernie wanted to add eight feet on either side, and it is a good-sized home to this day.

The prices we had to charge for the homes were going up too. All of us in the National Homes business had originally sold most homes for about ten thousand dollars, and the Cadet had actually sold for the hard-to-believe price of five thousand. By the mid- to late fifties, though, property taxes had gone up. We needed to have payments of a hundred dollars now, and it worried us. The market was able to bear the cost increase, though, and the concept endured. All of us in the National Homes business—on both the east and west sides of the city—had continued selling homes like popcorn, twelve hundred homes a year by 1956.

However, in 1959 Indianapolis and Marion County formed a Metropolitan Planning Commission, eventually the Metropolitan Development Commission. They placed increasing restrictions on all subdivision development.

It was all getting so complex. I knew also that the company was going to have to get much more savvy with the increasingly complicated world of financing. Bernie Landman fit the bill as our attorney very well: not only was he quite knowledgable in the world of finance, he knew the FHA regulations backward and forward.

At the same time we were still building some conventional homes; it's well to remember that. We had a project east of Shadeland in '58 and '59—the Glick East 21st Street Addition—between Shadeland Avenue and Franklin, with all the streets named after my daughters: Marianne Avenue, Arlene Boulevard, Alice Jeanne Court, and Lynda Lane.

But our projects in that area were jeopardized by "progress." Rather, call it bureaucratic stupidity. We had laid out several streets and put in quite a bit of the development's infrastructure in an area which the State Highway Commission was looking at for building Interstate 465 and its interchanges. The head of the State Highway Commission, who had formerly been head of FHA, sent a letter to FHA requesting that the agency not issue any commitments for loan guarantees for building in our subdivisions or in Tousley-Welch's. They might need to acquire the land for right-of-way for the highways. "Might" was the key word; they had no firm plan for taking this land for the highway.

Most of the people buying homes in this subdivision needed FHA mortgages. It put a crimp in our business. I couldn't believe an entire business venture would be held up, possibly ruined, because the state "might" decide to use this land at some time in the future. Our investment was large; we had bought the land and paid for it, streets and curbs were poured. We had to pay interest on the cost of the land and improvements.

Tousley, still involved to some extent at that point in his company, was concerned too. His venture was in the same area, and we spoke about a strategy to unlock these FHA mortgages. In his case, though, it wasn't vital; he was a man of means. It was like the story of the chicken and the pig walking down the street in a little Southern town and seeing a sign that says, "Ham and eggs, fifty cents." The chicken says, "Well, I guess we'd better go in and make our contribution." The pig says, "You'll make a contribution, but for me this is a TOTAL COMMITMENT!" And mine was total; I was the porker in this case. This was a situation where the state could do severe financial damage to us.

After hassling with the FHA representatives, I decided to go directly to the governor, Harold Handley (he was governor from 1957 to 1961). I went to his office and met his administrative assistant, and I said I wanted to see the governor. "What is it about?" the assistant wanted to know. I explained. "You can talk about this for three years and completely stop our development and at the end of three years say, 'Well, I guess we don't really need that ground.' In the meantime, we'll be in serious financial shape."

I failed to gain entry, but I kept coming back. Finally, I made so much noise in the outer office that they let me in to see the governor, a very helpful man, really. Some courteous letters came, saying the state intended to decide within a "short time." I wrote back, "In the meantime, you need to have your state people notify FHA that they can issue commitments." It didn't happen, though I was down there making noise almost every week.

One day I read in a national building publication that government agencies all over the country were having problems trying to deal fairly with people caught up in the decision-making process over the right-of-way for the interstates. One government agency, the article said, had decided that unless the taking of the right-of-way was "imminent and assured," other government agencies were not to take any action that would restrict an individual's free use of the land. Eureka! Carrying this article in my hand, I went to the head of FHA. The following conversation ensued:

FHA: Glick, what do you want me to do about this?

GLICK: I want you to issue commitments. When people want to buy homes, issue commitments.

FHA: Well, I don't know if I can do that. I have a letter from the state highway commission.

GLICK: Well, why don't we get together in a little meeting—the highway commissioner, the FHA attorney, the highway attorney, and my attorney. We'll have some interpretations here about this.

And when the meeting with Mr. Dawson from the highway commission occurred, this one:

DAWSON: Mr. Glick, the state is going to decide shortly.

GLICK: Shortly, hell! You people have tied up this land of mine without cause; we can be sure if it was your land and your political connections we'd have had a decision already.

FHA: We have the authority to hold on committing.

GLICK: What you are holding on is our ability to proceed and fulfill our company obligations. You no longer have the authority to do that. Have you read and understood this government regulation? This is the exact one, from Washington.

FHA: We need to think about this. We'll have to get clearance.

GLICK: Be sure you understand what this regulation means: Unless building the highway is "*imminent and assured*"!

Within two weeks we did have action—a letter from the highway commission stating that the taking of the right-of-way was imminent and assured. They were prepared to give us the shaft. At the proper time they notified us they had condemned the ground and gave us an appraisal—really low. Our appraisal was much different—higher. We went to a lawsuit over the matter, with a jury trial. The attorney general was committed to the low appraisal; the trial went on.

We had two expert witnesses. However, one of our "experts" was a gentleman with a drinking problem which we weren't aware of when we signed him on. He got on the stand, pretty thoroughly snockered, and was asked by the other side what his credentials were. He mentioned membership in some professional organizations and the lawyer pressed him: what were the credentials for getting in the organizations? Finally, after being asked "What were the credentials?" three times, our witness mumbled, "Two dollars and your name signed to the paper." So much for that.

But after five days of dragging the thing out, Jim Beatty, our attorney, called the attorney general and said, "This entire trial is idiocy. You have a preposterous appraisal. We had one of the most respected appraisers in the state give us a figure. Why don't you call another good professional and get him to review these two appraisals and we'll agree."

Within days the attorney general had received a corroboration of our appraisal and agreed to settle, calling the trial off. The judge said, "Mr. Glick, the jury has sat here for five days waiting to be called upon to possibly determine the amount of settlement. As a matter of courtesy, would you please tell them what your settlement actually was?"

"Your honor, I don't mind doing that. They deserve something. But first I want them to tell me what they might have awarded us if it had come to that." They did, and it was very close to what we settled for. What a waste of time!

But I had another condition for telling the jury the settlement figure. I wanted to ask them a few questions. It was a rare opportunity to look into the way the judicial system works.

"What was the strongest, and what the weakest part of our case? Start with the weakest," I suggested.

The jury mentioned the tipsy appraiser—our case went downhill after that. "We all thought at first you had nothing but a bunch of jerks to give your expert testimony." But then we also had Perry Meek's son, and he was decent-sounding, looking like a young Robert Redford and really giving a brilliant performance. "The state tore into him," said one of the jurors, "and that was not good to do to this nice young man. We were all on his side. When he refuted the state's counsel, made him look bad, we wanted to stand up and applaud! You went from the valley to the top of the mountain. He made your case."

Eventually the state used part of the property for the highway. But the rest it could not use, and under the law it had to offer it to the original owner at the price paid for the land. So it eventually did come back to us and was sold to smaller builders, because we were out of the single-family home building business by then.

I guess we were pretty tough and worked hard and creatively on these cases in those days. In the sixties we were like Israel, with our backs to the sea. Necessity made us lean and smart. With such business expansion continuing, and with such cash flow needs, we had to win or go bankrupt and that's a great incentive. An old saying, "A fat dog won't hunt," is about right. To paraphrase British diarist

Samuel Johnson, "When a man knows he is to be hanged in the morning, it really helps to concentrate his mind!" Certainly, the gallows sometimes loomed in those days.

There weren't many times when I thought we couldn't meet payroll, but a couple of incidents stand out. For a very brief time in the sixties, in the boom days of National Homes, we were using National Homes Acceptance Corporation. It was run by a respected man named Frank Flynn.

We had not received a construction draw, and I called Frank Flynn and said, "I've got to make payroll, and we need that construction draw to do it." He didn't have anybody coming to Indianapolis and without today's electronic transfers, he didn't see how I could get that money in time—even if he could find it. "Have the checks ready. I'm coming up there." It was winter, tremendously icy. "Surely you won't drive up here to Lafayette," Flynn said. Surely I'd better, or my people wouldn't get paid.

I slipped and slid all over that road, but when I got there, he came up with the money somehow. I could go make the deposit and pay the workers.

Later, we couldn't always wait to pay our people while the FHA or VA took us through the clearance and OK process to make a construction draw. I'd go to the inspectors and say, "Look, you've been out there, you know the job is at the correct point for the draw. I can't afford to wait two weeks until you get around to OK'ing us. I'm going to tell you the truth: I don't have any money. You can OK this now, sign while I'm here, please, and let me take this over to the bank." And almost without exception, they would agree. They had been to the site, and they agreed with me that payroll shouldn't be held up because of paperwork. They appreciated it when I told them the embarrassing truth. It took perseverance to overcome the difficulties of this period—and there were many, along with rewards, of course.

Though the troubles with the highway system were soon over for us and other builders, they were one more thing that pushed us away from the single-family home business. Taken with all the other hassles, the increasing complexity of rules and regulations, the restrictions on building homes on small lots, and the increasing costs of putting up homes, everything pointed us in a new direction: multifamily residential buildings—apartments or similar units.

In addition, the demographics were changing. By the sixties young people were needing housing, and many of them couldn't afford single-family homes, and many didn't want all the responsibilities that go along with home-ownership. Their only option to move away from the family was to live in an apartment. Multifamily rentals—that was a good direction.

As we had done in the past, we wanted to see what was being done in other areas. We traveled around the country, looking at the best apartments we could find—luxury apartments. Our purpose was to look at the luxury units and apply what we learned to the middle- to low-income units we'd be building. We never got involved in true luxury units, ever. We always took our greatest satisfaction in providing people of lower to middle income amenities found only in luxury units—along with tremendous financing.

One of the most instructive trips we took was out West, traveling from Colorado to California and Arizona. In 1961 I asked Bernie Landman to accompany me if his law partners in Bamberger and Feibleman would agree to it. After stopping in Salt Lake City, where a very interesting Mormon builder showed us around, we arrived in San Francisco. Later, in Los Angeles, Ray Watt of the California Home Builders Association met with us. He knew our wishes—to see the creative building projects. "Glick," he told me, "you won't learn anything from visiting my projects—they're just plain vanilla. You really ought to see the Huntington Beach Townhouses being put up by Eli Broad, a developer operating out of Phoenix." So on Saturday Bernie and I drove out to Huntington Beach. We wanted to learn from the people who did the world's best job how they did it—and how we could improve on it.

I'd never been to Huntington Beach and had very little idea how they did things in California. The streets were jammed, traffic impossible—but we finally arrived at the townhouse complex. The parking lot looked as big as the Speedway's but we couldn't get near it. We had to park five blocks away. As we approached the sales office, we heard a loudspeaker booming, "Attention all sales people, mark the following units 'sold.' " Then they called off the numbers of about twenty units. The people were one giant wave, pushing to get to the sales office. It reminded me of the Speedway crush just before the gates open, when tens of thousands of people move forward, en masse. I'd always provided a human shield, fearing my children would be crushed. Here they were, tanned Californians by the hundreds, driving forward to buy townhouses.

The crowd was funneling into the mousetrap—a passage through which they had to walk to get to the models, which it was necessary to pass through to get to the sales office. There was no resisting the forward thrust; this day we ended up in a direct route to the office, though what we wanted to see were the models.

Still, it was a gorgeous office. As we got shoved through the door, a voice rang out, "Well, God damn! Gene Glick! What are you doing here?"

It was Ron Phoell, one of the bright young stars from National Homes who had quit to join the California gold rush. "I'm here to get good ideas for units in Indianapolis," I told him.

"I can't believe the coincidence. Eli Broad wants to meet you. We were just talking about it." Broad had recently won a public housing contract in Indiana, and he wanted to meet the most knowledgeable contractors in the state to find out who were reliable subcontractors.

Broad was in Phoenix, and that happened to be our next stop. We made a luncheon engagement with the man by phone, then toured the townhouses outside the office. We loved them; they were solid, fresh and appealing, with pretty kitchens featuring dishwashers and garbage disposals. At that time no one else was selling townhouses: connected, but individualized, living units. Forty-year loans were available with the government, providing marvelous financing. They were organized as a co-op; unlike a condominium, where a buyer owns his living unit, a townhouse dweller bought into the co-op, selling his unit to the co-op board when ready to move. It sounded like a great idea!

At that Phoenix lunch, I recommended some subcontractors for

Eli to use on the building project he planned in Indiana, which happened to be at Fort Harrison. Then I said, "Eli, I liked your townhouses and would like to do something like them in my hometown. They're California—I couldn't use those fronts—but I think I could adapt them to Great Lakes tastes. Will you sell the plans?"

"No," he said, "but I'll give them to you on a handshake if you'll promise never to build them in an area where I'm selling." Soon we picked up the plans and used a key piece of information he'd given us—that we could find help in building the new co-op townhouses through an organization called the Foundation for Cooperative Housing. Thanks to this group of builders who were trying innovative ideas for the mass market, we were able to bring to Indiana and other places in the Great Lakes area the latest concepts in home development.

Our contact with Eli Broad enabled our company to be first in our area with the very best. I can reflect on other people who decided to have their product be the very best—best in finance, best in the marketplace—and they keep seeking to be better, thus not only helping their own products but providing a service to the public. L. S. Ayres and the William H. Block Company in Indianapolis were like that, and I know they traveled to the best department stores in the world to seek ideas and ask how those ideas could be improved in the local setting.

While it's true I gained a lot from Eli Broad, I think he gained something more from us than the reliable subcontractors list. He later told us that he'd read our ads in the papers, that they were the cleverest he'd seen, and he began using some of the ideas in them.

IN 1962, STILL AT WORK building single-family homes in the Sycamore Heights area, south of 38th Street and just west of Franklin Road, and National Homes too, we began our first apartment community. Williamsburg East, a colonial structure at 44th and Arlington, got under way, ushering in a new era for us.

We began building this eighty-unit apartment complex in the fall of the year. We wanted it to have the special touches we'd put in individual homes, so we planned and built carefully—for the people who would live there. Bernie Landman's parents were the apartment managers, staying in one half of the construction trailer. People were so eager to rent these units that we needed to have an agent on hand all day long while they were being built. The Landmans were our agents there for many years.

About this time Nick Smyrnis began to handle many of our real estate transactions, very competently. He optioned land for us from Arlington all the way to German Church Road. Nick was one of the most civic-minded people in the city, a Sagamore of the Wabash who was sometimes invited to the White House. Nick bought us a tract of land along 62nd between Allisonville Road and State Road 37, east of Keystone. This was to become Williamsburg North, built in 1965 under conventional financing.

This spot was a turkey farm which had enjoyed some small fame for years in northeast Indianapolis. Schoolchildren and families used to come out at Thanksgiving and Christmas and see all the gobblers running around waiting to get their heads cut off.

Nick remembers some minor problems getting possession of the land:

> *We had to find the time when the turkeys weren't hatching and when they could all be gathered together. The Jensens (the owners) were lovely people, and they were particularly concerned about the turkeys. They loved them. The property was some thirty acres east of Allisonville and north of Eastwood Middle School.*

Everybody was sorry to see the turkeys go, but they were also interested in the project as we began to put up various phases of the 318-unit complex. Phase I was completed in 1964, Phase II in '65, Phase III in '66. Marjorie Bradford was the efficient manager of Williamsburg North, and it attracted many renters. Among the special features were several four-bedroom units, very rare in Indianapolis. These have always stayed rented, even to this day.

My mother had died in 1960, making this phase of our life a little sadder. She had a cancerous growth on her colon and was facing drastic surgery. My father had made up his mind not to tell her what the result of her surgery would be: she would live the life of a colostomy patient. But the surgery never materialized. The doctor said, "There is no sense in putting her through the turmoil and pain of major surgery. She is going to die soon anyway, we believe. She has severe hardening of the arteries."

In what we considered a great blessing, she died not long after that while watching TV with my father. She was spared much suffering, but the loss still left a void for me—even to this day, so much of my life relates back to her, and I am who I am at least in part because of her. It was a comfort to know my father's so-called "declining" years were anything but declining for twenty more years. He was one of our most active and most successful salesmen, and I was pleased to see him travel for the first time in his life. As a company we'd win trips to Italy or France, and I'd give them to him in recognition of his sales success—and because I wanted him to enjoy new vistas and experiences.

What a long and eventful period his life had spanned! Here he was jetting to Europe in hours. As a young boy in the 1890s, he told me, he helped his father harness the horse to make all-day trips to Greenfield, Indiana, a suburb you can drive to in fifteen minutes on the interstate today. He had seen it all—the advent of the automobile, telephone, moving pictures, airplanes, lived through two world wars and gone from oil lamps to nuclear-generated energy. Man had experienced fantastic growth in my dad's lifetime, and it is exciting to think that this change will continue on into the future at what will probably be an accelerating rate.

LIFE GOES ON in the building industry as well. Using the ideas of Eli Broad and relying on our association with the Foundation for Cooperative Housing, we built the first co-op in Indiana. Its attractive units became the talk of Fort Wayne, and our open house in 1963 drew crowds which were an Indiana version of what we'd seen in California. Seeing pictures of that event makes me smile to this day. That project was followed in 1964 by Yorktown South in Indianapolis, at I-465 and U.S. 31 South. Then a second co-op project was developed in Fort Wayne and then one in Mishawaka, near South Bend. The company went on to develop more co-op projects on Indianapolis' east and west sides, in Hammond, Indiana, and down in Louisville, Kentucky. After all, it was only across the river, and we had confidence we'd know that market, too.

One of the kingpins in the cooperative movement in America who helped mentor us was David Krooth, of the law firm of Krooth and Altman in Washington, D.C. Krooth had been one of Roosevelt's advisors on housing and helped forge federal housing policy. He and FDR believed that homeowners were the backbone of America, providing strength for the economy and character for the nation because they had a direct stake in the country's prosperity. Dave Krooth was instrumental in creating legislation to enable FHA to insure cooperative housing, providing shelter for the poor and the disadvantaged. These citizens could not otherwise have afforded housing.

The Foundation for Cooperative Housing was a not-for-profit agency working in cooperation with FHA. It had a modest budget with few staffers, so sign-ups which went through FCH were slow, and we helped a good deal in expediting the process. Processing the applications was, of course, vital; we'd be closing on sixty units and couldn't do that unless the paperwork for all the units was completed with the FHA. Many other people gave up on the FCH process, saying it was too long, but we put our principles of persistence in play, and they worked.

We often used the "TNKA" process then—and still do—when necessary: Take names and kick posterior. These more complicated building projects demanded increased efficiency. I realized how necessary it is to get good people, teach and instruct them, and then to follow up, follow up, follow up. With some people, when jobs aren't done, excuses flower like trees in spring. If the person can't do the job on time, it's necessary to part company with him or her.

THOUGH THE CO-OP CONCEPT was exciting and occupied us fully

during the mid-sixties, there were problems with it. The main difficulty came in the marketing because builders had to rely on the FCH to do it. We'd be tied into payments which depended on the units being approved by the Department of Housing and Urban Development (HUD) and sold. But in reality that part of the project was out of our control because it was under the aegis of the FCH.

Let's take an example: if we were building a hundred and fifty-unit project, and the project was divided into three phases fifty units each, we could have an initial closing and draw on construction loans after we had half the units sold in any one of the phases. It was up to the FCH to sell those units—fast—but they were a not-for-profit agency with limited funding and manpower. The people on the staffs of not-for-profit agencies are often underpaid and overworked. So there we were, well along in construction, and the units either weren't sold or the processing wasn't completed, and so we did not have a 50 percent approval.

So we became disillusioned about the co-op ventures as businesses. We began to look more carefully at our success with the conventionally financed projects such as Williamsburg East and Williamsburg North. People really were interested in small, neat places with amenities and the ability to leave when they wanted to. This promised to be a large market, especially for those with limited incomes. For this grouping, which always interested us, there was a new development—subsidized housing. The straws were in the wind and we wanted to be able to pick them up.

We began to look beyond co-op to apartment building, with government assistance. We didn't yearn to put up fancy apartments—there were plenty of people to build deluxe units. My interest wasn't piqued just because the government was giving money for subsidies. That old philosophy of my mother's, taking care of the poor people out in the yard, came into play. I wasn't interested just in the marble bathroom trade. I remember once Bob Whipple, who's had a business and personal relationship with us for years, said to me, "My father is moving out of his home and he can't find any good luxury-level apartments. There's probably a great economic

Our Co-op Projects and the Dates of Completion:

PROJECT	DATE	NUMBER OF UNITS
Jamestown Homes Fort Wayne	3/31/65	212
Jamestown Homes Mishawaka	3/31/67	160
Yorktown South Indianapolis	3/31/67	154
Three Fountains East Indianapolis	3/31/68	342
Three Fountains West Indianapolis	3/31/69	300
Three Fountains Fort Wayne	3/31/69	257
Townhouse East Mishawaka	3/31/69	204
Sutton Place Indianapolis	3/31/70	360
Colonial Square Louisville, KY	3/31/70	329
Georgetown Homes Hammond	3/31/70	108
Cambridge Square Mishawaka	3/31/70	232
Tara Fort Wayne	3/31/70	278
Mayfield Green Indianapolis	3/31/70	344

4,000 At Glick's Opening

CROWDS ATTEND OPENING OF MOUNT VERNON TOWNE HOUSE APARTMENTS
Five Different Floor Plans Available, Beginning At $49 A Month

More than 4,000 persons last Sunday attended the formal opening of the $6 million Mount Vernon Towne Houe apartment complex at East 38th Street and Post Road.

The huge crowds resulted in the largest single day of business ever recorded by the Gene B. Glick Company in the firm's 17-year history.

GENE B. GLICK, company president, said Towne houses and apartments totaling $405,000 were sold on last Sunday's opening day sales which prompted the company to announce that it was starting construction immediately on the second phase of the 510-unit project. Phase two will contain 124 units.

The Mount Vernon project brings to Indianapolis an entire new concept of apartment living which combines the advantage of home ownership with carefree living that is associated with apartment rentals.

A ONE-BEDROOM apartment in Mount Vernon can be purchased for $49 a month and the prices range upward to $73 a month for a four-bedroom, 1½-bath Towne house. There are five different floor plans available.

Each unit has its own front and rear entrance and each unit has its own screened patio.

FAMILIES living in Mount Vernon will enjoy the use of a new swim and cabana club built by the Glick Company. It will be ready for use this spring.

Other extras provided with each Mount Vernon unit are bathroom vanities with marble tops, ceramic tile baths, de luxe kitchen cabinets and brick and aluminum exteriors.

Mount Vernon is open from 11 a.m. to 9 p.m. week days and Sundays and 9 a.m. to 6 p.m. Saturdays.

opportunity to have apartment complexes at the high end of the scale on the north side."

I thought a while, and said, "Bob, you're probably right. Somebody is going to make a lot of money doing that. But that somebody isn't going to be me. There will always be enough people to provide rich people with houses. My place here is to take care of some of the poor people."

The first multifamily units we built after the Williamsburg projects were owned by Gene and Marilyn Glick and other officers of the company. They were:

(100 PERCENT OWNERSHIP GLICK COMPANY 221 D3 PROGRAM)

Carriage House West I completed 6/12/68
Carriage House East I completed 1/31/69
Carriage House West II completed 6/19/69
Carriage House East II completed 10/10/69
Carriage House West III completed 5/19/70
Carriage House West IV completed 3/31/71

These projects created tax losses which offset the income earned by the development of the cooperatives. We were phasing out of the co-ops and were therefore generating income we needed to shelter. But we soon realized we needed larger capitalization than we could provide within the company. We were reaching for the stars, with high goals and many units in mind. Luckily the government would help with the sort of units we wished to build—at least it did for a while. Lyndon Johnson wanted to lead the country into what was called "The Great Society." He was waging war on poverty, and part of the effort would be to find affordable, decent housing for the poor and elderly. There would be rent subsidies for these people as well as food stamps and enhanced welfare aid.

It sounded attractive: It would enable us to serve the underprivileged as we liked to do—and also to expand our business. The problem was that Indianapolis wasn't buying the "Great Society." Indianapolis has always been a conservative town, and we were so far-right during Johnson's era that you could almost feel the city tilt right off the planet. There wasn't any way the town was going to take government money, but we needed it to do just that if we were going to do the type of building we envisioned.

Central to our problem was the position of *The Indianapolis Star* and *The Indianapolis News*, which had always been conservative publications. *The Star* editorialized that Indianapolis should not be receiving any federal government "handouts"—period. *The Star*'s publisher, Eugene Pulliam, was exercising his proper right as a publisher to take a political stand with the paper.

Still, I was going to do my very best. When John Barton was running for mayor, Jim Beatty asked me to support Barton. I could go either way in any election—my dad had been a Republican and my mother a Democrat. "What position does he take on this federal aid?" I wanted to know. "Let me meet him, and if he's planning to take the lock off the money the city should be getting, then maybe I'll do it."

I met the would-be mayor and he told me that if he was elected he was indeed going to introduce legislation that would let the city accept federal aid.

So I supported Barton and he was elected. But time passed, and after a year or so, still no federal aid. I called Beatty and I said, "What's going on? This man promised we'd have a change."

"Well, Gene," said Beatty, "you may have a chance to ask Mayor Barton yourself. Lyndon Johnson is coming into town for a rally and the mayor will be there on the lawn of the governor's mansion."

The day came, I went to the garden party, and I met the mayor. "Mayor Barton," I said, "we had an understanding that if you were re-elected you'd change the rules here and Indianapolis would be able to accept federal aid. You're only hurting the city by not doing it."

He said he agreed; the problem was that they were so short-staffed that there was nobody to write the legislation.

I thought a minute. "Well, it doesn't say a legislator or city employee has to write a proposed law. I'm sure some of us could hire somebody clever and civic-minded to write the law for you." We contacted a very bright attorney named John Neff; he wrote a good piece of legislation to enable the city to accept the funds, and the city attorney reviewed it. The city council passed the law, and they filed the request. The federal government approved the city's application and soon hundreds of thousands of dollars started pouring into the city, creating a flow of jobs and well-being.

But of course it helped us too. Before this, we had been unable to build any subsidized housing, and so the new policy really was a breakthrough, not only for us but for anybody who wanted to build subsidized housing. If it hadn't been Barton who accepted federal money, it would have been someone else—the time had come and it was monumentally important to the economy and the social and economic health of the town.

We felt at that time that we were breaking new ground, and it wasn't always the most pleasant of feelings. We took the lead when public opinion was fixed in a different mold. Being out front, you're always aware of a cold wind at your back, blowing pretty strongly. As Niccolò Machiavelli said, "There is nothing more difficult to conduct or more uncertain in its success than to take the lead in the introduction of a new order of things." And taking aid from the federal government in our town and state was something radically new.

At this point, it's appropriate to comment a little on Jim Beatty. When Bernie Landman was with Bamberger and Feibleman I commented that, unlike other major law firms, they had no one on staff with political clout. It may have been as a result of that comment that they subsequently hired Jim, who was an honors graduate from the University of Michigan.

When Bernie left Bamberger and Feibleman, he formed a partnership with Jim, called Landman and Beatty. Jim has been active through the years in local politics, including serving as Democratic county chairman. He also ran against the incumbent Democratic mayor for his party's mayoral nomination in 1967 and later was the Democratic nominee for lieutenant governor in 1968. He is very bright, articulate, and capable. In addition, Jim is creative and "tells it like it is," a quality that I admire in a person.

We began working with HUD, which insured the funds allocated for subsidized housing. We met their people both in Indianapolis and in Washington, D.C., and grew to understand them well.

Taking the bull by the horns, or in some cases by the tail, is a mark of successful entrepreneurial management. Or perhaps it's just having the guts to go get what you need. We tried to cut through government red tape whenever we could, and I remember all the times we needed to process our HUD funding applications, and the rules and regulations needed to be cut through. The man who did the expediting was named Eugene Gulledge, the assistant secretary of HUD, a very capable man who operated out of Virginia Beach.

It wasn't easy to track him down. We'd call on the phone, and they'd say, "Sorry, sir, but the man who can help you on this is Gene Gulledge, and he's out of town." He was always out of town; he travelled all the time. One time when we were calling on a particular matter, I think I got a little desperate. "Where in the hell is this guy?" I asked my people. "They say he can't be reached. He's going to be speaking to a convention tomorrow in California."

California? What could I do? I know what I did do. I got on a plane and flew to California, to San Francisco, to the convention. I had no other reason to go, but I went to see him. I listened to the speech and milled around in the crowd clustered around him asking questions at the end of the speech.

Finally they went away, and I said hello to him. We knew each other of course. "What are you doing at this convention, Glick?" he wanted to know.

"I'll tell you the honest truth. I came out here to see you. That's the only reason. I've got some things only you can solve, and as soon as we finish, I'm flying right back."

Surprised, he said the least he could do was talk to me over coffee downstairs. We weren't asking anything unusual, just the removal of some anchors that were holding back our projects, and he agreed to do that rather routine but stalled work. Then he said, "Any time you want to reach me, just call me at this number."

I went home, began work again, called the private number, and it never worked. He was always gone. The next time a logjam appeared in the work, he was in Key Biscayne. "That's it," I told myself. "I'm going to Key Biscayne." So I hopped another plane.

When I arrived at the hotel this time he was in the middle of his speech. I went to a phone booth to make a call, and as I started to dial, there was a "tap-tap-tap" on the window. I looked up to see a matronly, sixtyish woman, and I knew her.

On an earlier trip, this same woman had approached Bernie Landman and me and asked for a ride. She seemed friendly and chatty, and since I needed to be let out, I left her and Bernie in the car together. He returned angry, and in his usual blunt way with me said, "You are so naive! How could you sic her on me? Don't you know she's a streetwalker?" I was astonished. A woman of her age and matronliness? It didn't seem possible.

But here she was now, in Key Biscayne, waiting for me outside the phone booth. I was desperate to get inside the hall and meet with Gulledge. What if he should come out and see me conversing with this aging prostitute I had met only in doing a good turn? What would he think?

She was hungry, so I took her inside the coffee shop and bought her some food, telling her I needed to meet an important man, that she couldn't stay with me, and so forth. Finally she got the hint and said, "I can tell when I'm not wanted." That was an understatement. I paid for her food and left her eating.

Gulledge came out and I cornered him. "I don't believe you've done this again. I'm on my way out of town," he said. "You can come up and watch me pack and tell me what you need." I went to the elevator with him, all the time looking over my shoulder to see if the old gal was following us!

We went up, he packed, I talked, we exited. "Please, Lord," I prayed, "don't let her show up. Not only will he think I'm a bad man, but he'll think I have terrible taste too." That was the last time I followed anybody from HUD around. We managed to get our own contacts all through the subsidized housing network.

Chapter 8

Housing for the People—With Government Help

There is nothing more dangerous than to build a society with a large segment of people in that society who feel they have no stake in it, who feel they have nothing to lose.

—Dr. Martin Luther King, Jr.

IT IS IMPORTANT to describe in some detail the financing of subsidized housing, because it became both the philosophical and economic lifeblood of the company. For some of the information on this subject I am grateful to Max Thurston, who has taken the time to analyze the complicated financial history of the company.

Max was raised in Mishawaka, Indiana, the child of educators. He went to Northwestern and Harvard Business School and signed on with Ernst and Ernst, coming to Indianapolis in October 1960. He was assigned to our account shortly after that and began to modernize our accounting system. He left Ernst and Ernst to go into private practice with Bob Whipple. It was then that he began comparing estimates with actual construction costs and doing tax planning for us. I asked him to become absentee controller, and he worked with us closely but not as a direct employee from 1965 to 1971.

As I've said, we tired of the risks of the FCH market and the burdensome process of cooperative unit sales, and we wanted out of them. We began to use a new kind of financing for the subsidized housing we were beginning. The government was insuring mortgage money for our projects; but there was money to be raised beyond that. "Limited dividend" seemed the way to go to get that extra capital. Max Thurston describes the technical process of limited dividend partnerships in this way:

> *We learned that there was a market of investors interested in the tax losses generated by 236 limited dividend projects. There were incentives to an investor. Since the government was providing assistance to the residents who qualified, they needed to restrict the amount of cash—or dividend—the project owners could receive. Thus the term "limited dividend" came into play. Other investors were needed, and there was little risk to those investors. Because there was government assistance available, many potential renters would qualify and the units would stay rented. So long as the tax law and the investor's income remained the same, the investor had little risk. Local accountants asked if we had ever thought of bringing in these investors. We decided to try to find them with Carriage House East III, the first 236 limited dividend project to be completed in the United States.*

We would be "syndicating" or grouping several investors to benefit from the limited dividend system. We would own a minority share; investors would own 80 percent.

As for the "tax loss" part of it, John Hart—who was also involved in syndication at the time, though not for us—details the process in his own down-to-earth way:

> *The whole theory was involved with finding somebody who was a high-income taxpayer—that professional person who had a private business and wanted to make an investment, probably to shelter some income. The syndicating operation would go to this person and say, "If you will put twenty-five thousand dollars into this syndication over a four- or five-year period, we will give you tax losses each year three times the dollar amount you're putting in." The person would look at the situation and see that he had seventy-five thousand dollars in losses, so he had a negative capital account of fifty thousand. Once the project was sold, or went broke, then the so-called limited partners had to pay a capital*

gain on the deficit account, the amount they had all previously written off.

The object was to create a program with no defaults or serious cash flow problems. The Glick team, carefully selecting sites and project types or make up, produced achievable cash flow projections. The company was highly rated nationally as a safe investment. Glick projects soon had syndicators waiting in line for new projects.

Even with double-digit inflation, Glick projects were normally within budget. In 1986, when Congress retroactively killed the feasibility for new syndication, Glick projects continued to be attractive because of their strong management concepts.

By 1969 Max Thurston was spending most of his time on our account. He worked with two strong new people—Steve Valinet and Kent Poore—burning the midnight oil, putting down monetary and tax assumptions, running numbers into the future to see what the tax losses and other benefits to the investor would be. They'd all complete a project package, and then Max would want to try another couple of assumptions. Steve and Kent would have to hand calculate the whole package over. When it was finally complete, Tom Ringer took over, ready to present the idea to investors.

Tom Ringer became a master of presentations. He and his wife had returned to Indianapolis to be near her ailing father, and we hired him as controller. Tom had come from IBM, where he had been well trained by IBM President Tom Watson himself to do excellent presentations. He told a story that illustrates Watson's insistence on perfection in presentations in meetings.

Ringer had prepared a big flip chart with various pages, all of it fascinating material, perfectly memorized. Watson came in. Ringer started his presentation on page one and Watson interrupted. "I don't give a damn about those first pages. Where are the facts?" Ringer went on to the second page and Watson interrupted again. "Those aren't facts. I want facts." So Ringer got confused and started searching through the pages for "facts." Watson got up and left abruptly. "Call me when you get facts," he said.

Fortunately, a company vice president came over to console Ringer or he would probably have jumped into the river. "Don't think it's you," the company officer said. "Mr. Watson does that to everybody the first time he makes a presentation to emphasize that those flip charts should be fact-filled."

Well, now he was with us, and his presentations were not only fact-filled but also appealing sales vehicles, smoothly made and convincing. We were ready to use them in a new phase of our financing. What we needed to do was find investors and convince them to put their money into the projects we were building.

We gathered executives from Eli Lilly's, Hook's Drugs, and other places where large salaries and big tax liabilities were common. Everybody listened carefully. There were, however, questions. It all sounded a little iffy. A couple of conservative souls wanted to know if the government wasn't about to change the tax code; there was talk of that in 1968. If the tax laws were changed, the funds they were investing might not be sheltered anymore. The government would come after them and claim taxes. We didn't think that would happen soon, and we worked hard to reassure the skittish prospects.

The investors, particularly the people from Lilly's, were also concerned that the projects might be considered future slums, casting the investors as slum lords. That obviously wouldn't be good from a public relations standpoint. Over the years we have been proud that our subsidized developments are virtually indistinguishable from the unsubsidized housing in the same neighborhoods. The result is that our investors have been proud to have taken part in building them, and have told us so on several occasions.

But there, in those early days with Carriage House East, they backed off, uncertain. Except for one man. Max Thurston, who was there the day of the signing, tells the story:

The man's name was Richard Bearss. The closing was down in Bernie Landman's office with Bernie, myself, and this Richard Bearss. It was a three-payment deal and we'd signed all these papers, and it was time to sign a check for $33,333.33—that was the amount. Richard signed a check, then ripped it up. He got *out another check, then ripped up that one. Bernie and I looked at each other. Was the deal falling through? But no. "Would you please have your secretary type this?" he asked. "I can't get thirty-three thousand three hundred thirty-three dollars and thirty-three cents handwritten out in this space!"*

So we breathed a sigh of relief and had our first closing. Still, if this thing was going to work, we were obviously going to have to take a slightly different tack.

We needed syndicators capable of finding investors on a more widescale and professional basis. Fortunately, Josiah Child, founder and then-president of Boston Financial, contacted us at that time of need.

Max described the specifics of that first negotiation with Boston Financial:

We had been contacted by a number of New York firms offering us 10 percent of the mortgage for 95 percent of the partnership and its benefits. After working on the numbers for Carriage House East, I kept saying that the project was worth more than 10 percent. Nevertheless, construction was beginning on several projects and occupancy of the units would not be far behind. Depreciation benefits would be lost to investors if they weren't in place before occupancy began. Fred Pratt, now CEO for Boston Financial, and Dave Hewett, a couple of bright young men in their twenties, came to Indianapolis to negotiate for the changing of the mortgage percentage. Ultimately we settled for 16 percent of the mortgage instead of 10 percent. It became the starting point for a very long working relationship with Boston. As demand for tax losses grew, investors accepted lower returns and eventually the proceeds grew from 17 percent to 22 or 23 percent of the mortgage.

Fred Pratt has told us that at one point, as a smaller and rather new company, Boston nearly decided to go with a developer who wasn't such a "tough" negotiator—who didn't ask so much so quickly. They had another developer in mind who wasn't quite so demanding. They came out to Indianapolis to see us with the intention of ending their relationship with us, but after the meetings they went away with plans not only to finish what they'd committed to, but to join with us in future ventures. "It's good we did that," Fred Pratt said, "because in a couple of years the other fellow went into bankruptcy, and over the course of many years, we did over a hundred transactions with Gene Glick." Tough, fair negotiation is a real part of successful business.

Another lesson in perseverance came from Josiah Child. If it were not for his persistence, we would never have established our relationship with Boston Financial, which, as Max has noted, has been mutually beneficial throughout the years. Jo was told by a New York law firm that the Glick Company drove a hard bargain and it would not be to his advantage to pursue the relationship even if he had a chance of getting it. He did so anyway, and the rest is history.

Clearly Boston Financial was a primary force in our early HUD years. We would tell them how much we wanted, needed to raise in the way of equity, and we would discuss with them the terms and conditions and they'd sell it. I don't believe Boston would have sold to anyone whose interest was less than twenty-five thousand dollars, and for the most part people were investing fifty thousand to a hundred thousand.

Boston, or Paine Webber, which was associated with Boston through their worldwide network, would take most of these opportunities. Mickey Maurer also played a role in bringing investors in; his own high standards and integrity, substantiating those of the company, gave potential investors confidence in us. Eventually we had investors from all over the U.S. and several foreign countries; we've been gratified with their confidence in us and pleased with their success. I recall one interesting name was Madame LaSalle de Toulouse-Lautrec, the great-great-granddaughter of the painter. She lived in the south of France and became a Glick investor.

Mickey Maurer, who worked full time locating land for the

Projects Built Under 236 LD Financing

NAME/SITE	DATE COMPLETED
Carriage House, Mishawaka	10/7/70
Carriage House, Elkhart	12/23/70
Carriage House South, Indianapolis	3/29/71
Carriage House North, Indianapolis	3/30/71
Carriage House West IV, Indianapolis	3/31/71
Cambridge Square, Ft. Wayne	5/4/71
Cambridge Square, Grand Rapids, MI	5/12/71
Carriage House of Muskegon, MI	10/29/71
Cambridge Square II, Mishawaka	11/8/71
Cambridge Square North, Indianapolis	12/28/71
Carriage House, Minneapolis, MN	3/31/72
Mount Vernon Apartments, Louisville, KY	5/8/72
Cambridge Square II, Grand Rapids, MI	6/1/72
Carriage House of Atlanta, GA	9/8/72
Carriage House of Columbus, OH	11/1/72
Cambridge Square of Hollywood, FL	11/5/72
Mount Vernon Apartments II, Louisville, KY	2/1/73
Colonial Square, Indianapolis	3/21/73
Cambridge Square of Ft. Wayne II	6/1/73
Carriage House of Florence, KY	7/18/73
Plymouth Arms Apartments, Grand Rapids, MI	12/7/73
Cambridge Square, Monroeville, PA	1/10/74
Carriage House of Decatur, IL	2/28/74
Carriage House, Greenwood	5/6/74
Cambridge Square, Hialeah, FL	5/10/74
Carriage House, Flint, MI	5/31/74
Sutton Place Apartments, Amherst, NY	9/16/74

company for a year in 1969, and who served us for several years afterwards in setting up syndication opportunities for select clients, came to us in an unusual way. I had met him at a dinner party and asked him to come to work for us. He hit the construction business cold; he is an attorney and an accountant. Working with Max Thurston, he came to understand the technical aspects of this complicated business, but more importantly, he firmly shared our beliefs in integrity and honesty in dealing with everyone. He and Max developed in detail the economic feasibility of these arrangements. He and Bernie Landman developed packages describing the cash flow and tax benefits investors would receive. We bent over backwards to present it all fairly.

By 1969 we needed an increasingly complex office management system, and Lois Morris came to us to help professionalize the growing operation. Jan Metcalf was my secretary at the time, and since she would be leaving, she asked Lois, who was working at Hall Neal Furnace Company, to apply for the job. Although she flunked the typing test (it was on a memory typewriter she'd never seen), Lois began working for the company in February of 1969, and has been the cornerstone of the office operation ever since.

I'M PLEASED TO SAY that almost without exception the investors in the syndicated projects did as well if not better than we thought they would do. That was true as long as the federal government didn't change the rules.

But the real benefits came to the people who would be living in the units. Our units began going up all around the eastern U.S. The possibilities for us to expand were unlimited because we could get sufficient equity under the limited partnership to make a development economically viable. The syndicated limited partnership sales were the vehicle, the financial engine, that enabled us to take on projects in several states outside Indiana.

Of course, in our syndication days, financing was only one important step. We also had to have some land to build the apartments on in these far-flung states. As we have said, Mickey Maurer became instrumental in our land-purchasing needs. And after he left, the right person joined the staff to scope out and purchase land—no easy task. Rick Wells, who served us admirably for many years, came on board in a unique way.

Five of us—Jim Bisesi, Bernie Landman, Max Thurston, John Grogan, and myself—were having one of our long review and planning meetings in a little, all-brick, single-family home out near 38th and Post Road. It was a pleasant place to have our meetings, which often went into the wee hours.

It was about 12:30 in the morning and Jim said he had to go get something from his office. He wasn't gone a minute when he came in and shut the door. In a hushed voice, he said to us, "There's some guy sitting out in the outer office."

"At this hour?" I asked incredulously.

"He's been waiting to see you since 6:30."

"What kind of guy will sit six hours to see me?" I decided I'd better find out.

"He wants a job. He knows Mickey Maurer and Bill Schloss at Morris Plan. Name's Wells."

I went into the outer office and sure enough, there he was. He explained he'd been determined to see me and when the receptionist left at 6:30, she'd told him I was in a meeting. He thought he'd just read a while until it ended. Time passed and he just stayed.

"We'll be meeting another two hours anyway, and I don't want you to have to stay, so I'll take your number and call you. But I'll tell you this: I'm impressed with your perseverance. I like you already."

Mickey Maurer recalls that meeting:

Actually, Rick started with the company on an independent-contractor basis, as my assistant. We went together a few times before he found land on his own. I suggested that he show up at the Monday night meeting because I knew Glick would really flip. I didn't tell anyone that because I wanted Glick to be impressed with Rick, who was impressive in his own right. He was aggressive and a quick study. When I stopped finding land, Rick went full time. I liked Rick and I'm sure he did as good a job as I did—perhaps better.

While I was with Glick, on the advice of my wife, I negotiated that the company would pay me a thousand dollars per contract and a percentage of the purchase price of any land I found that he would buy. I had a whole file drawer full of contracts that Glick entered into for land that I had found around the country. I used to fall asleep calculating the money I would earn if he purchased all of that land—it was hundreds of thousands of dollars. I was in my late twenties.

One day President Nixon abruptly put an end to the land development program. I literally emptied my file drawer in the wastepaper bucket. My "future fortune" was gone. Glick called me in to discuss this matter and offered to pay a thousand dollars each for some real estate parcels that I had secured but he could never use because of the Nixon moratorium. I used the money to make the down payment for our first house.

Rick's job, now that we were selling the limited partnerships well, became finding the land in cities where we'd determined we'd be able to build.

How did we decide where we wanted to put up these units? We could have spun our wheels by sending him to areas we thought were growth areas, boom areas where apartments were going to do well. We were dealing primarily with subsidized housing, though. HUD was guaranteeing our mortgages, and we needed to go where HUD was going to approve subsidized housing.

In any given area we'd first meet with the HUD officials. We'd ask them to check with Indianapolis HUD to determine if we were high-quality, reliable builders, people you could depend on. We'd ask them straight out whether they wanted us to come into their area to build subsidized housing; sometimes they'd have plenty of builders available who could do the job, and in that case we wouldn't go there. Actually, we had the advantage in the subsidized building field. Most of the apartment builders in that boom time were making so much money building conventionally financed apartments that they didn't want to fool with complex government programs. You've got to know one thousand and one rules, dot all I's, cross all T's. It was much easier to go to mortgage companies who were anxious to put out money for conventional building—the profits were greater.

But we were operating under the premise that we were going to concentrate in areas where we had expertise, where we were gaining success. By this time Bernie and Max and the rest of us knew all of the rules and regulations, all of the pitfalls, and most of the complicated ways of the government in all its wisdom. So we were operating in an area of our specialty, and where the field was narrowed.

If HUD said they didn't want us, we'd walk away from that project. If they said, "Yes, come talk to us," Bernie or whoever was available would go and have a little dog-and pony-show—pictures of what we'd done, testimonials of how good we were, our integrity and honesty. And pretty soon word got around in the various HUD offices. If you want good subsidized housing, that Glick organization does one hell of a job. Whatever they tell you they're going to do, they do it.

It was a handshake and our reputation. We bent over backwards to never cause any embarrassment to any of these officials in anything we built, said, or did.

I think we eventually wound up knowing the rule book even better than these officials at FHA and HUD did, because Bernie was such a gifted attorney, and because we had such a need to get it right. Frequently these people would consult with us about the interpretation of a certain regulation or procedure. We developed access to the people in Washington who wrote the rules, and we'd call and say, "We think this is what you meant, but we want to make very sure." They'd clarify and we'd convey it to the local office. We didn't want to make any mistakes.

After we had established that HUD approved of our building in a certain place, we'd send Rick out to get the land. He'd have to scout the terrain thoroughly, contact the owners, see what encumbrances existed in the titles. Rick was extremely persistent, just as he'd been in our outer office that late night. If he had to track down people in different parts of the country, he'd do it. He'd talk fully and persuasively and get things done quickly—that was a real selling point. Certainly we compared favorably to the competition, who dragged their feet. Rick promised them early closing. We'd always try to deliver on his promises, but somewhere between his pie in the sky and Max's perfect, long-drawn-out closing times, we'd make it.

They came to trust us in Michigan, Kentucky, Florida. As the years went along, we gave our operating manuals to the offices in the states where we built.

We also were cautious in other ways. We believed in the Ten Commandments, but we had some of our own, too. One was "Thou shalt not buy land nor commence construction without a construction and takeout commitment"—which meant that you had construction financing and permanent financing before you began. The one time we did not observe that and began construction with only the construction financing, we were burned. More than one contractor began work with only the short-term financing and left a project unfinished. We didn't do that.

Only once did this relationship with HUD break down, and that was a major flop. We had gone into Ohio to seek direction for our land-location efforts there. The director of HUD suggested the possibility of placing a 236 project in Dayton. We found land and the director indicated they would fund a project there as soon as funds were available. But the land owner became impatient and wouldn't extend the option. We decided to go ahead and buy the land—after all, the director had committed verbally. Then he transferred to another office.

The new director told Landman, "I don't care what the previous director told you. Just submit your proposal and we'll consider it." They didn't fund it, and the director blew it off by saying, "I don't like that area." That was that. We held onto the ground for ten years and eventually sold it in an auction. By then the area had changed. The land cost us about $345,000 and the auction brought us about $30,000.

Steve Valinet was a kingpin in market research and feasibility, as well as in the land-locating operations which were so crucial to the company. Here's how he described those years:

We attempted to identify the areas and major cities where growth was occurring. We wanted to be near major schools, all white-collar oriented, high-income areas near regional malls, if possible. We did market and economic feasibility studies in over a hundred and fifty U.S. cities from coast to coast. (Many of these reports were in excess of five hundred pages each.) Most of these cities were not funded, because politics intervened. These reports included not only the above factors, but also analyses of population, incomes, household formation, wages, growth trends, and so on. What was important was not only where the development would be positively situated, but also that the property would have long-term residual value. Most people were building in the inner cities in those days. We had done extensive research and found out that most of these inner-city HUD properties were in default—they were totally unsuccessful. Mr. Glick wanted the properties we built to be in the best suburban growth areas, so they would have long term real estate residual value. And that was the correct stance—the tax laws changed in the eighties and those projects that stayed in the growth areas over twenty or twenty-five years are actually more valuable today than they were then.

There was also feasibility analysis. This consisted of what the rents should be by type of unit, what the proposed mix of units was, estimated return on investment calculations, estimated operating costs, and construction costs. Also analyzed were how many units we would build and land cost. We developed a formula to estimate construction cost, profit centers for each type of activity, and whether we could make it work under a given set of standards. We would try to duplicate the same mix and product in as many areas as we could, so as to reduce our risks by relying on previous actual historical construction and operating costs.

Every time I would run the set of numbers—euphemistically referred to as "The Front- and back-door Approaches to Feasibility"—my immediate superior, Max Thurston, would review them and if these numbers did not meet the desired profit contribution level, we would not proceed. We ended up putting in ap-

plications in many more places than we actually got funded—in Texas, Massachusetts, and California, for example. And sometimes HUD got very definite about the site. "You either build here or we won't fund you," they'd say, so we'd settle for a little less sometimes, but not often. We wanted good neighborhoods.

In the 1970s Steve Valinet also brought in four additional bright individuals (with masters degrees in real estate, appraisal, and investment analysis) from his own graduate school experience at the University of Wisconsin. Steve was one of several young men during this period trained by the late James Graaskamp, a nationally known professor of urban land economics and real estate appraisal and investment. Jack Lynch was also one of these bright young men. Jack was responsible for the development and construction of several of our projects in Florida and subsequently the management of them.

It was also in the sixties that Jim Bisesi came to us and began demonstrating the intellect, strength of character and versatility he would use to enhance the company for the next forty years.

Jim grew up in Indianapolis and worked for Paul Cripe's engineering firm while he was attending Purdue University. We were one of the clients of that firm, and Jim came with our company in 1959 and has been here ever since.

He began by punching out the National Homes, getting them ready for inspections by the authorities. Soon, though, he began coordinating the engineering of land development activities.

I remember the tight squeeze we were all in when he was just starting out with Cripe—in '57 or '58. The Cripe organization was designing subdivision plans for our single-family developments. All of this is done on computers today, of course, but in those days all of us in the building industry were dependent on good engineering plans.

I was doing my usual thing of going down to the company and saying, "Now when are you going to start? What are the phases of completion? What are the dates you'll commence and complete each phase?"

I never yelled. I'd just go down and say, "You said you'd be started on this and now you're not." There were stacks of work from lots of us waiting to be engineered. One of their men who had a sense of humor listened to me ranting about getting this work done and said, "There is this much work down here, and only so much room in this place. I tell you I'm going to get the job out for you, but hell, every time I turn around there's another group coming in, waving papers with another project. I just tell them to get over there in line." Jim observed the bottleneck we were having and told me privately that he could work on his own on our designs and expedite them. He did it, and we hired him.

To know Jim's work through a number of years for us is to understand the history of the housing industry, at least as we have practiced it.

Engineering and land development were very important in all we did, and Jim was instrumental in this area. He saw us through from the time where we did fairly standard subdivision development, where we put in streets and sewers and curbs without much design, to a more sophisticated era. Grid patterns evolved into curvilinear streets and cul-de-sacs, with a variety of sizes of lots and homes.

He helped supervise the engineering through the multifamily phase, which offered more flexibility to the designer and fewer regulatory hassles. As we progressed from co-ops to apartments, he focused our efforts on superblocks, with buildings arranged around large green space in the center, enabling everybody to walk to recreation without crossing streets. Parking in the sixties was generally at the rear of the building instead of the front. As tenant preferences became known, we moved parking to the front.

Jim originated and supervised further changes which incorporated paths and sidewalks to take residents to recreation or shopping areas. Then he designed for environmental management, in response to public concerns and new laws mandating that the company consider relationships of water and land use. Jim has said this about those days with the environmental movement:

In the mid-seventies there was a much greater emphasis on intro-

ducing water into our projects. Initially it was a result of the regulatory changes that required a builder to provide detention or retention of storm water on the site, by use of dry or wet ponds. We soon came to realize that these ponds were a real aesthetic attraction, and designing for them became not a detriment, but an asset. We began to introduce water into the projects even where we didn't need it for storm water management. Williamsburg West is a good example; in it we voluntarily created a lake in the housing project.

Jim's job kept him traveling more or less constantly through several years—at one time two thousand units in twelve states—overseeing the projects from start to finish in a variety of ways. He would locate suitable land, get it to the point where it could be developed, work to get it zoned, design the project and supervise it through construction. And he also flew his own airplane. Quite a lot of responsibility!

In the seventies the company was stretched to capacity to meet the needs of these days of intense building. In January of 1971 Steve Valinet, who was area manager for our project in Muskegon, was called by the construction superintendent, who said he needed three large roof vents, each weighing three thousand pounds. If the company didn't get the vents up there immediately, the various trades on the job site would have to leave. "Do what you have to do to be sure nobody walks off the job," I told him.

That was always our main worry—that the trades would walk off, leaving the schedule in a shambles. Steve rented a large truck with a metal screen divider and found a supplier in the Indianapolis area who had three of the enormous vents. With all nine thousand pounds of them loaded into the truck, he climbed behind the wheel and headed north on I-69 as the winter weather grew increasingly harsh.

Steve was also carrying a fifty-thousand-dollar check to deliver to Steve Fuson, who was leaving Muskegon and heading for New York to meet a subcontractor there and deliver the check.

Steve tells the story this way:

As I was driving this big truck, with nine thousand pounds of sheet metal roof vents, near Kalamazoo, I slid off the road and the truck turned over sideways. I climbed out of the cab on the driver's side and clambered down over what seemed like fifty feet of truck beneath me. I left the truck and thumbed a ride with a trucker going all the way to Detroit. I got the check to Detroit Metro about ten minutes before Steve Fuson was due to leave.

I hitched a ride back to the truck and got a wrecker, which came and pulled the truck upright. It was getting late and I was exhausted and starved. Still, I had to rush along, through the continuing ice and snow. The men would walk off the job.

Words can't express what I went through over this twenty-four-hour period. When I got there, about 9 P.M. the superintendent said he'd found another supplier in Grand Rapids that same day and my vents weren't needed. I wanted to scream, but after a minute I realized the job was going on, and that was what counted. I think this was something that was quite a bit beyond the call of duty, but for the Glick company I would have done anything.

In those days of intense construction, working with HUD to manage the insured mortgages demanded a lot of careful analysis. We had to provide cost certification on each job before HUD would insure the mortgage so it could be sold to Fannie Mae (the Federal National Mortgage Association). John Cottrell recalls those days:

Our mortgage company provided the construction financing to the projects we were developing. Once the last building passed inspection, the cutoff date for doing the cost certification was established. The interest rate the prospect paid dropped to 8 percent, but the mortgage company was paying at 18 to 20 percent. Each day was important because we had seven or eight projects going.

Now, you're in a hurry to get these cost certifications completed and force HUD to act on them real quickly to get them accepted and then get them off to Fannie Mae for them to buy the *mortgage. I remember many a night, back in '74 or '75, I think, sitting at midnight at my kitchen table reviewing these cost certifications so we could speed the process up. Sophisticated electronic transfers were not known in those days, and we were talking a spread of eleven, twelve points on maybe $5 million. It was worth it to us to have somebody take a plane to Chicago, go to Fannie Mae, pick up a check, come back and get it in the bank that day.*

John Cottrell, another of our young Ernst and Whinney (later Ernst and Young) superstars, was proving himself indispensable. He eventually became chief financial officer of the organization, vice president in charge of accounting and auditing. He has been a perfect "company man" and helped us develop the reputation of producing the necessary tax information for all of our investors earlier than anyone else—and as error-free as human beings can make this type of financial reporting. John has been largely responsible for our reputation of producing quality accounting records for state, local, and federal governments, and for our employees too.

Through the years we have been impressed with the professionalism and high quality of the work performed by our accounting firm, Ernst and Young. In fact, we have been fortunate to hire many of the Ernst and Young associates who were assigned to our account. One good way to observe someone's work is through seeing them on an assignment. Many of our key associates came to us in this manner, including Max Thurston, John Grogan, John Cottrell, Denny Edmonds, and Anita Smith. We have also been very fortunate to have high-quality individuals as the managing partners of E & Y, including Bill Carter, Clarence Long, and Jack Shaw.

I have not yet commented on John Grogan and his contribution to our organization. John took great pride in whatever he undertook and accomplished every task with professionalism and creativity. To his credit, he helped to develop the skills of John Cottrell, who replaced him when he retired to go into consulting.

John Cottrell has been ably supported in the accounting department by Denny Edmonds, vice president and property management controller, and Anita Smith, vice president and corporate controller. Because of their capable assistance, John has been able to assume the responsibilities of overseeing our complicated computerization.

THE EARLY SEVENTIES were busy, but troubling signs were in the wind. Richard Nixon was re-elected President and in 1973 was proposing to change the tax law. He put a moratorium on 236 limited dividend projects. So that part of our business went on hold. There was a gap in construction starts of subsidized housing from '73 almost until '77. We had other, market-rate projects going.

A new opportunity eventually opened up though: Section 8, a modified form of responding to requests for proposals through HUD. Max Thurston explains the system:

> *Under the Ford administration subsidized housing was revived but in a new form: NOFA—Notification of Fund Availability.*
>
> *HUD would say, "We want to place a project in Muncie." They'd notify you and you'd barrel around trying to find ground in Muncie, with all the competition barreling around too. You would submit a proposal to them by such and such a date to build this given product on this site for these rents and operating expenses. You'd win or lose. That was it. No more suggesting to HUD how and where we'd do the projects.*

It meant a shift in staffing to try to meet these quick-deadline do-or-die bidding opportunities. We were definitely entering a new age, and quickly. We cut back on personnel, to the bone. We kept a nucleus who would be good at negotiating—fast-response people to meet the demands of this new NOFA program—but many others had to go. It's enough to say that Jim Bisesi's "department" was Jim alone.

In 1976, HUD shifted gears, having statewide NOFAs for both family and elderly Section 8 projects. We had three weeks to respond. Max continues the story:

That Indiana NOFA was really one of the highlights of my career because of the teamwork that was involved and the success we experienced. We called it "Operation Firecracker" because the submission was due just after the Fourth of July weekend. We figured that HUD would prefer having submissions in cities and towns that didn't have subsidized housing. Rick Wells located eighteen parcels of ground and tied them up with the owners. Jim Bisesi checked out basic engineering requirements. The sites we picked often were good for the elderly as well as families, and for these sites we decided to submit three separate proposals: elderly, family, and a combination of both.

Marge Harper from accounting came over to help put together the feasibility study. She had come to us in 1961 and had moved up in the company through her own hard work and night-school courses, eventually becoming office manager and then controller. At the time of the NOFA Independence Day effort she was a proficient accounting person. We had our copier supplier on standby that weekend for emergency service. On the morning the submissions were due, we had fifty one-inch-thick application packets in various stages of completion with none complete. I remember Jim Bisesi and three or four engineers draped over a drafting table, putting together a site plan on our last submission. Somehow by 3 P.M. all fifty packets were complete. Our mail person delivered three dolly-loads of documents to HUD. A few weeks later, we learned we had won seven projects!

Marge Bauer Harper tells a story which illustrates the value we place upon personal and professional development. We have always tried to help our employees advance their careers and gain the necessary education and experience to enable them to do so.

When I first came with the company I did some minor jobs, but then was offered a job as bookkeeper. One night Gene came back around seven. He sat at a desk by me and said, "I know you have been offered this position, and I also know that you hesitated be-

cause of not having formal knowledge or training. I want to know how you feel about this."

"I am willing to work real hard," I answered. "I believe I can do it, and I will put forward my best effort."

Gene responded, "Marge, that is all I wanted to hear. The job is yours." And eventually, I became office manager.

RAPID GROWTH, though, has its problems, and they seemed accentuated under Section 8 building. Marilyn and I retained roughly 20 percent of each partnership with other key associates. Our company was the builder. We guaranteed we would build a project for a specified price. If the project cost more than projected, we swallowed it. And we swallowed some pretty good bites. Sometimes inflation sacked us, and materials were always in short supply. To get the material we needed to finish, we would have to pay a premium. Subcontractors would sign a contract with us for, say, a million dollars in material and labor, then come back and say, "I can't do it. My material prices went up. I've got to charge a million one hundred thousand." What could we do? Go back to the next highest bidder and say, "We'd like you to take it now for the million"? Of course not. We'd tell the contractor, "Do the best you can. We'll have to make it work." Many contractors went bankrupt then because they were held to the contract. We usually just ate the increase ourselves and didn't go back to the investors to tell them we couldn't live with the costs we had projected. These overruns could affect the profitability of the project, lessening the investment return. Had we not absorbed these shortfalls, we would have ended up misrepresenting the project, and we weren't going to do that.

Partnerships suffered in many parts of the country because builders wouldn't do what we did—absorb contractors' overage costs. Partners were getting bills over and above the "guaranteed" construction costs. They might have a hundred-thousand-dollar investment and were getting an additional bill for eighty thousand dollars.

If the builder went bankrupt, the projects would go bankrupt

Projects Built Under Section 8 Notification of Funding

NAME/SITE	DATE COMPLETED
Carriage House of Evansville, Evansville, IN	5/78
Village Apartments, Mishawaka, IN	6/78
Island Wall Cooperative, Reston, VA	7/78
Fairington Apartments, Louisville, KY	7/78
Fairington Apartments, Clarksville, IN	7/78
Cambridge Square of Anderson, Anderson, IN	7/78
Cambridge Square of Bedford, Bedford, IN	8/78
Cambridge Square of Marion, Marion, IN	8/78
Jamestown Square North, Indpls, IN	8/78
Cambridge Square of Muncie, Muncie, IN	9/78
Carriage House Apartments, Virginia Beach, VA	9/78
Carriage House Decatur II, Decatur, IL	9/78
Woods of Fairfax, Washington, D.C.	2/79
Fairington Apartments, Lexington, KY	7/79
Cambridge Square of Richmond, Richmond, IN	7/79
Edsall House, Ft. Wayne, IN	7/79
Carriage House of LaPorte, LaPorte, IN	7/79
Briarwood Apartments, Toledo, OH	7/79
Jamestown Apartments, Seymour, IN	7/79
Fairington Apartments, Lafayette, IN	7/79
Cambridge Square of Hamburg, Hamburg, NY	7/79
Cambridge Square of Bloomington, Bloomington, IN	7/79
Northwood Apartments, Franklin, IN	7/79
Jamestown Square Apartments, Washington, IN	7/79
Jamestown Square Apartments, Vincennes, IN	9/79
Cambridge Square of Beech Grove, Beech Grove, IN	9/79
Fern Creek Arms, Louisville, KY	9/79
Oglethorpe Apartments, Savannah, GA	10/79
Jamestown Apartments, Valparaiso, IN	10/79
Briarwood Apartments, Lexington, KY	10/79
Fairington Apartments, Ft. Wayne, IN	10/79
Fairington Apartments, South Bend, IN	11/79
Carriage House Apartments, Bowling Green, KY	11/79
Cambridge Square Apartments, Chesapeake, VA	12/79
East Ocean Square Apts, Stuart, FL	2/80

too. When the mortgage company foreclosed, it was disastrous for the investors. Whatever depreciation they had taken would be recaptured, putting the investor at a very substantial loss. We took great pride in the way we dealt with these national trends. Almost all of our investors got everything they were promised. If they didn't, it was as a direct result of changes in the tax laws, over which we had no control.

Toward the end of the seventies we had a lot of jobs to build and manage, but our staff was spread thin. In particular, 1978 showed just how far we were stretched. Some contractors failed and we were having to hire construction superintendents very rapidly. Max describes that year this way:

> *We had some newly hired negotiators building new communities where we hadn't built before, often with new construction superintendents. In these situations some subcontractor or employee failures are going to occur. Sometimes our reliable subcontractors from other communities could bail us out at a minimum cost, but they had travel costs to add to their material and labor costs. Often we had to pay huge premiums to competent local subs to get them to complete the work for those who failed. Still, it was cheaper than continuing with the incompetent subcontractor. I think this was the only year we lost money.*

In the early 1980s, funding for suitable Section 8 projects dwindled and died. For a while we had funding for market rate projects containing 20 percent Section 8 units. The GNMA Tandem Program had some 7.5 percent forty-year loans available, but funds under these programs were limited. It was announced that Ginny Mae would open its window until the funds were exhausted; applicants had to have a HUD commitment to a given stage.

Anticipating the rush for funds, we set up phones in the accounting area with automatic redial features to them. About ten accounting clerks were on the phone, getting busy signal after busy signal. Finally one would get through to Ginny Mae. That person would quickly call for Bernie, who would take the phone and say to the Ginny Mae representative, "I want to make a commitment for such-and-such a project." People put forth extra creativity and effort, and it paid off—several projects were funded with favorable financing.

I OUGHT TO CLOSE this discussion on our subsidized housing units by commending HUD. I know it isn't usual these days to praise the government, but our relationship with this federal housing agency was usually quite good. Through the years Indianapolis was fortunate in having an outstanding HUD office. Kentucky's was also exceptional. I recall in the mid-seventies the head of Indiana HUD, a man named Armstrong, called a number of developers together for a general discussion on what his agency could do to help expedite the developers' processing. He talked for about fifteen minutes and then he looked at me and said, "Well, Mr. Glick, you are doing as much as anyone with HUD programs. Do you have any suggestions on how we could improve?"

I said, "Mr. Armstrong, I can't tell you how to improve, but I do want to make an observation. Through the years we have done business with twelve or fourteen FHA or HUD offices, and we cite the Indianapolis office every place as an example of professionalism and efficiency. Our hats are off to you and the people in your office for their dedication to the people we all intend to help! You've recognized your responsibility, and fulfilled with integrity your obligation to the people we're supposed to be serving well." People were applauding, so I guess they agreed. Bernie Landman had the last word, though: "Don't let that go to your head because you don't know the incompetence of the other offices!" True enough, but the local HUD office still deserved the praise.

These were high-tide days for the company, and Bernie himself deserves a good deal of the credit for the success of this period. Far-sighted, exacting, brilliant in negotiations, he had the ability to see through a problem to its solution and to handle difficult problems with extraordinary skill. He could be irascible, often was hard-nosed, but he also had a fine quality of humanity which surfaced when it was needed.

One Sunday in the early sixties, Bernie and I were out inspecting properties. I told Bernie that I had read in a builder's publication that Indianapolis businessman Louis Moeller was in the hospital, desperately needing blood—Type B-positive.

Both Bernie and I knew from our Army days that we had that rather rare blood type, and though he didn't know Louis well, Bernie readily agreed to go out to the hospital then to give the blood. Later, I went to see Louis as he was recuperating. You had to know Louis—he was Dutch, hearty and red-faced as they come. He said, "I really appreciated having you and Bernie Landman give me blood. I've always thought of myself as a good businessman, but now with two pints of Jewish blood in my veins, I'm going to be unbeatable!"

That's what all of us were trying to be in those days. I think it's still a good goal.

My father's health had begun to decline, and in 1972 we hired a companion to stay with him. In spite of all the problems he had, his spirit remained strong, and at this time I sent him a little piece by Douglas MacArthur called "A Thought":

> *Youth is not wholly a matter of bright cheeks, red lips, or supple knees. It is temper of the will, a quality of the imagination, a vigor of the emotions, a freshness of the deep springs of life. It means a temperamental predominance of courage over timidity, of an appetite for adventure over the love of ease. Nobody grows old merely by living a number of years. People grow old by deserting their ideals. . . . You are as young as your ambition, as old as your doubt, as young as your self-confidence, as old as your fear, as young as your hope, as old as your despair.*

My dad was, in those last years, as young as his self-confidence and his hopes, which were always high. As far as his power to inspire the rest of us, that knew no bounds. May we all have that said of us in what's called "old age." He died peacefully in his sleep in 1980.

Dad loved to travel. This photo was taken when he was on on one of his many trips to Europe, around 1965. He also enjoyed dancing, which he did here with Marge Bauer Harper at a Christmas party.

(*Left to right*) Jim Price, CEO of National Homes, Roger Branigin, former Indiana governor, my dad, and I. We were celebrating our successful marketing of National Homes over a number of years, and recognizing my dad as one of the outstanding salesmen.

CHAPTER 9

FROM BUILDING TO MANAGING APARTMENTS

The height by men of achievement reached and kept
Was not obtained by sudden flight
But they, while their companions slept
Were toiling upward in the night.

—After Henry Wadsworth Longfellow

OUR MONDAY REVIEW and planning meetings, which got into high gear in the early 1960s and continues through the present, were dubbed "the Notorious Night Meetings." I suppose that name reflects both the intensity and the productivity of those grueling sessions. I also hope it reflects some of the fun and camaraderie I think we all shared as we built the company together. A lot of the company's energy was generated in those meetings.

I've always worked at night, of course. When it was just Marilyn and I, we'd work days supervising construction and then sit up at night at the kitchen table, doing the books or the schedules or the payroll. Though I liked getting to bed by 2 A.M., I was willing to see the sun rise if necessary.

Marilyn remembers that on one night before the children were even born, we'd set a goal of updating the books. We started in the night and needed to finish by 3 or 4 A.M. She got so tired she started to cry. We went out and got coffee and then came back home and finished it. But for me, the night-owl shift was second nature.

The Monday meetings began during our single-family-home days at the suggestion of Kelly Snow, our marketing consultant. We'd meet each Monday to review the results of the past week—what worked, what didn't, what competitors had done—and to plan our advertising and other efforts for the week.

As we moved into multifamily development, we continued the practice, first meeting with Jack Dickhaus and Jack Kline and later Bill Minner on marketing issues. Then Max Thurston, Jim Bisesi, John Grogan (the vice president of finance during this period), Bernie Landman, and I discussed our progress and bottlenecks in our developments. We covered everything from land location, zoning, engineering, HUD, and construction to floor plans and rents of certain units.

I guess I knew the value of eating well to break and refresh. People have to eat. We often hired a caterer named Minnie Campbell to come out and fix dinner right there and serve it to us. That way we could eat and talk.

If we didn't have Minnie to cook, we'd break at eight and go out to dinner. We'd go to some nearby place, taking a few papers with us so we could continue the discussion while we ate, then we'd return to the office. These meetings would go on late, very late, sometimes. A few times I'd just be getting home and the sun would be rising. I told myself maybe that was a sign, that perhaps I'd managed poorly.

These meetings were—and are—invaluable both from a strategic and tactical standpoint. They allowed us to review long-, medium-, and short-range objectives. They provided regular contact with all of our key people. And by the time the meetings were finished, each person had a clear idea of what the goals, objectives, current assignments, and responsibilities for the coming week were.

The meetings were very informal in those early days, with no set hierarchy. Bernie Landman was marvelous at getting things done, laying out agendas, and seeing that we moved through them. He was practical as well as intelligent. In the marketing meetings, when they split off, it was my custom to go around to each one and say, "Okay—what was your assignment and what did you get done?" And each person would make a report.

One night Bernie said, "I know you want to move these meetings along, and you've just asked me to make a report on what has happened with this assignment, so I'll just say NAFT."

"NAFT?" I asked. "What does that mean?"

"*Not a F—ing Thing.* I don't want to waste time talking if nothing has been done." We all laughed, but NAFT became a common term in those early meetings.

Others in positions of business responsibility may feel it's unnecessary to meet weekly, or maybe they communicate in other ways, but there is something special about an eyeball-to-eyeball meeting with everyone involved in the decisions. It reminds me of a wartime situation, where great armies realize the importance of each soldier's depending on the other. The thing that creates fighting spirit and convinces everybody of the importance of the sacrifices at the front is the feeling that you want to help your buddy survive. We all agreed to our assignments, and we wanted to succeed, not to let one another down.

We were a team working together, each participant contributing his own bit of genius.

By the late 1970s, as the management function increased and construction was phased out, the meetings would last even longer. We moved our office to the north side in 1976. One night in the office at 91st and Meridian we'd stayed long, and Bernie and I remained even after the others had left. I had reminded him earlier that I needed a ride because my car was in for service, but as the night dragged on we both forgot and he left without me. Fifteen minutes later I started walking home. It's interesting how wide a berth cars give a man walking in a business suit at four o'clock in the morning. Nobody was interested in offering help. It took thirty-five minutes before I walked up my driveway.

Around 1970 we broke meetings into two sections: management on Mondays and operations on Tuesdays. The meetings still went late, and we would be eating late in restaurants like the Glass Chimney, tables cluttered with our papers.

The management group during this period included Jack Kline, Bill Minner, Frank Basile, Jack Dickhaus, Dave Williams, and me.

Dave, an upright type of man who never gave into the "cussing" urges many in the company practiced, ran Division III, which we added as we moved into construction in other states.

Operations people were Max Thurston, Bernie Landman, John Grogan, and Jim Bisesi. But always all of us came back and shared ideas at the weekly meetings. They bound us together.

I wouldn't be honest if I said the meetings were always even-keeled. Sometimes there was friction, but even that was helpful, to let off steam, to vent and try to reach common ground.

I remember when Mickey Maurer served his stint with the company. He recalls that a couple of his bosses at the time considered him—rightly so—a newcomer with little knowledge of the construction process. Mickey asked one of them, because he really needed to know, "What's spackle?"

They gave him a scornful look, as if to say, "Here's a guy hired to work in construction and he doesn't even know what spackle is." So he got razzed.

Mickey believed he might get put down at the Monday meetings because all the old pros would be there and he had shown himself to be a greenhorn. So he went to the library and looked up spackle: everything you could possibly want to know, who invented it, where it was first used, what its chemical composition is. He came to the Monday night meeting and, sure enough, the razzers got on him: "Well, did you ever find out what spackle is?"

Mickey recited spackle till nobody could stand it anymore, but everybody had a laugh. It probably cleared the air in a way nothing else could for a new kid on the block.

AS I'VE MENTIONED, towards the end of the seventies we had a lot of jobs to build and manage, with people spread thin. Some subcontractors failed, and we were having to hire construction superintendents very frequently. With so many apartment projects going at once, we had troubles keeping control, both supervisory and cost. We were forced to hire general contractors for various jobs, and superintendents to supervise the general contractors. Earl Bradford, a

(*Clockwise, from top left*) Frank Basile, Max Thurston, Steve Valinet, and Jim Bisesi at a "building" time in the company's history.

human resources man experienced at General Electric, interviewed people for us and hired "qualified men." Even so, there was simply too much for us to keep track of.

We were at that time building on an unbelievably hilly terrain in Covington, Kentucky. I'd visit these sites when I could, trying to keep an eye on things. I said, "We're spending too much money on earth moving on this site. I know there's a lot of earth to move, but this general contractor we've hired has billed us for work half done and I want to be sure where the job stands." From the reports we'd had, the job wasn't nearly half done.

That contractor had earth-moving equipment the likes of which I'd never seen. But when I arrived, the machines were just running back and forth over mounds of earth, aimlessly. I went up to a couple of the operators and said, "What in the hell are you doing?" One said, "Well, the contractor had to go get some stakes to set and he told us he didn't want us just sitting around, that we needed to run the machines back and forth while he was gone." Billable hours. The contractor was billing us not on how much work he'd finished but on how many hours he'd put in. I told the operators to stop that immediately. I spoke to the supervisor. "Why are you approving this sort of billing?" I asked. "He needs the money," was the answer.

We hired four or five general contractors during this fast-growth period, and we ended up having to finish every job ourselves, hiring our own superintendents and taking them there to mop up others' work. In that period, 1979 to 1981, prices skyrocketed and help was hard to get. The financial failure rate was high—the meat wagon was picking up bankrupt contractors every day. People used to ask how we survived during that period, and I'd say, "By damn hard work, conscientious watching. Watching, controlling, watching."

We had more projects under construction during this two-year period than we ever had in the past or since. Dramatic cost overruns or loss of control at any one project could spell disaster and bankruptcy. Jim Bisesi and I set up a war room in my office, and every Friday, from early morning until late in the evening, our superintendents would call in and give their weekly progress reports. Jim and I reviewed the progress and budgets, and while we had the superintendents on the phone, we would try to give directions to eliminate any bottlenecks and keep the jobs moving forward on schedule, while still maintaining quality construction. I'm certain that this tight control and weekly check-ins played a major role in ensuring that the "meat wagon" didn't find our people—or our projects—lying at the side of the road. Believe me, if you didn't have a headache when you began this process, you'd have one when you finished listening to problem after problem and wracking your brain with the site people to solve them.

We had to do some firings in the late seventies, of course. Parting company is difficult, and I've always sought the advice of others before I take that step. Sometimes I think someone is doing a poor job, but others who know better will say, "No, he's doing fine." I'm honest and straightforward if someone has to leave the company. I try to reinforce the feeling that each individual has talent and ability, or we wouldn't have hired him or her in the first place. But sometimes the situation simply isn't workable at the company. We try to be fair, giving severance pay and/or letting him or her stay on the job until a new job is found.

AS I'VE SAID EARLIER, the government decided to put a moratorium on the 236 program. We completed the projects under construction, and began developing our first market-rate D4 projects. They were as follows:

PROJECT/SITE	DATE COMPLETED
Village Apartments, Mishawaka	11/15/74
Briarwood Village Apartments, Elkhart	1/31/75
Briarwood Apartments, Indianapolis	12/31/75
Washington Square Apartments, Indianapolis	7/15/75
Williamsburg West II, Indianapolis	7/15/75
Briarwood Apartments II, Indianapolis	8/78
Cambridge Square, Greenwood	9/78

In 1981 the tax laws changed, affecting our syndication efforts. The changes in the law made it beneficial for a new group of investors to buy into the project. We "re-syndicated" the project, making new projections. The new group of investors paid the old group the value of the partnerships by assuming mortgage liability, paying cash over a period of years, a portion of which was interest. A purchase note was issued, due upon sale, refinancing, or at the end of fifteen years, whichever came first.

An appraisal was done, with several factors about the project's viability and value taken into consideration. Physical assets were transferred from old to new owners, and the funds continued to be supervised by the accounting department.

Further tax law changes occurred in 1986. John Cottrell describes the situation:

> *The biggest change was the definition of passive activity. By definition the law calls real estate a passive activity, and you could now only deduct passive losses against passive income. Obviously, there's not enough passive income in the world to go around. We had investors who still had substantial installments to pay. They could no longer deduct the losses that their investment was generating. So all of a sudden, the investment changed. The tax benefit, which was the most significant part—it was gone. This change had a tremendous effect and dried up most types of real estate syndications. They now required guarantees of cash flow. We decided that the cash return that the investors wanted guaranteed was not acceptable to us, so we stopped syndicating. We built only five projects after 1986.*

And so a new era dawned, one as significant for the company as the change from single-family to multifamily dwellings had been. We quit building apartments and went almost full time into managing them.

Not that management was new to us. We had been managing our own projects for years and in the seventies thought that we'd try property management for others and sought that kind of business.

It didn't work very well. Max Thurston describes the process of trying to get apartment owners to sign up with us for management:

> *Invariably, when you made your call to try to obtain the business, the owner was satisfied with the management agent or was under contract for a given period of time. Then, when you did obtain the business, the projects were in deep financial trouble. We frequently spent as much time with these projects, if not more, than we did with our own projects. When we succeeded in turning the project around, the owners then sold it and we lost the management. In other cases, the owners felt that they were now perfectly capable of managing the project—after we had turned it around. The best that could be said about this experience of managing for others was that we purchased Goodlette Arms and Canterbury House as a result.*

A rather funny incident involved a man who owned a rundown apartment complex here in town. This builder, who admitted he'd let things go downhill, came into Jack Kline's office one day and dumped a bushel basketful of invoices, leases, and all the records of the project on Jack's desk. "Here are leases, invoices—I'm sorry they're all messed up," he explained. The worst thing about it was that people were living in these units without leases. We rehabbed the project, repainted it, replanted the grounds and cleaned it out to give it a fresh start. A month after the cash started to flow, he came in and said, "I think I'll manage it myself." There's no permanence to these arrangements, so we soon concentrated fully on managing our own units.

IN 1975 FRANK BASILE joined the company. He had sound ideas about apartment management, and they came from personal experience. When he was working for the Ford Motor Company in Indianapolis, he lived in an apartment. It was obvious to him that it was poorly managed: things weren't fixed on time, infrastructure was rotting out. He asked the apartment manager how she was trained to manage the complex, and the woman replied that somebody came over from Columbus once or twice a month, chatted, dropped off some forms, and left. Frank knew there had to be a better way of running things:

> *With a high interest level in the subject, I sent out a few resumes to people I'd identified as the major apartment developers in the city. Mr. Glick thought that Max Thurston was playing a practical joke on him, because just the night before they'd discussed needing to hire someone to direct and organize the growing management function of the company. They had identified a list of characteristics the prospective manager would need to have. When Mr. Glick saw my resume, so the story goes, he wrote across the top of it: "This is the human being you and I discussed last night."*
>
> *Max is a thorough person, and he was extra thorough in checking me out. I think the interview lasted four hours. After that a friend of mine, Jim Lloyd, said, "My God, Frank, you'd think this guy was checking you out to marry his daughter instead of coming to work for the company." Little did we know at the time that that actually was going to happen—but when you're hiring somebody to run a portion of your company, you're not just hiring somebody for eight hours a day. You're hiring a person who is going to represent you in the community and nationally within the industry. On September 8, 1975, I came to work for the company.*

At the time Frank came to the company, we had twelve thousand units under management and were getting ready for another building boom. I knew that we needed more professionalism in the way we managed. Though we had some procedures in place, they needed to be committed to paper and consistently practiced. We had two divisions, and their policies varied. Frank's job was to be sure that the procedures were uniform throughout the company, that they were in writing and disseminated and maintained through the years. That's the way it worked out—our procedures are recognized as the best in the industry. In fact, they're the basis for the textbook that the National Association of Home Builders uses in training property managers.

Two people headed the management divisions. Jack Kline was in charge of central Indiana and Bill Minner headed out-of-state. Bill was a former Army officer who came from a family of actors. He appreciated and cultivated people better than almost anyone I know. Bill was a soft-sell salesman who believed that the quality of his presentation and of our product would "make the sale."

The management philosophy centered around one thing: quality service to the resident in every unit we managed. Not only did it serve our main concern of making the customer happy, it also was good advertising because satisfied people told others that Glick was good. Frank has described our focus on excellence well. He found out early and caught on fast.

> *The first week I worked for Mr. Glick, I learned to what extent he'd go to insist on quality in his projects—and that extended to management. Old-timers told me that on an inspection tour, spotting a serious defect in construction under way, he got out of his car in a pouring rain and in his Gucci shoes he sloshed through the mud and slush to make a close-up inspection and discuss the problem with the superintendent.*

We also hold our projects to a standard of excellence by evaluating them according to a standards manual that contains exacting photographs of how projects should look. Those not meeting "Gene Glick Management Standards" are timetabled for improvement.

And we don't stop there:

- Project financial goals and reports are stringently monitored for accomplishment. We have a 95 percent accomplishment of project cash flow goals through the years.
- We hire people of excellence through an organized screening and testing process, and then train them meticulously.
- Regional property managers live in the area of their highest unit density for close project supervision, which provides the

advantage of a locally managed company.

- Monday meetings with Frank, the division managers, and myself, and detailed weekly operating reports ensure careful monitoring of company progress.
- Compensation plans including bonuses provide incentives for employees to achieve their share of company objectives.

Our goal has always been to hire people of excellence, to ensure that they are well trained to do their jobs and to provide the type of environment that inspires and motivates them to do the best they can. Our supervisors treat each and every employee as a human being, the same as they would want to be treated themselves. This combination of hiring the right person for the job, training, and ongoing compassionate supervision encourages excellent performance and long tenure. We have been very fortunate to have one of the lowest employee turnover rates of any organization in the property management industry. Illustrative of the type of people that we hire who perform in an excellent manner over the years is Mary Clark, who is an assistant property manager, and who has been with our organization since September 5, 1972.

In line with the value that we place upon our human assets, we have a human resource department which is headed by Mike White, our vice president of human resources. Mike is the type of person who has both the knowledge and compassion to represent our associates and to ensure that our policies and actions are designed to help them grow and develop, both personally and professionally.

When Mike first came on board I told him that his primary responsibility was to assist property management in hiring and training people of excellence to operate our projects and serve our residents. One of the key areas in which he is directly involved is establishing and administering our fringe benefits package. My goal has always been to provide the best package in our industry to help ensure that we attract and retain the people of excellence that we desire. One of the key components of our package is our retirement/profit-sharing plan in which we set aside roughly 15 percent of corporate earnings for each qualified employee. The typical industry average is somewhere around 3 percent. With the exception of only two years, we have been able to meet our goal. In 1975 we were unable to make the full contribution and in 1979 we made no contribution because the company suffered a substantial loss.

In line with our policy of developing people to move up in the organization, we also ensure that we have replacements when key people either resign or retire. Such is the case with Max Thurston, who retired as executive vice president on December 31, 1996.

Max had the foresight to hire Dean Donnelson, a man with the credentials and background to assume many of Max's responsibilities. He was hired in 1992 and was groomed to provide a smooth transition as Max became a consultant, leaving full-time employment to pursue other personal interests.

Another important constituency within our organization is our investors whose function has been capably handled through the years by Bev Taylor, another of our longtime employees, having started with the organization in January 1969. She has now progressed to asset manager, helping Dean Donnelson oversee the management of our apartment projects.

Perhaps most important of all are the yearly visits we make to every one of our sites. They give us much-needed insights, including general impressions and opportunities for improvement. But most of all, they're symbolic. They show that the people who have the ultimate responsibility care about every individual serving the company, every customer and every unit we provide. The bosses aren't at headquarters. They're on the spot to show they care.

I really believe that this sort of symbolic imaging is important in our business. Frank tells the story of Avis president Lynn Townsend, the man responsible for the turnaround in Avis from substantial loss to profit, who wore the uniforms donned by car jockeys or rental clerks to show in a graphic way that there's not much difference between the president and the person behind the counter. That's really true. Frank demonstrated this as soon as he came to the company—he was casting around for some way to really learn the business on the front lines.

On my first day with the company I reported to the maintenance garage at Carriage House North. I'll never forget the maintenance superintendent. His name was Danny Carberry. I introduced myself and said, "I'm coming to work for the company." He looked at me warily and said, "Our offices are over there. Not here." I said, "I know where they are, but I thought I'd work here for a week in maintenance." He looked at me again skeptically, and then told me he was getting ready to sweep the garage. So my very first job with the company was sweeping the garage at Carriage House North. All week I worked with maintenance. They tolerated me. The next week I was in the rental office. The third week I showed up in the home office. . . . No matter what we do at 8330 Woodfield Crossing, the main impact happens at the site—primarily with the property manager and the maintenance superintendent. If you don't have good people on site, you don't have a good operation.

That says it all as far as I'm concerned.

When Frank came, he initiated specific changes which evolved into a new system for management of our rental properties. First of all, we reorganized the on-site supervisory responsibilities. Before this, the property manager and the maintenance superintendent had equal authority and reported directly to the regional property manager. That caused problems; only one person should be in charge on site. But putting the property manager in charge, changing the coequal relationship, didn't happen overnight. It took five years to make this work well. A lot of follow-up was necessary to ensure that the property manager really was empowered to direct. Issuing a directive is 5 percent of the job; seeing that it's carried out is 95 percent.

We want to know the condition of our projects, both good and bad. That is the only way we can continue to improve. Frank tells an interesting story which demonstrates the importance we place upon marketing as well as "telling it like it is."

In late 1987 there was an overbuilt condition in apartments throughout the country, and occupancy was about to go down. In anticipation of this situation, we decided to hire for the first time a director of marketing to provide overall direction to our marketing effort.

Furthermore, the goal of property management is to increase the value of the asset—the apartment project. To do this we must increase net operating income (NOI) since the capitalization method is used to determine value. If we are to increase NOI, we must either increase income and/or reduce expenses. There is only so much you can do to reduce expenses and generally we have good expense control. In fact, in some cases a further reduction of expenses could be counterproductive to the marketing effort. Therefore, the significant upside potential for NOI is to increase income. This is accomplished through raising rents and increasing occupancy. Thus, marketing is essential.

We had three finalists for our newly created position. I asked each one to visit three projects, one of which we knew was not up to our usual standards. Two of the applicants reported what they thought we wanted to hear, that the project was in great shape. Only Jennifer Nevitt reported the facts as they were, and we hired her! She was with us for eight years and did a great job in helping us to become more marketing oriented.

When Jennifer, who had been with us for seven and a half years, left the company in 1993 to pursue her entrepreneurial ambitions, we were again fortunate to have someone join us with similar marketing and leasing skills—Brenda Coons. We did not miss a beat as we moved from our first director of marketing to our second.

I'VE SAID BEFORE that it's important to really listen to people. The turtle cards are one way we do that. We are proud of the fact that we get very few cards rated other than "excellent" or "good." For the most recent twelve-month period (1996) we responded to 142,960 service requests, which resulted in 105,600 cards being returned to the home office, an impressive 74 percent. Of these, 88 percent were marked "excellent," 9 percent "good," .8 percent "average," .027 percent "below average" (29 cards), and .034 percent "poor" (36 cards).

Particularly because of this superb service-request handling, we were able to launch a new concept in apartment marketing with a full-page ad in the Sunday edition of *The Indianapolis Star*. The ad announced the first money-back guarantee in the apartment industry and read

> *The Glick Guarantee: We're true to our word. If for any reason you are not satisfied within the first 30 days of occupancy and move, we will cheerfully refund all rent monies and your security deposit, providing there has been no damage to your apartment. No questions asked!*

This promotion, which we continue to use, turned out to be highly successful in attracting and keeping quality residents. In the long run, it has cost the company very little because the records show that few people have taken advantage of the guarantee.

Complaints aren't always easy to take, but listening carefully to them is one of the primary public relations tools we employ as business people. I recall a time early in the company's history when we were building single-family dwellings. We were small potatoes in the construction business; acting as general contractor, we were building just sixteen houses a year. The larger developers were building two hundred, so of course the subcontractors would go to take care of their building needs first, working us in. We'd work out a schedule. They'd tell us when they were going to finish, and people would buy a home and we'd promise to finish it if the contractors lived up to their agreements with us.

Out in the Ritter neighborhood, seven women called me one day. We were building their homes and they had all met each other at the construction sites, chatting as new neighbors, and they had all discovered we were behind schedule. "We're all just as sore as we can be," they said. "You gave us a move-in date, and you're six weeks behind now. We want to come over and see you now."

We set a time and, at the appointed hour, in came the seven irate women. They began to give it to me. One would say, "We've had to get out of our apartments and you are not delivering for us on time." Then another would speak up. "You're not living up to your promise." I didn't say anything. I was listening. So when they finished, I said, "You know, you ladies are absolutely correct. If I were in your place I'd be even more vociferous than you have been. I did tell you two months ago that you'd be in in a month and I have no fault with your complaint. Every night I sit up till 2 and 3 o'clock calling these subcontractors to get them over here. I don't want to rush the jobs on Ritter. I insist these subcontractors send us only their most capable men, and sometimes we have to wait. But you're right—you're not in. I want to tell you that we are going to do everything in our power to get you in just as soon as possible. I am sincerely sorry for what has happened."

The ladies looked at each other. One of them finally spoke up: "We wanted to be mad at you when we came over here. You've taken the wind out of our sails. We thought you'd yell at us about bothering you." I told them I was talking to them as I'd want to be talked to, and I asked them to have a cup of tea with me. I told them the various definite steps we were taking to move the projects along, and then I said, "Soon after you move into your new home, you'll forget about the extra month it took to build, but you will always be aware of the quality." They nodded and left, satisfied.

It's better to admit you're wrong when it's necessary; it's the best way to deal with legitimate complaints. We still try to sincerely listen to our customers' concerns and to take appropriate action. Sometimes it's difficult, but the same methods work: listen carefully, respond with sensitivity, showing them you care and answering with facts, and implement a satisfactory solution as soon as possible.

Recently we remodeled our condo in Florida. We tried to follow the same general pattern. As always, we were working against time, and the contractor was trying to meet a bonus deadline. The marble people were working day and night for him, weekends too. Some of the neighbors were subjected to a lot of racket from the beginning of the project, wheelbarrows running up and down the halls, framing from scratch in two units—pounding and clomping and all of that. At the management meeting we explained the rush to complete the units, but a woman who lived two units away was very angry. She said she was going to call the police if there was any work on Friday or Saturday.

I tried to remain calm and said to her, "We do have the right to be there. We followed all the rules and regulations of the condo association and obtained all the permits from the city of Palm Beach. I know you have been inconvenienced, but the workmen have made every effort to be considerate, putting runners down to decrease the noise and so forth." But she wouldn't be mollified. Another woman, who lives right next door to the job, had a different approach. "Gene," she said, "I know you have the right to do this and I appreciate your need to work weekends. But I am having a bridge group in here this weekend and it would be a special favor if you didn't work on Saturday. Could that please be arranged?" How nice that sounded. I found ways to answer both complaints by asking my men to gather everything up and be out by Friday night that weekend.

One time I didn't listen to complaints, and the union came in because of it. During the early 1970s we had some very demanding maintenance supervisors. A couple of them, loyal to the company as the day is long, but overzealous, caused irritation. The maintenance men grew disgruntled. It never came to my attention, and so I could never do anything about it until they had voted in the union in the Indianapolis area.

It had happened on my watch, so it was my responsibility. If I'd known, I'd have had someone go to the maintenance men at the various projects and find out what was bothering them, to walk in their moccasins, as my mother used to say.

Frank has said how important maintenance is in apartment management. He couldn't be more right. Wayne Pio had been with the company for some years as a construction superintendent when we asked him to be in charge of maintenance supervision. He was a dedicated, hard-working company man who loved his job, and a very religious man as well. He was also a strict disciplinarian. Sometimes that seemed harsh to some employees.

I approve of unions in general, but I believe in an open shop so that people have a choice. The last time we were drafting an agreement, I said, "I want this to be an open shop." I thought that was best for the company. We now have an open shop and it works well for everyone.

Henry Ryder, a partner with Barnes and Thornburg, was the perfect labor attorney to persuade the Teamster's Union representatives to accept our open-shop proposal. For many years Henry was our primary labor attorney. He has always had a natural ability to deal with people and to arrive at negotiated settlements that were good for both sides and did not leave any residual bad feelings. This was very important in our union negotiations.

A company like ours needs to constantly be alert to employees' concerns. That's why we implemented conflict resolution procedures to be followed by all staff in dealing with disputes, whether among employees or between employees and residents. Conciliation requires great skill.

Sometimes it isn't easy. In Naples, Florida, we had a standoff between the property manager, who was really competent, and a difficult resident. This was the resident from Hades, a maintenance person's nightmare, the very personification of Mrs. Difficult. HUD was giving us flak, and even the city said, "Why don't you pacify this woman?" The complaints were petty, but we finally fixed them all anyway. Then she moved, and later it turned out that everywhere she went she was Mrs. Difficult—she lived that way.

Occasionally, conciliation doesn't work and you have to go to court. Especially in construction it can be very costly and aggravating and tie up the company endlessly. One of those failed general contractors I was talking about went bankrupt. It was a pity because he was the third generation head of a very respected company. As many of these firms did during the boom-and-bust period of construction, he took on more business than he could handle just to pay bills, with no cost controls or self discipline. He couldn't finish, and we were stuck with a huge cost overrun and an incomplete project.

It was a bonded project and finally we took the bonding company to court. We hired an expensive Washington law firm, Arnold and Porter, and eventually the case went to the American Arbitration Association. Testimony showed that the contractor was a playboy who had frittered the company away, and our project along with it. But the cost of the project had mounted to $2.2 million more than the contract. The bonding company wasn't square with us—they'd represented to us that the contractor was not a risk, that he'd be able to finish our job. They knew better. Eventually they settled, but we had to eat much of the cost overrun and pay enormous legal fees.

Not everyone in the company is gifted in conciliatory talk. Bernie Landman, one of the best executives in our company's history, was a tough negotiator and very direct. During one period we were putting up houses with a sweat-equity program. Some of the purchasers had special skills—maybe they were good carpenters, or could do hardwood floors. Or they'd clean up the job site, doing away with the need to send people in to do that. Marilyn and I went away on a trip, leaving Bernie in charge, and some of the purchasers were not getting their sweat-equity jobs done on time. Contractors were calling Bernie, saying, "These people are holding up our operations." Bernie was his usual direct self. He called the buyers and said, "You have got to go in there and do this work immediately or we'll do it for you and charge you." More complications with the program followed, and he got so mad that he abolished the program then and there, without consulting me.

But when I returned I told him we needed to resume the program because we needed to stick to our commitments. We'd promised sweat equity—we should deliver. So everyone has his own best territory, and very few are ombudsmen. Still, everyone is a unique spoke in a wheel whose center is service to our residents.

We try not to stir up trouble in the neighborhoods we enter. Zoning has always been a major hurdle, of course, because people incorrectly assumed that when we zoned for low- to moderate-income projects with HUD we would put up shoddy buildings for undesirables, something that would downgrade the neighborhood.

Neighborhood residents and local officials of all sorts would try anything within the law (and sometimes outside it) to stop what they perceived as a bad step for their area. Jim Bisesi recalls difficulties with our zoned properties:

> *I think we went on with a zoning hassle in Florence, Kentucky, for about two years. Finally we got it approved and built and of course it's one of the nicest things in Florence—much nicer than a lot of the conventional projects. In Lauderdale Lakes, Florida, we bought a piece of property that was already zoned for multifamily, so there wasn't much anyone could do, though they wanted to. When they knew we had additional land for subsequent phases, to expand the project, they changed the building code to require larger units than those we were building. So we had to amend our architectural plans to build larger units to comply with the zoning ordinance.*
>
> *Another good example where local government tried to keep us out was Bowling Green, Kentucky, and that's probably one of the nicest projects in the city today.*
>
> *Our company was an exception to what you would normally think of when you talk about subsidized housing. People often stop in our offices trying to rent, not realizing the units are subsidized. Some of them get very insistent when they're told they can't rent. We don't have the visual stigma, if you want to call it that, and I think that's a result of Mr. Glick's philosophy and our own design. We would seldom select a site for a subsidized housing project that we wouldn't also build a conventional project on. We weren't out looking for cheap land in bad areas.*

PEOPLE HAVE OFTEN SAID that we have created beautiful living areas which enhanced their communities. Jim hired Bill McKee, who for a long time did the majority of our architectural work, and he hired very wisely. Many agencies, including numerous HUD offices, Illinois Housing, and Kentucky Housing, and municipalities tell Jim that the plans and specifications we submitted were superior to anyone's. Bill McKee's plans were so detailed and excellent that there was never any fumbling or uncertainty in our presentations at agency meetings. We've flown all over the U.S.—from Minneapolis to Washington, D.C., Florida, and the states in between—and it's this Johnny-on-the-spot treatment that has helped define the company and ensure its standards of excellence.

NOT TOO LONG AGO AT LUNCH I told someone that through the years we had built over thirty thousand units and now managed over twenty thousand. In addition, we have provided homes for an estimated half-million people and provided over 15,000 jobs in connection with their construction, and another 650 ongoing jobs for the past thirty-five years in connection with their management. He seemed surprised, and of course it is noteworthy. Quite honestly, it surprises me; it makes me realize what a long road it has been from those days in the baseball fields near my neighborhood on Salem Street.

Truly, though, it really is not that far removed. I loved the rough-and-tumble kind of baseball we had then, the organizing and team-building skills it took to get a squad on the field, the competition with the boys from the other neighborhoods on those lots along Meridian Street, the satisfying crack of the bat, and the risk as the ball sailed toward somebody's window. The only trouble was, my team didn't win a lot because I had friends and relatives on it instead of the best players.

Today all the elements of that earlier competition are there, but I do have the winning team—there's the difference. The best, most dedicated and ethical people we could find have, over the years, made the Gene B. Glick Company what it is. And if they have become my friends, that's all to the good.

Thanks to our seven-hundred-plus employees, our success has carried us into the nineties strong and viable as a company. We are one of the largest privately owned housing development and management companies in the nation. We have built more than four thousand single-family and twenty-six thousand multifamily homes in twelve states from Minnesota to Florida, with a total value exceeding one billion dollars.

It is humbling and extremely gratifying to know that we are the standard in the industry. In 1992 the company received the prestigious Property Management Company of the Year award from the National Association of Home Builders. My own election to the National Housing Hall of Fame, my selection for the Master Entrepreneur Award for Indiana (1990), and the Indiana University School of Business Distinguished Alumnus Award reflect credit on everyone in the company. Most recently, in 1997 I was inducted into the Central Indiana Business Hall of Fame, and received the Lifetime Achievement Award from the National Association of Home Builders (this has been awarded only once before); also in 1997 I received the Lifetime Achievement Award from the Louisville HUD office, the Kentucky Housing Corporation, and the Southeast Association of HUD Managing Agents.

Of these honors and accomplishments we're very proud, and we'd like to see everyone in our profession achieve this level of performance. That's why we readily share our operations manual; all that any of our competitors needs to do is call and ask and pay for the printing. The more professional we all are, the better we serve the public, the better the reputation the industry enjoys, and everyone benefits.

Still, we can't rest on any part of our reputation. I recall, and sometimes share with the people in the company, the prayer that is attributed to President Eisenhower:

> *Oh, Lord God, when Thou giveth unto Thy servants to undertake any great measure, grant to us also the wisdom to know that it is not the beginning, but the continuation of same until it be thoroughly finished that yieldeth to Thee true glory.*

The excellence one demonstrates today should be nothing compared to the excellence to be demonstrated around the next bend. Naturally, we've progressed into the nineties with minority hiring and the advancement of women in the company. How could a father of four daughters want anything else but excellent opportunities for females? Eleven of the fourteen division and regional managers are women, and we have scores of other women serving in positions of responsibility. We now have two female vice presidents. One is Deana Wilson, who has been with the company for over twenty years and began her career as an on-site manager, and Anita Smith is the other. Both of these women are true professionals and have made major contributions to the advancement of the company.

We did have a bout with a sexual harassment suit. In the mid-eighties, a property manager at one of our northern Indiana projects filed suit, claiming she was being harassed by the maintenance superintendent and the assistant maintenance superintendent, also by the regional manager and probably a couple of others. She was asking a hundred thousand dollars in settlement. The insurance company advised us to settle. Our attorneys were Virginia McCarty, a former federal judge who had graduated first in her law school class at IU, and Jim Beatty, with Bernie available, of course.

Listening to the plaintiff, our attorneys doubted her story. It was bothersome: should we let our insurance company settle or fight? No one wants sexual harassment to occur. Were our policies being ignored? I wanted an explanation. Bernie went up for the deposition stage of the testimony and came home convinced the woman was lying. He recommended that we absolve the insurance company, let them out of it, and assume responsibility ourselves.

The testimony seemed to favor us, with the woman admitting she was intimately involved with two of our maintenance men. A third relationship started, and conflict ensued, with epithets thrown by both the woman and her former lovers—there was bad blood. We thought we had the suit won, but we lost in what has become a textbook case of sexual harassment. What I learned from that is that when the insurance company says settle, you should settle.

But there was an interesting sidelight. Our family went on a cruise on the Italian Riviera later, and on the boat a man came up to me, introduced himself, and said he was a lawyer for the firm that had represented the plaintiff. "We were really surprised when we won," he admitted. "We fully expected to lose that case." But he was not as surprised as I was. To this day, when I read the transcript of the trial, I still can't find a shred of evidence indicating sexual harassment.

THERE ARE MANY ELEMENTS to the success of the Gene B. Glick Company—with the caliber and performance of each person in the organization being the primary cause of our gratifying results.

Second only to that is the system of property management we established to ensure staff professionalism and excellent service. Training is primary and we have been fortunate to have Chris Wolfe as director of training since 1985. She started with the company as an on-site manager in 1970. The company was cited for having the best training program in any industry in 1990 by the Central Indiana chapter of the American Society for Training and Development, the premier organization of training professionals.

Frank Basile, as vice president of property management, received the 1983 Property Manager of the Year award given by the National Association of Home Builders. Chris received the same award in 1991. Also, in 1983, Frank won the Professional Builder Apartment Management Achievement Award, given only when the staff of *Professional Builder* magazine feels that there is a person deserving of this recognition. It has not been given since then.

Careful monitoring of all programs and projects has been, and always will be, a key to our success. The three division managers have been with the company anywhere from four years to twenty years. Besides Deana, our other two capable division managers are Jim Lyons and John Hancock. Regional property managers report to the division managers and are responsible for hiring, training and supervising the on-site managers. Our detailed standards of excellence in maintaining apartment projects—and follow-up to see that these standards are enforced—fulfill the "95 percent factor" of success: seeing that things get done.

There are five levels in the rating scale for the projects: superior, above average, average, below average and poor. We inspect each property once a year—traveling either in our own plane, piloted by Jim Bisesi, or in a chartered helicopter. With our years of experience, we can roam a project and from our sampling extrapolate the condition of the rest of the project. Generally Jim goes with the maintenance people and I go with the rental people, meeting in the office afterward in what I call "executive session." Jim will put down his rating and I put down mine and we'll compare; rarely do we vary more than one level. We take careful notes, and before we leave we tell the managers what we've found. Then a detailed report is sent to them, listing the areas of improvement needed. If they get into the superior range, they all go to dinner on the company. If improvements are needed, Jim does the follow-up after the report. As usual, 95 percent is follow-up to see that improvement is made.

Running a top-notch management company isn't easy. We're in twelve states, and getting and keeping people of excellence is very demanding. It's much easier to operate an office building. There you have only a few tenants. If you have General Motors or Hewlett Packard as a tenant, all you really need are some top-quality maintenance people to keep them happy; one check comes in to you for the rent. But in residential you may have five hundred checks coming in from one apartment project—five hundred people to satisfy, and they're much less tolerant of management's mistakes. Residential apartment management is very, very labor intensive. We have set a standard in handling these difficult challenges that has made us the envy of the industry.

We must be ever alert to changing needs and continue to monitor cost controls. During preparation of the annual project budget, we compare budgeted expenses with expense standards at each project and review actual expenses monthly to be sure we stick to the budget. This system has always worked: we've realized 95 percent accomplishment of our cash flow goals through the years.

Independent appraisals, and those done by Steve Valinet's team, have helped us accurately assess the value of our properties. We have not been satisfied with accepting government tax assessments and paying them automatically. Instead, we've developed machinery to contest them when we think they are inaccurate.

Steve does his job well and he's certainly intense. Once, while doing an on-site analysis in Florida, he was focusing on dictating some facts he'd gleaned about the competition's operations, and he walked right into a concrete wall. Blood trickled from the wound; he'd suffered a concussion. As they tried to take him away to get medical help, Steve kept saying, "I've got to get this report out and back to Glick." I can see giving your all for the company, but your blood? That is too much.

These days, we focus especially on safety. Frank Basile heads a committee to study and investigate ways the company can keep our people safe on the job. As a result of their work, we've substantially reduced on-the-job injuries and incidents where our valued employees get hurt—as well as lowering premiums we must pay.

In the early years of our organization every nickel that we accumulated was plowed back into the business as we continued to grow and build. In later years, as our building slowed down, we had some excess funds which had to be properly invested to secure the best returns. It became necessary to employ someone to oversee the management of our investments. Fortunately, we had the right person at the right time for the right job. This was Tom Grande, who has done a fine job of not only managing our investments, but also handling our risk management.

The building business is risky enough without assuming additional risks outside of our normal business, such as fire, liability claims, and accidents. For this we must make sure that we have proper coverage to protect our investors and associates. Again, this function has been capably managed by Tom, with the assistance of Doug Porter and the folks at Wells and Co.

We are constantly looking for opportunities to increase our company's profitability while at the same time providing superior products and services to our projects. As a result, we have added such ancillary services as alternative phone and cable systems, leasing of laundry equipment to the projects, and a service division. Our director of purchasing, Tom Blandford, has assumed responsibility for coordinating our ancillary income activities along with his primary purchasing job. In addition, Frank uses Tom in many different capacities as the need arises. He is an excellent "utility infielder," to borrow a phrase from baseball.

The rating—superior, above average, average, below average, and poor, with pluses and minuses on either side—is a monitoring device and a behavioral incentive. The top rating cannot be achieved, of course, without the people of excellence I've spoken of so often. The property managers and the maintenance superintendents are the keys to a superior operation. They work where the rubber meets the road.

Above the people on site, the property manager and maintenance superintendent, are the regional property managers and division managers; it's their responsibility to see that people of excellence are managing these sites and to monitor the continuing effort to stay superior. Rental rates are closely watched in relation to local market factors, and advertising and promotion is in the hands of the people on site. After all, they understand their own neighborhoods. They use the operations manual to aid them in making their decisions. The manual is important, but what good does it do if it just gathers dust on a rack? They must follow it—and we must follow up on them.

What happens when, after repeated review, a given property can't seem to improve its rating to "superior"? Is the problem the policies and procedures? Probably not now—we have revised them to the extent that they really represent the best and most practical path to excellence. No, when ratings don't improve, it's obvious somebody isn't following the policies and procedures. The few projects which don't stack up, remaining below "superior" over a period of time, are usually the most difficult ones we have. A variety of people inhabit our units, including some elderly people whose apartments could grace the pages of a magazine, spotless and tasteful.

But some residents are simply irresponsible. Some have had two or three cars up on blocks, with oil oozing out onto other people's parking spots. Certain apartments seem to be damaged repeatedly. Certainly there's a bit of truth to the managers' complaints that some people act like slobs. However, if the people in charge on site were implementing the policies and procedures correctly, these problems wouldn't linger. You wouldn't hear excuses; you'd see results. They'd know who the problem residents are and how to work with the local police to take care of them.

For example, our people in Lauderdale Lakes, Florida, fixed some very thorny issues by working to overcome problems at the local level.

When I was in Florida to inspect our projects, I would visit them by helicopter; Marilyn would look in the Yellow Pages and contract the copter providing the lowest bid. On one trip we chartered a very plush copter and flew to Lauderdale Lakes, which at that time was in the heart of a heavy drug-trafficking area.

When we landed we were immediately surrounded by police and sherrifs' cars. The officers threatened the pilot, shouting that landing any place but an airport was prohibited. I was positive they were going to arrest him. I managed to go on to inspect the property, and when I returned about an hour later the policemen and deputies were taking turns sitting in the helicopter. It turned out that the copter belonged to actor Burt Reynolds, which we hadn't known. We found out later that there was so much dope being smuggled inland from ships offshore, that the police were certain our helicopter mission was drug-related.

When Rae Ezzo became the manager of Lauderdale Lakes, she worked with the police department, the sheriff, and the city fathers to get rid of the drug dealers and other people who didn't want to live like decent human beings in a safe environment. She turned a real hell-hole into an oasis, creating a model project at Lauderdale Lakes—one that's won all kinds of awards.

It isn't easy managing an apartment project in this day and age. What we need on site is a person who loves people and sincerely cares about them, who has the brains and courage to evict people who should be evicted and encourage the rest of the residents to support civilized behavior.

We set a goal of having all of our apartment properties earn superior ratings during our annual inspections of 1997, on our fiftieth anniversary as a company.

What difference does it make if our project is rated superior? Well, I can tell you it makes a lot of difference to the people who live there. These apartments are their homes; we want each resident to take pride in that home. I take pride in bringing my friends and my family to my home, and I want our apartments to convey that same feeling.

Chapter 10

Giving Back to the Community

Perfection is not obtainable; but if you chase perfection you can catch excellence.

—Vince Lombardi

He who helps a child helps humanity with an immediateness
which no other help provides—
nor in any stage of human life can possibly give again.

—Rev. Phillips Brooks

I BELIEVE IT'S APPROPRIATE as I conclude my comments about the company to relate the mission statement of our organization as it exists today, which is basically a management entity:

> *Our mission is to continue to be one of the best apartment management companies nationally by hiring and training people of excellence to accomplish the following goals:*
>
> 1. *Provide quality housing and excellent service to our residents.*
> 2. *Maintain our properties to our high standards.*
> 3. *Accomplish the cash flow and other objectives of our property owners.*

Of course, not everyone in the organization is directly involved in accomplishing these goals, but this is what we are all about. Many play a supporting role to those who *are* responsible for delivering quality service, maintaining our high standards, and accomplishing the cash flow goals.

Our mission statement does not differentiate between conventional and subsidized housing. Residents in subsidized housing deserve quality housing and service. True, these projects may not have the same amenities as conventional projects, such as a swimming pool and tennis courts. However, all residents are entitled to a well-maintained property and excellent service.

I derive a great deal of satisfaction when people—both industry and non-industry—comment that our projects look as good or better than conventional ones, either ours or our competitor's. When I hear this, I know that our on-site personnel are accomplishing our objectives as defined in our mission statement, which is color-blind when it comes to type of projects and residents.

In fact, the satisfaction achieved by our subsidized housing personnel can be even greater because they realize that, were it not for their excellent performance and the existence of that project, their residents might not be enjoying the kind of quality housing now being provided.

Property management people who have occasion to view our projects and our policies and procedures manuals will sometimes ask to see the manuals for our subsidized projects. My answer has always been the same: we manage them *exactly* as we do our conventional projects. Our procedures governing the way we handle service requests, maintenance, cleanup, community inspections, and preventive maintenance are identical for all of our projects regardless of whether they are conventionally financed or HUD-assisted, and that's the way it should be.

Regarding goal number one, as mentioned earlier, very few returned service cards are marked "average," "below average," or "poor." This, of course, is our ongoing way of keeping track of the service we provide to our residents, who are our customers.

Regarding goal number two, when Jim Bisesi visits the projects during the annual inspection tour, he applies the same objective standards to all properties. During his 1996 tour, seventy-seven projects were rated "superior," which represented 79 percent. Eighteen projects were rated "above average."

And as for goal number three, we accomplished our cash flow

goals at nearly all projects which were not adversely affected by market circumstances over which our personnel had no control.

Finally, we know that we are accomplishing the preamble to the three goals of our mission statement because our company was selected Management Company of the Year by the 160,000-member National Association of Home Builders, which is the largest trade association in our industry. By staying focused on the three goals of our mission statement, we ensure that we *remain* among the best management companies in the country!

DURING OUR FIFTIETH YEAR of both our marriage and the Gene B. Glick Company, Marilyn and I are reflecting on the apartment communities we've built through the years and experiencing a special sense of pride in them. We'll be adding to the landscape areas we set up in 1990 and creating new ones in each of our communities.

To further demonstrate our pride, we have made a financial commitment to the community foundation of each city and each neighborhood where we built homes. In addition, we're working through the Metropolitan Indianapolis Board of Realtors, the Indiana Builders' Association, and the Apartment Association of Indiana to provide scholarships based on need and merit. These scholarships will be ongoing and I hope someday the students earning them will be celebrating the one hundredth anniversary of the company—even though we won't be there to see it.

Helping people get college educations is such a rewarding experience—and it benefits the entire society. We've also supported the Jane Addams Fellows program, which provides graduate school opportunities for very bright young people who wish to make contributions to society. These young people are inspirational; their true desire after they get an education is to help their fellow travelers on Planet Earth. Every time Marilyn and I share dinner with these young people at the beginning and end of their graduate years, I learn things I never thought about before.

When we give to charitable organizations, I feel as if each and every person in the Glick Company, and not just Marilyn and I and our children, is giving something back. We've all received so much; we can ill afford not to share. Albert Schweitzer said, "The only ones among you who will be really happy are those who have sought and found how to serve." Sometimes that service comes as we give our arms and hearts and wisdom to some cause in direct service; other times we can give resources to help the cause.

Giving is one of life's great joys, and most people discover and live that truth by the time they get a little older. Marilyn and I are enjoying the opportunity to intelligently contribute much of what we have earned to worthwhile causes. I hope we have a lot of years to do that: Robert Browning said, "Grow old with me, the best is yet to be. The last of life for which the first was made. . . ." I'd agree with that now that I've "arrived."

In 1982 Marilyn and I established the Eugene and Marilyn Glick Foundation for charitable, educational and religious purposes. Its purpose mirrors the philosophy of Maimonides, the medieval Jewish scholar and philosopher who believed there are eight levels to giving, with self-serving or easy charity on the lower levels. At the highest is teaching someone to take care of him- or herself: That's the best way to serve a needy person. Some important causes and groups which encourage personal responsibility as the basis of successful living include

- CHILDREN: Ultrasound equipment on the MOM Mobile, which goes into low-income areas doing ultrasound readings on pregnant women at risk. PRO-100, a career guidance program for low-income young people.
- EDUCATION: The Next-Step program, which stays in touch with the PRO-100 young people during school years to help provide support toward a strong educational background, and the Wells Scholars program at IU.
- MEDICINE: Contributions to various health foundations, the Indiana Society to Prevent Blindness, and the Sigma Theta Tau nursing honorary's Center for Nursing Scholarships.

THE ROAD FROM MY CHILDHOOD on Salem Street may seem a long one, yet many of my interests remain the same. The young boy who skipped piano lessons to play baseball became a man who loves both music and sports.

I was on the Indianapolis Symphony Orchestra board for years, involved in three endowment campaigns, both through the foundation and through individual gifts. I recall Mary Jo Bradley headed the first campaign, Tom Moses the second. He died during the campaign and Henry Ryder came on to serve in his place. It was a pleasure to serve with these civic-minded citizens.

As our foundation considers future gifts to the orchestra, I would like our contributions to be used for educational purposes, perhaps with an interactive TV project that connects schools in a study program to excite and educate kids about music, for example. I can still recall those music appreciation sessions at School 60, with the rich, erudite voice of Walter Damrosch teaching us about Beethoven and Bach. We must be sure our children also develop an understanding of the arts.

Marilyn has devoted time, energy, and financial resources to assembling and managing one of the nation's finest collections of glass art. Bret Waller, director of the Indianapolis Museum of Art, and Barry Shifman, IMA's curator of decorative art, have organized a show, complete with catalogue, for what they consider to be a masterful collection. Many of Marilyn's pieces are now displayed at the museum, on whose board I've also served.

I like to stand in the gallery amidst the items from Marilyn's collection, to watch wide-eyed schoolchildren go through and point, amazed, at some masterpiece of glass. One Swedish piece, a boat, is suspended from the ceiling. As visitors view it, they can see White River Valley through the large glass windows immediately behind the boat. When Marilyn and I are gone, the entire collection will go to the museum. The credit for selecting and displaying this collection is all hers; I pay bills and admire, which reminds me of an old joke: Two men were talking one day, and one said, "You know, my wife made me a millionaire." "Really—what were you before?" the other responded. "A multi-millionaire!" came the reply.

Most of all, though, I think, our continuing interest has been in the character-building activity of sports. My great love has been the program called PRO-100, mentioned earlier in the foundation's support list. The program began when I attended a meeting of the Greater Indianapolis Progress Committee, which I served as a director. State Representative William Crawford, a Democrat from Indianapolis, had come to the meeting in the mayor's office in the City-County Building. He surprised me by taking the mayor and those of us in the business community to task for our failure to respond to the plight of unemployed teenagers in the Indianapolis area. He went on to describe the devastating effects of joblessness on young people—on their own lives, neighborhoods, and the community at large. He said we'd failed to take action on what had to be one of the city's most crucial problems.

When Mr. Crawford left the meeting, I followed him downstairs and, catching up with him at the front door, introduced myself. "What you described a few minutes ago to the group upstairs confirms what I read about in recent publications," I said. "I agree with you—we have a severe problem. Do you have any recommendations about what we could do to find a solution?"

"I know the problem," he replied regretfully. "But I'm afraid I don't have the solution." Perhaps, I thought later, we could provide summer employment for jobless young people in low-income areas. An idea came to me. That summer, Indianapolis was to be the host for the United States Amateur Golf Tournament at Eagle Creek—the "Publinx" tournament. They would surely need caddies. We quickly organized a group of people willing to train these young people to be caddies for the tournament.

We were to pay a minimum wage, and the golfers themselves could provide tips for their caddies. The golf pro at Eagle Creek, Jerry Hayslett, agreed to give the kids some basic instruction in golf during their off time. He had some old golf clubs he could let the kids use. The program began to expand, and the students started to draw payroll checks for sprucing up the landscaping at the public golf courses, which really could use the help in those days.

During this time Marsha Oliver, executive director of the Private Industry Council, suggested that we create a public-private enterprise, of which the Indianapolis Network for Employment and Training could be the administrative arm. INET would verify the young people's eligibility, write checks and save us from the details of administering such a program.

So the government, under the Comprehensive Employment and Training Act, worked with us in a joint venture. The act now governing the PRO-100 program is the Job Training Partnership Act, cosponsored by Senators Ted Kennedy and Dan Quayle. Thus, Indianapolis created what is considered by many to be the best summer youth employment program in America. By 1996 INET was no longer actively involved in the administration of the program; that role has been assumed by the Children's Bureau of Indianapolis.

During the fourteen or fifteen years that we worked with INET, we developed an excellent program for training disadvantaged, primarily inner-city youth—white, Hispanic, and black, but primarily black, and that continues to this day. About 100 to 120 interns, as we call them, are screened each year for eligibility. Each must be a member of a family whose income is below the poverty line. They work at Indianapolis public golf courses and at Indianapolis Public Schools sites, planting shrubs and trees, grooming lawn areas, cleaning up trash, and improving and beautifying the premises.

PRO-100 operated originally from plans drawn by two well-known landscape architectural firms: Browning Day Mullins Dierdorf, and Mark Holeman. These firms identified tree and shrub gardens and rest areas that over a ten-year period could be dramatically improved to add to the beauty of the golf courses. Some of this plan proved impractical, so alterations were made.

Nowadays we use a yearly plan devised by the landscape architects, a plan which takes into account the kids' skill levels and the amount of resources the foundation has to expend on the summer's projects.

Barbara Gunn heads the Glick Foundation. She describes the workings of PRO-100 this way:

We have had the program evaluated three times since I've been with it. In one of the evaluations it was suggested that kids could probably relate well to public school sites. We began to include them, but we continue to focus on public golf courses, because Mr. Glick believes golf is an important recreation, one that can teach lessons and will be good for lifetime fitness and sports enjoyment.

Serious training goes on all summer. We have added computer work where kids can sit at the computers and explore their career choices. What we've found is that minority kids who live at the poverty level have unrealistic perceptions of work in society. For instance, someone may say he or she wants to be a doctor and yet not be interested in education after high school at all. They don't want to hear our counselors tell them that, but they seem to accept advice when the computer gives it.

When Purdue University officials evaluated the program, they said they believed teaching horticultural skills to young people helped them become contributing members of society, giving them a clear sense of accomplishment. I can see the truth of this by observing the kids' progress over a summer. Each day they generally work five hours on planting and beautification and spend an hour on instruction. They are learning about employer expectations, how to apply for and keep a job, how to set standards and take personal responsibility. We tape a job interview rehearsal with them and help them analyze it for improvement. Their "coaches" are Indiana high school and college teachers hired for the summer.

I try to meet the new interns at the beginning of the summer, and I can see their hesitation. I shake hands with them. Typically there's no eye contact. The boys shuffle around nervously. The girls giggle. They're assigned about ten interns to each coach, and their daily instruction with the coaches is very important. They're taught to address people by name, to feel confident in expressing themselves. They role-play work situations and learn conflict resolution.

But more than that, they learn practical life lessons that expand their horizons. They go out to hospitals, such as the IU Medical

Center, for a firsthand look at the various employment opportunities in the health-care field. They meet nurses' aides, technicians, occupational therapists and general health-care maintenance people. They visit colleges so they can see what a campus is like and understand the variety of subjects taught and the expectations.

Successful people like Bill Mays of Mays Chemical and Herman Blake, a vice president at IUPUI, talk to them about how to achieve success. I remember one such talk by Herman Blake. "Pay attention!" he demanded. "Look at me straight in the eye! I know you're thinking, Oh, here comes a college man, and he's got it all—a great background. Well, I want you to know that I came from a Chicago housing development, and if you think Indianapolis is tough, you've never lived in a Chicago housing development. That's the environment I came out of. No matter how bad you think you've got it, I had it worse. I overcame my difficulties, and you can too!"

I speak to them too, trying to touch the right chord to inspire. Recently I spoke of the life of Simon Haley, father of *Roots* author Alex Haley, as an example of a goal-setting person who saw education as a way to a meaningful life. "Simon's family scrimped and saved to send him to school, but finally he had to drop out. He became a Pullman car conductor." I asked the young interns to raise their hands if they knew what a Pullman car was, and nobody did, so I explained.

Then I went on: Alex's father Simon made up his mind to be the best Pullman car conductor anybody had ever seen. He rendered outstanding service for each Pullman passenger and became their friend. One wealthy man was so impressed with Simon's outstanding service that he sent a check for five hundred dollars to the school which Simon had attended, providing an anonymous scholarship for the young man. Simon went back to school, graduated, and raised several sons and daughters, all of whom became professionals: schoolteachers, artists, writers, doctors, and nurses.

I told the interns to set their goals high, to reach for the moon, to set specific goals on paper and to make that summer the first step toward realizing those goals.

And I tell the coaches that they are the leaders, the vanguard of a

A Sampling of Glick Foundation Grantees

Arts and Museums

- Arts Council of Indianapolis
- Creative Glass Center of America
- Dance Kaleidoscope
- Indiana Humanities Council
- Indianapolis Art Center
- Indianapolis Civic Theatre
- International Violin Competition of Indianapolis

Civil Rights

- United Negro College Fund
- Indiana Civil Liberties Union

Education

- Nine Universities and Colleges
- Ten Secondary School Systems
- Numerous Scholarships

Health

- Action on Smoking and Health
- Crossroads Rehabilitation Center, Inc.
- Mothers Against Drunk Driving (MADD)
- Noble Foundation, Inc.
- Riley Hospital for Children

Religion

- Anti-Defamation League
- Jewish Community Center Association
- Christian Theological Seminary
- Interfaith Homes

Seniors

- Indianapolis Senior Citizens Center
- Meals on Wheels, Inc.

Special Groups

- American Red Cross
- Gleaners Food Bank of Indiana, Inc.
- Pleasant Run Children's Home
- PRO-100/Next Step

Sports

- Indiana Special Olympics, Inc.
- Indianapolis Junior Golf Association

Youth

- Big Brothers and Big Sisters of Greater Indianapolis
- Indiana Juvenile Justice Task Force

Miscellaneous

- Hudson Institute
- Greater Indianapolis Progress Committee
- Madame Walker Urban Life Center
- Indiana University Center on Philanthropy
- Humane Society of Indianapolis

new generation. I share with them Doris Lessing's quotation: "Humans anywhere will blossom in a hundred unexpected talents and capacities simply by being given the opportunity to do so." And I give them John Gardner's idea that "it may seem paradoxical, but if you have some respect for people as they are, you can be more effective in helping them to become better."

Teachers, coaches, all of us who come in contact with young people, have tremendous impact. The famous educator Chaim Ginott said, "I've come to the frightening conclusion that I am the decisive element in the classroom. It is my personal approach that creates the climate. It is my daily mood that makes the weather. As a teacher I possess a tremendous power to make a child's life miserable or joyous. . . . In all situations, it is my response that decides whether a crisis will be escalated or de-escalated and a child humanized or dehumanized." These coaches in our program truly take their jobs seriously!

At the end of the seven weeks we take a helicopter trip to greet the graduates of the program. I used to take Mayor William Hudnut, and on this last trip Lieutenant Governor (now Governor) Frank O'Bannon accompanied me. We're also joined by the head of the city golf courses, the parks superintendent, and others.

Likewise, Mayor Stephen Goldsmith has supported many of our activities. He presented a proclamation to me declaring June 30, 1992, as Gene B. Glick Day, in honor of the forty-fifth anniversary of the company. This was in connection with a party and parade at the Williamsburg North apartment project in Indianapolis. Mayor Goldsmith also spoke at our dedication of land at 42nd and Mitthoeffer as a nature preserve.

As we approach the young people, their progress is immediately obvious. They will come right up to the dignitaries and introduce themselves and say, "Hello, sir. It's a pleasure to have you out here today. Let me show you what we've accomplished this summer." The dignitaries respond: "Glick, we weren't expecting too much, but we were really amazed at how articulate these kids are and what has been accomplished. They really have made these golf courses and school grounds more beautiful, more pleasant for everyone."

A plaque is placed by each garden the young people have improved or created, with all of the team members' names on it. I tell them, "Now here are the trees you planted. Someday you can come back and sit under them with your children and enjoy the shade they create. Bring your families, now, to see what you've accomplished." And they will do that, showing Grandma and Grandpa the trees and flower beds. We've made arrangements through the Indianapolis Parks Foundation for those plaques to be there a long time, so we all can feel the continuity.

One of the nicest features is the donation we ask each team to make at the end of the session. We will have informed them about Indianapolis' charitable institutions, and each team can choose which charity they'll make a donation to. About five dollars will be donated from the last paychecks (although they sometimes raise more), and Marilyn and I match the contribution. A letter comes back to them, thanking them for the contribution. After all, they need to develop that spirit of giving, too.

Though the summer programs are good, we found that what was really needed was a yearlong follow up and support program for the grads of PRO-100. We needed to, as the Lilly Foundation said, "nag the hell out of them to stay in school." So we established "Next Step" to give them advanced support and counseling. There are sessions on college choice and advanced vocational advice. They're encouraged to call any of the coaches who have worked with them and get advice on how to choose a college, how to use athletics for life and advancement, and maybe just a simple "hang in there." We do follow up on what has happened with our interns, and it is gratifying to see their success. We have business workers, college students, and even one at West Point.

Some people may be surprised at the variety of our philanthropic projects. We try to think carefully about our charitable giving, remembering the long-ago comment of the uncle of the young man who was getting a loan when I was a loan officer. Perhaps that uncle had taken his sentiment from Aristotle, who also said, "To give away money is an easy matter and in any man's power. But to decide to whom to give and how much and when and for what purpose, and how, is neither in every man's power nor an easy matter." Barbara Gunn expressed the philosophy of the foundation very well:

> *During an interview with* The Indianapolis Star, *Mr. Glick quoted Andrew Carnegie: "Anyone who dies with a substantial estate dies in disgrace."*
>
> *"I don't intend to do that," Mr. Glick said. They want to be sure to the greatest extent possible that the endowment funds leverage other funds, preferably government funds, but that's getting harder to do. He provides challenge grants stipulating that when a certain amount is reached, then his contribution kicks in. He also likes audited statements of the financial status of these agencies to which the foundation gives. He's very careful. He doesn't just throw his money around. Still, I have eight pages, single-spaced, of the various charities this foundation has given to. My own tabulation shows 21 percent of their gifts have been to support religious activities, 30 percent for educational and arts activities, 32 percent for charitable activities, 10 percent for health-related causes, and 5 percent for sports activities.*
>
> *Mrs. Glick is a central force in all the giving activities. She has a love of giving that goes back years. She was the youngest volunteer for the Jewish National Fund Flower Day in Detroit, at seven years of age. She's served on the boards of her Temple Sisterhood, Hadassah, the National Council of Jewish Women, and the Jewish Federation. As co-chair of the annual Borenstein Home Guild (now Hooverwood) raffle she raised the level of giving from thirty-four hundred dollars to over forty thousand. She has been active in founding the People of Vision auxiliary for the Indiana Society to Prevent Blindness, as well as serving as an integral part of fund-raising activities for United Way, Young Audiences, the Indianapolis Museum of Art and the Indianapolis Art League.*
>
> *I was touched one day when a friend was interviewing Mr. Glick for the* Indianapolis Business Journal *and asked what was the wisest decision he had ever made, and he answered, "Marrying Marilyn." I mentioned that comment to Mrs. Glick and a*

> *beautiful look came to her face and she said, "That's really touching. And you know, my wisest decision was marrying him. The longer we're married to one another, the more we admire and respect one another."*

That's true, even on the golf course, where some couples don't always admire each other.

Barbara goes on about the philosophy of our foundation:

> *Mr. Glick wants to "teach them to fish," to enable people to make their own way, and he won't support enterprises where people don't carry their own load. I think the best example of this philosophy of joint responsibility was his experience with Little League.*

Of course I wasn't affiliated with Little League in my youth, and I still think the experience we had forming our own sandlot teams was the best. We learned responsibility. We certainly learned financial management—whoever could afford a bat brought the bat, and we all brought whatever cheap softballs we could get, generally popping out at the seams. And we learned leadership and the drive toward excellence.

John Hart accuses me of sidelining players on my team who wouldn't perform to my standards of excellence. He says we were down to three players sometimes, and I suppose that's true. We learned risk-taking, especially as the ball soared toward some apartment window on Meridian Street. We knew a building superintendent or an angry resident would soon emerge, intent on revenge.

But times have changed. Little League players today learn lessons of life and character in a different way, and we have supported this program for many years. The Little League teams came to me in 1962 and wanted to know if we could provide a place to play. We gave them the Bel East Field, on the south side of 38th Street, just east of where I-465 now is. When the interstate went in, we had to move over to 38th and Post Road. There, the Fort Harrison marching band would participate in the opening day Little League parades, also furnishing frolicking clowns. We had five hundred to seven hundred youngsters playing ball in those days.

In 1997 we'll mark our thirty-fifth year of participation, with the field now being located on the west side of German Church Road north of 30th Street. We intend to have the Little League continue playing on this field through an arrangement with the Children's Bureau, which now holds official title to the ground.

I make it a point to attend the openings of the Little League at Bel East Field, which now has eight or ten grades playing, boys and girls. I throw out the first ball, and when I can't go Marianne goes in my place. She has a pretty good pitching arm. Our arrangement with them stipulates that they must keep the grounds up to certain standards of excellence. Jim Bisesi visits the field each year to make sure that the facility is well maintained and an asset to the neighborhood. Their maintenance is good, especially when they have a well-organized and effective president.

Not long ago the Little League president came up to me at one of these events and asked, "Do you remember me?" He'd been in the Pee Wee leagues when we first sponsored the field, and now he headed the organization. One year they called me a bit late for the opening day, and I'd already made reservations to go to Florida. But I told Marilyn I'd take a later flight and arranged to have a helicopter fly me over the field, so I could drop the first ball from the air.

I told the kids that they were to stand in their places, and I'd drop the ball. Whoever was nearest to where the ball dropped could tell us what improvements the field would need, and I'd donate a thousand dollars to seeing that those improvements got made. Well, of course, the best laid plans of mice and benefactors often go astray. When I dropped the ball, a mass of humanity converged on the spot, and I had to tell them I'd communicate about the improvements by mail. My dealings were with Allan Rummel, a Little League activist for many years, and Jan Hartzell, secretary to Peoples Bank president Bill McWhirter. Jan has been active in the Little League for years, arranging functions and openings and generally serving as the glue holding that organization together.

In the late eighties Mayor Hudnut asked me to come to a meet-

The PRO-100 and Next Step programs have a clear-cut mission, stated in the front of the brochure that tells about the programs:

> *A chance. It may well be the single most valuable thing you can offer to an individual and the community: the power to change a bleak before into a promising after.*

It taught me more leadership skills than anything. You are the one. You have to show some type of leadership.

—Twana Ellis
Full-time student
1986–87 PRO-100 Intern

Society looked at me and thought I couldn't make it. My PRO-100 coach looked at me and said that I could.

—Donny Hinkle
Groundskeeper/Motivational Speaker
1989–92 PRO-100 Intern

PRO-100 offers young people an alternative to the streets and a place to build confidence in their own ability.

—Duane Turner, Cadet
U.S. Military Academy
1990 PRO-100 Intern

Of all the handicaps that can stand in the way of success in a person's lifetime, perhaps the biggest handicap of all is economic disadvantage.

—Eugene B. Glick

I've always enjoyed meeting the kids and talking with them. Here I am at the South Grove Golf Course during a helicopter tour in 1996.

Courtesy Indianapolis Newspapers Inc.

In 1989, Mayor Bill Hudnut presented me with an award given by the Indianapolis Parks Department for our contributions to the parks system.

Mayor Hudnut and I inspected the work done by PRO-100 interns during the summer at city golf courses, 1984.

ing in his office. Little League officers had come to Indianapolis to talk to citizens about the possibility of creating a central regional headquarters for Little League in our city. Knowing of my keen interest in baseball and our support of Little League, he wanted me to be present, along with Jim Morris, then with the Lilly Endowment. We were to meet Creighton Hale, president of Little League Baseball then and later chairman of the board.

The Little League officials believed Indianapolis was the right spot for their regional facility. We are in the middle of the region's fourteen-state area, which would help minimize travel for training and for the regional playoffs. After the teams play each other at the regional level, they journey on to Williamsport, Pennsylvania, where the national headquarters is located and where the Little League World Series is played.

The officials made their presentation, then left, and we got down to business. Mayor Hudnut and Jim Morris said, "We want you to head up the drive to bring Little League to Indianapolis. They want the headquarters here, and you're the man."

That gave me pause. I cleared my throat and said, "I do like baseball. I think the regional headquarters is a marvelous idea, and we will make a contribution. We will give the ground for the new facility."

They said that while they appreciated the offer of the ground, what they needed was somebody to head up the campaign to raise funds. I argued that I had no idea who in the area would support the drive. I didn't want to take on a drive that had so many uncertainties and a chance of failure.

"I'll tell you what I will do, though," I said. "I'll take it on if the Lilly Endowment guarantees that after I've tried my best to raise these funds, the endowment will make up any shortfall."

No, that couldn't be done, they kept insisting. I stood firm about the guarantee, which they would not give. "Very well," I said, "we will stand by our offer to donate the land, subject to the raising of the funds—by somebody." We left, and Jim Morris asked for a ride to 49th and Pennsylvania streets, where his car was being repaired. As we drove along, both of us agreed on the project's merit.

It would be wonderful for the town to have a regional headquarters of Little League, a tremendous influence on the lives of young people. They would be building five baseball diamonds, dugouts, practice fields, a swimming pool, and a summer camp where young people could learn baseball from experts. The city would be putting up some of the money.

"Again, won't you please head this drive?" Jim asked. "We need you."

"I will do it on the basis I outlined. If we fall short, I want Lilly Endowment to intervene and put up what is necessary."

We got out of the car and shook hands, and as I was preparing to drive away, there was a tap on the window. It was Jim. "You've got a deal," he said. I headed the campaign, we built the facility, and it is beautiful.

There were people who were generous. Al Stokely has been active in Little League for years; his nephew made a major commitment, and they named the main field Stokely Field. Many of the contributions, though, came from dedicated people of modest means who loved Little League and contributed twenty-five dollars. We appreciated them all. But the solicitation was long and sometimes difficult. I learned a lot, since I was doing a lot of one-on-one solicitation. If someone won't commit right away and says he or she needs to think about it, that person is probably afraid to tell you no. They're not interested; you've just wasted their time and yours. I came to respect the person who would say no right away if he or she wasn't interested.

We have landscape architects visit the fields regularly, and Jim Bisesi goes out there with a to-do list. We want to make the facility an asset to everyone in the community, and the last few times I went out there it was impressive. The playing fields are gorgeous, and flowers have been planted around the facility—it looks like a big league park.

We are also involved with Little League in building a challenger field for physically challenged children. In the challenger program regular Little Leaguers work with those in wheelchairs. For example, the wheelchair-bound kid bats and his partner pushes him in the wheelchair to the bases. The Little Leaguer fields the ball and hands it to the kid in the wheelchair so he can throw it. There are certain regulations for dugout height, wheelchair accessibility, and parking accessibility for the challenger fields.

Little League headquarters made a movie to promote the challenger program, and it really melted my heart. It was a marvelous movie, inspiring but not at all cloying. Not-for-profits have learned to make good presentations when they appeal for funds, a skill not always available to them in earlier times. Our contribution to that fine program is to be called Bernie Landman Challenger Field.

Other causes attract our giving as well. We have been especially pleased through the years to contribute to the Wells Scholarship Fund, not only because it has enabled us to help young people, but because it has allowed us to interact with Dr. Herman B Wells, one of the greatest Hoosiers of this century. Dr. Wells, more than any other person (and there have been many), has been responsible for making Indiana University a truly great university. I've enjoyed gargantuan lunches with him, appreciating his brain power and eclectic brilliance. The Wells scholarships may lack the renown of the Rhodes scholarships, but they are just as important and rewarding to the recipients. Twenty or thirty outstanding students are selected on merit each year to receive the grants.

Each one of our four daughters also has a scholarship in her name. Arlene, Alice, and Lynda graduated from IU, and Wells scholarships are set up in their names. We are now conferring with Butler, Marianne's alma mater, to set up a similar scholarship fund there in her name.

Marilyn was busiest, I think, in her work with the People of Vision, an auxiliary of the Society to Prevent Blindness. No human being ever worked harder on that program than she did. I'd come home from the office at three or four in the morning and the lights would be on in her office as she typed prospect cards. She served as the group's first president, built up the membership roster, and continues to work on membership and fund-raising. She is justifiably proud of the group's local vision screenings and national research programs.

My main contribution to the board of Methodist Hospital was linked to my long experience as a builder. I was on the board during the time when the hospital undertook a major campaign to transform the facility from a couple of buildings on Capitol Avenue to the large regional hospital with campus-like grounds that exists today. When bids for the building were being reviewed, the board was about to reject the lowest bid because it came from a local firm that was relatively small. Board members thought the local bidder lacked the experience for such a large-scale project. I objected vehemently. If the bidder didn't have the experience, why was he allowed to bid? I wanted to know. "You completely wasted this company's time. But more importantly," I asserted, "I'm convinced this low bidder is fully capable of doing the job. They would take pride in doing it and therefore render an especially good job."

The majority did finally side with me, and the job was given to a fine Indianapolis firm, Geupel Demars. It is interesting that one or two board members, by virtue of their experience in a certain field or on other boards, can swing the votes of others. Ultimately, the expansions were successfully completed, and at a substantial savings.

When I was on the Children's Museum board, a similar situation occurred. They were going to enter into a construction management contract, and I said, "Invariably, in a construction management contract you pay more. The best way to have your building cost the least is to insist that your architect prepare top-quality plans and specifications that are crystal clear, so anyone can read them and bid. Then choose the lowest bid." That view did prevail, and the lowest bidder came in almost a million dollars less than the building manager's "guesstimate." Other members of the board were glad to have nearly a million dollars for other purposes at the museum.

I was the building committee chairman for the Hulman Pavilion at the Indianapolis Museum of Art, a position I'd accepted at the invitation of the late Bob Ashby. When he first asked me to head the building committee, I'd wanted to decline. I told him that I was swamped, but finally agreed to do it if we hired supervising architects to monitor the building progress. I didn't have time to go to the site much, but I could give them the time- and money-saving advice I'd gained through experience.

The board agreed to that arrangement. As is often the case, some people on the board seemed to think that the most brilliant people in the world all live out of state. They wanted to import an architect to do the plans for the pavilion. I argued for local people who understood the architecture of the buildings already on the Lilly property, but they decided to give the contract to an architect who had designed the Dallas Museum of Art. I lost big on that one. It wasn't even close. The chosen firm, Edward Laraby Barnes, was a fine one headed by the man who gave the company its name. These architects had real experience with museum design, but when I called the sites of their completed projects, the universal report was: "They're brilliant, but whatever your original estimate is, it will be doubled by the time they're finished."

I met with Mr. Barnes and said, "Sir, we have $11 million to spend on this building and that's all. We will have to enter into a contract that stipulates that in the event the plans you prepare come in at a cost in excess of $11 million, it will be your obligation to redesign the plans until we can find competent contractors to build what you've drawn for the price we can pay." Mr. Barnes demurred; he insisted he'd never entered into a contract like that and he didn't intend to do it with our project. But I'd told the board about my contacts with the other museums and they backed me up completely. When Mr. Barnes saw we were firm in our determination to have him guarantee he'd "get it right" for the contractors, he signed. And today Edward Laraby Barnes can take great pride in the fact that he drew a magnificent set of plans and specifications that resulted in a great addition to the museum—and he did it for the dollar amount the client had to spend.

Supervising architects visited the site once or twice a week to make sure the contractor was following the plans, and the architects submitted reports to me on a weekly basis. Unfortunately, Bob Ashby died during this process, so he never saw the beautiful pavilion. Bob was a gifted attorney and a citizen of Indianapolis who is truly missed in the arts community.

The Glick Company has also been involved in supporting

projects of the Jewish Federation. In early 1990 Mickey Maurer first made me aware of the plight of Jewish refugees from Russia. Some of these people were coming to Indianapolis. They were reasonably well-educated, but they needed temporary funds to set up in a new land—to buy tools of their trade and so forth. Harry Traugott, who ran his own small-loan company, operated the program. We provided no-interest loans to the immigrants from a revolving fund set up through the Federation.

The Russian émigrés had no credit, of course, and among the first things they needed were automobiles. A short while later, a second fund was set up to help the refugees pay rent. The number of refugees coming has now declined, and as the monies are returned, they are going into the Jewish Federation fund again.

The Hooverwood home was a project my mother very much loved. She would go to visit the residents, bringing them news of the outside world. There is a favorable mix of Jewish and non-Jewish residents, and I think I can take some credit for that. When the facility was built, many years ago, I headed the committee overseeing the construction. It was my belief that we could do twice as much with the facility if we could qualify for the federal Hill-Burton programs, which had allocated funds to build extended-care nursing facilities. One of the stipulations was that admission could not be restricted to any particular religion, race, or creed. That fit my own belief that these facilities should be open to all, serving all kinds of needy people. We qualified for Hill-Burton money and as a result developed a facility far superior to what could have been built had we relied solely on local funds. In the past few years, Hooverwood has been substantially improved. An Alzheimer's wing has been added and sections have been renovated.

We made a contribution to the facility and named the dining room in honor of my mother. Fresh flowers go on all the tables in honor of my grandmother. Building that facility was really a time-consuming experience; Lois, my secretary, said she'd quit if we ever did anything like that again. The file was enormous.

We have also been involved with the Indianapolis Hebrew Congregation Cemetery. My grandfather had been involved with the

Jerry Goldberg Photography

A good friend since childhood when we played ball together, Bernie Landman joined me in celebrating the fortieth anniversary of the Glick company in June 1987.

One of the children's softball teams that we sponsored around 1992. My granddaughter Laura, Arlene's child, is in the front row, second from the right.

The groundbreaking for the Regional Little League headquarters at 42nd and Mitthoeffer, September 15, 1988. The participants were (*from left*) Al Stokely, myself, then-Mayor Bill Hudnut, the late Mike Carroll, Little League president Creighton Hale, and Mrs. Edward Harris. We donated thirty acres of land for the facility.

IHC and at one time served on the cemetery committee for the Hebrew Cemetery at Meridian Street and Bluff Road. He was also president of the congregation from 1916 to 1920.

In the late 1980s IHC obtained land on the far north side for another cemetery west of Ditch Road at 161st Street. The site became the source for a bit of morbid humor.

The first time I went to this cemetery was on the occasion of Leonard Larman's death in 1990. At the funeral, when they lowered the casket into the ground, I looked in and could see water at the bottom. I asked the people at IHC responsible for the cemetery to correct the problem, and I hired an engineer to inspect. He suggested installing field drain tiles to run water to a drainage ditch on the south side of the property. We hired engineers to design the drain field, providing drawings showing what depth to put it and what tile and gravel to use. We gave the plans to IHC and even took bids. But nothing happened. We were dealing with a bureaucracy.

When my old buddy Bernie Landman died, we went out to the cemetery again. We looked in the grave, and it was the same situation—there was ground water under the casket. I said to Jim Bisesi, "I know Bernie is now saying, 'God damn it, Glick and Bisesi! Get me out of this water!' " We had to do something.

We worked more with the cemetery committee, and eventually they did do something, but it made things even worse. A committee member suggested a cheaper, less complicated solution. They tried it and it didn't work. We kept trying to submit our plans and suggested they go ahead with them, and I believed they were finally going to solve the problem. When I asked why they were delaying, I was told that an engineer on the board had said, "What the hell's the difference if there's water in the graves? What do they care? They're dead!" I pointed out that, had their loved ones wished to be buried at sea, most relatives could have made that arrangement.

A few years ago I met with Rabbi Jon Stein of the Indianapolis Hebrew Congregation to suggest that the congregation start a program to provide a hot meal once a week to the hungry. It was my suggestion that this program be administered in conjunction with other church groups actively involved in feeding the hungry. I suggested that when the congregation's children are bar or bat mitzvahed, they could help with the food program. So our young people began journeying to the food kitchen on Indianapolis' south side to help prepare and serve food. I'm sure they learned a good deal about compassion and responsibility—and at a crucial time in their development into adults. Many parents and grandparents have told me they appreciated this well-timed, broadening experience. Recently we made a substantial contribution to the endowment fund of the food program to ensure that it continues.

CHAPTER 11

REFLECTIONS AND LOOKING FORWARD

A good deed is the best prayer, a loving life is the best religion.
—Robert G. Ingersoll

FAMILY FOCUS began this book; family solidarity and love continue unabated still in our lives. There are several factors involved in the happiness we're experiencing in these later years.

Thank God I have had good health through all these years. I don't recall missing a day because of a cold or headache in all these years in Indianapolis. Sometimes I would go in late to work, living with the cold or headache. It wasn't a macho thing; I simply didn't like staying at home when I was ill. I forget about the aches and pains while on the job.

In 1961 I happened to be reading a magazine called *Executive Health*. An article said that some of America's major corporations were sending their executives to a place called Greenbrier in White Sulphur Springs, West Virginia. I told Marilyn that it sounded like a good idea; we hadn't been getting regular physicals and perhaps it was time. Our corporation would send us. In 1962 we went to Greenbrier for the first time. They do a marvelous job; all the tests are done right there, and they have excellent golf courses, more than thirty-six tennis courts, horses and carriages. The food is wonderful. We went every two or three years for a while; lately, once a year.

One time in the early years of our Greenbrier visits a doctor came out and held up my X-rays and said, "Your X-rays show that you have a polyp." I didn't know what that was, but he told me it was a benign small growth that can sometimes become cancerous. "You need to have surgery to have it removed," he said.

I'd never been sick, and I was shaken up. I went home and

checked with a doctor I'd known for years, Dr. Leon Levi. He was an avid reader and kept up on the latest things in medicine. "There's something new," he said after hearing about my diagnosis. "A Japanese doctor in New York is removing polyps with a new instrument called a colonoscope. Why don't you consult him?"

I had Bernie Landman call an attorney in New York who was on the board of a New York hospital; it just happened to be the one where the Japanese doctor practiced. The attorney said he could recommend this doctor highly but cautioned that the process was experimental. I began to put out some feelers locally.

The doctors I knew socially in Indianapolis thought I was crazy to even think about this procedure: I was considering going to a quack; I could damage my colon.

Still, it sounded attractive to me and I decided to get some more opinions. I chartered a jet for the Mayo Clinic. I was just going to appear there, no appointment. What did I have to lose? I walked into the clinic, holding my X-rays in my hand. The nurse said, "Surely you have an appointment . . . ?"

"No," I said, "but I've got to get some advice. I'll pay you anything. I know you're a great facility and I want one of your specialists to look at these X-rays and tell me what to do." The young woman looked at me like I was an idiot. After all, this was a place where you made an appointment six months in advance. "Let me have the films," she said, and took them and left.

When she reappeared she said she couldn't believe it but Dr. So-and-So would see me—for five minutes. So I went on back. He was a nice-enough man, and he was looking at the X-rays. "I'll give you just five minutes. Tell me what you're planning to do," he said. I explained that I was faced with surgery but I had an option of going to the highly recommended doctor in New York who was experimenting with the new instrument called a colonoscope. He looked at me. "We know all about that colonoscope but we're not using it here. You're very foolish in even considering it. Do you know that after they remove the polyp, the area is cauterized? They cut it out. The colonoscope has a light and a snare, and during the cauterization of the polyp there's an electrical charge. You could explode." He had a straight face. I assumed he was serious. I looked at him, eyeball to eyeball. "Doc," I said, "I have just one question: If I explode, will the doctor go up with me?"

He gave me a sort of condescending look. "I believe your time with me is up," he said. "I recommend you not do this experimental thing. If you want to be a guinea pig, no one can stop you. But I say, have the operation."

I went back to Indianapolis and tried one last time to get advice. At Bernie's suggestion, I called one of the leading gastroenterologists in town, but I didn't get to talk to him. I asked the nurse to have him call me. A message came back from the nurse. "He doesn't need to talk to you. He doesn't know anything about the machine and he doesn't want to know anything about it. Have the surgery. That's all there is to say."

But I decided I would be a guinea pig. I went to New York, leaving about noon on a Friday and taking my golf clubs and Marilyn's clubs with me. I checked into the hospital, and the golf clubs had to come up to my room because there was no place to check them; I carried the two golf bags to the room myself.

The next day I had the procedure, with no anesthetic and only slight discomfort. They removed the polyp. I did not explode. I went back to my room. Soon I was talking to Thurston and Bisesi on the phone; the next day I carried out my golf clubs and we left to go to Carling Lake, Canada, to play a few rounds.

And talk about chutzpa—about a year later the unreachable doctor from Indianapolis called. He wanted to know if I'd talk to him because he had a patient who might need the procedure! We don't need to stand around with blinders on—even in medical matters. We need to have our eyes open always to the best creative options to solving problems.

HOW ABOUT THE FUTURE? I want to continue living the way I have been, with my interests focused on the business and my community ties. Whatever we do, it should be important, ground-breaking. That's been our way for all of these years. We've followed architect

Daniel Burnham's dictum: "Make no little plans. They have no magic to stir men's blood and probably themselves will not be realized. Make big plans. Aim high in hope and work."

Jim Bisesi wants us to consider development again. We own a piece of ground in Florida that we picked up some years ago, and we're taking a look at it now to see whether it can be developed or should be sold. Naturally, he hopes we can get back into those creative times again—which I, too, would love to do, although we do have a good deal of challenge just managing what we have.

I want to continue my deep involvement in strengthening and appreciating our family. One's values mellow after seventy years; perspective grows sharper. If the saying is true about growing older that "Candles burn dimmer, martial drums are muffled, and pain is not so keenly felt," then it is also true that like a beacon, the light of family affection burns brighter as years pass. The trip to Europe to relive my World War II experiences was wonderful—unique—and I'll never forget it.

Friday night was always reserved for the family to have dinner together. In the early days both Marilyn's mother and mine would join us and our growing family, but my dad didn't come. He had lodge meetings at the Elks Club, and I think secretly he was happy not to spend so much time around "all those females." This tradition of Friday night dinners, which began when Marianne was born, continue through today, and when they're in town, our daughters and their husbands, the grandchildren (and hopefully someday the great-grandchildren) still gather around our table to celebrate family night and usher in the Sabbath.

Luckily we've had fine help at home for many years. Syvaline Miller prepares breakfast for Marilyn and me, fixing the oatmeal with orange juice on it that I like. She cleans and even dusts Marilyn's art glass. Edith Shelton continues to cook delicious Friday night dinners when we all get together. Syvaline and Edith tell us that being with our family is like being at home, and the only complaint they have is that Marilyn won't send them back to the Pritikin Longevity Center—they didn't stick to their diets. "You're a bad investment," she tells them.

Fitness hasn't been a bad investment for me. Marilyn and I have both tried out an exercise program developed for use in nursing homes, and it has made us both stronger, I think. I've always tried to keep myself in shape, though I got a real test of whether I could hold my own about three years ago in Palm Beach. I was mugged, and police later told me I could have been killed, though I didn't think of it at the time of the incident. We were taking some friends to a French restaurant, and I was carrying about seven hundred dollars in cash, because Marilyn and I knew the restaurant hadn't taken credit cards in the past.

When the bill came, though, I was told I could pay with a credit card. That left me with an unusually full billfold, and perhaps the doorman or somebody knew that, because later, when I decided to take one of my middle-of-the-night walks along the Intercoastal Waterway, somebody grabbed me from behind. I was thrown to the ground and we began to wrestle. I gave whatever I could in the fight, and soon it was over, with one man running away.

But the odd thing was that another young man stayed. He looked at me and began to apologize for what he'd just done. We walked along A-1A and he told me his story. He said he was in cooking school in Del Ray, studying to become a chef, and he and his buddies were out of money. I told him if he'd just come up and told me that story, I might have loaned him the money. "You're making me feel this big," he said, putting his thumb and forefinger together. He asked for my forgiveness and even told me his name.

That night, while showering, I saw how bruised and beat up I really was. The next day I met with a policewoman who listened to my story and took down the name the young man had given me.

The police pursued the matter, and finally these two men were brought to trial. The judge came back to me for my input, as the victim, in the sentencing process. "They're both crack cocaine users. You could have been killed," he told me. "The one man confessed to police he apologized to you only because he saw a police car around. He thought it might look like he was an innocent bystander if he was seen walking around talking to somebody. Three years is the general time they draw."

"What good will that do?" I asked. "They'll only get worse in prison. Why not send them to some sort of penal camp, where they can get treatment for the crack and learn a skill? I'll pay to have the man who apologized taught to be a chef." The judge agreed and they did go to the boot camp, though the results weren't great. Looking back, I know I was lucky. Many people have been killed in muggings like that. Truly, as I say so often, Fate is the hunter.

But I was secretly pleased to see that I was still fit enough to tussle with those teenagers and hold my own, and I know my fitness today pays off. It has definitely improved my golf stroke. I've worked the last few years with a golf pro named Rex Arnett. He gave me lessons, videotaped my swing, and then worked with me at the house. As a result, I've had some not-too-bad rounds at Broadmoor recently. Rex says that to achieve success in golf you must gain consistency, and for the person who doesn't play regularly that's very difficult to achieve.

Lately, though, my eyes haven't been good enough for much golf. I have given it my best shot all these years and have sometimes had good games, often had some good shots—I should be grateful for that. Perhaps Buddy Hackett was right when he said, "Jews weren't meant to play golf." Arlene certainly continues to be a fine golfer, though with all the child-rearing she's had to do, she doesn't get out as often as she might. Still, she won the 1996 Broadmoor Women's Golf Tournament—and that was her third time!

We're all still basking in the glory of the day she shot a hole in one at Greenbrier. It was July 7, 1995, at the old White Course there. The third hole is a par three for women, 167 yards. She hit a fine shot, and Tom, her husband, said, "You've either gone over the green or in the cup. I can't see the ball." We all walked towards the green and eventually began running to the cup. "Let her look in first!" I said. Sure enough—a hole in one!

I wrote to Jack Nicklaus, mentioning that my daughter, an admirer of his, had made her first hole in one on the same day he'd made his seventeenth—in a seniors' tournament. Could he write a word of congratulation? A couple of months later Arlene and Tom received a letter from Nicklaus. Thrilled, they opened it up—only to find a letter addressed to another couple in Hawaii congratulating them on their fiftieth wedding anniversary! Tom got on the phone and soon the misdirected letters were switched.

Our whole family loves to go to Greenbrier, and when we're gone, the memories of these outings and all the family times together will be part of the legacy we leave them. That legacy will exist in a world of great change and tremendous progress, which I believe is occurring exponentially. This has to be one of the most exciting times to be alive in history. The average citizen in America lives better as far as creature comforts are concerned than kings and queens in the richest empires of the past. We can only hope that our fellow travelers on Planet Earth will gain knowledge of our deep interdependence in the years to come, so universal peace may come about. We all have an obligation to each other to help realize our species' destiny, though no one individual can complete everything.

Frank Basile sent me an article by Robert Artman from *Better Life Journal*, and I think it has a very interesting rationale about what one leaves behind:

> *Isn't it ironic that we leave so little of the value systems which helped us become successful people? So often, the hardships we suffered, the mistakes we made, the joys, the triumphs, the tragedies and how we dealt with and learned from them all go with us to the grave.*
>
> *It's hard to believe that any thinking person would consciously decide to allow sixty or seventy years of learning experience and thought to be tossed out like last night's dishwater—wasted—gone forever and for naught. What a loss in each case. And yet, unless each of us makes a special effort to leave a record of our lives, that will be the case. Sadly, we will be remembered only for what material possessions we have accumulated—not for the flesh and blood we were—not for the wisdom we may have accumulated or the intangibles we contributed to society in general.*

I embrace this idea completely and it is a major reason why this book has come into being. Yes, we leave buildings behind as visible monuments, and they are tremendously important in improving the lives of many of our fellow citizens. But the ideas, the ideals, and the basic tenets of belief which caused these homes to be built can be revealed and expressed only by our words and preserved for consideration by those who follow us by the printed documents which mankind has created for this purpose.

So through these many words I have told of the principles which I've tried my best to maintain through my life, and which were interpreted by actually constructing and providing comfortable, safe dwellings for our fellow human beings.

Has my life experience left me cynical, doubting our continued prosperity in the future, or optimistic, thinking of the better life for us all? Permit me to quote myself, in remarks I made recently when I received several honors as a home builder and businessman: "How fortunate we all are to live in this time, the most exciting time in the history of man. The engine that has driven and is driving this dramatic improvement in the lives of not only people in America but throughout the world, is the American free enterprise system and ingenuity and creativity of American entrepreneurs."

The noted global investor and philanthropist, Sir John M. Templeton, says it so well:

> *My friends, the future is bright! Who can imagine what new benefits will result from discoveries yet to come? The more we learn the more we realize how little we knew in the past, and how much more there is still to discover. So, as I look into the future I cannot help but be positive about our prospects on this great planet of ours. Each of us should be overwhelmingly grateful for the multiplying multitudes of blessings which surround us now, and for the prospect of even more wonderful blessings for our children and grandchildren.*

In my heart today and what I want to express to you, is what a marvelous journey this last fifty-plus years has been. Leaving the merciless death camp at Dachau and devastated Europe, then coming home to America to witness and participate in a small way in the greatest economic miracle and building boom in man's recorded history, was an unparalleled experience.

Allow me to recap some of what you may have read already; parts of my life which have been so important to me, and which form the basis of the optimism I endorse. To come back from the death and destruction of the war and find work at Peoples Bank running the VA mortgage department was a most fortunate start. Then one day, freshly turned earth and new lumber, the precursors of a new dwelling which would hold such promise for those for whom it would become a dream home, caught my imagination and that evening I told the charming girl I was dating, who would become my dear wife and partner, that I had found my life's work: I would become a builder. What a wonderful sequence, what good fortune! To come home from the devastation of a great war, to find a worthwhile job, to fall in love with a wonderful girl, and to find my life's work . . .

What more could a man ask? Marilyn and I consider ourselves two of the luckiest people on this planet. We have been blessed with four great daughters and thirteen grandchildren, with talented and caring business associates, and many, many longtime friends.

As we ponder the needs of this and other communities and how we can best contribute to the general welfare, to relieve pain and suffering, to provide for equal opportunity, to advance research in science and medicine, we are sometimes overwhelmed by the enormity of the problems. Herman Wouk, in his book *This is my God*, examined the problems facing humanity and became discouraged at times; but he took heart from the ancient words of Rabbi Tarfon who said, "The work is not yours to finish, but neither are you free to take no part in it." So we, too, have taken that commandment to heart and through the Eugene and Marilyn Glick Foundation are doing what we can to improve the lives of our fellow travelers on this Planet Earth.

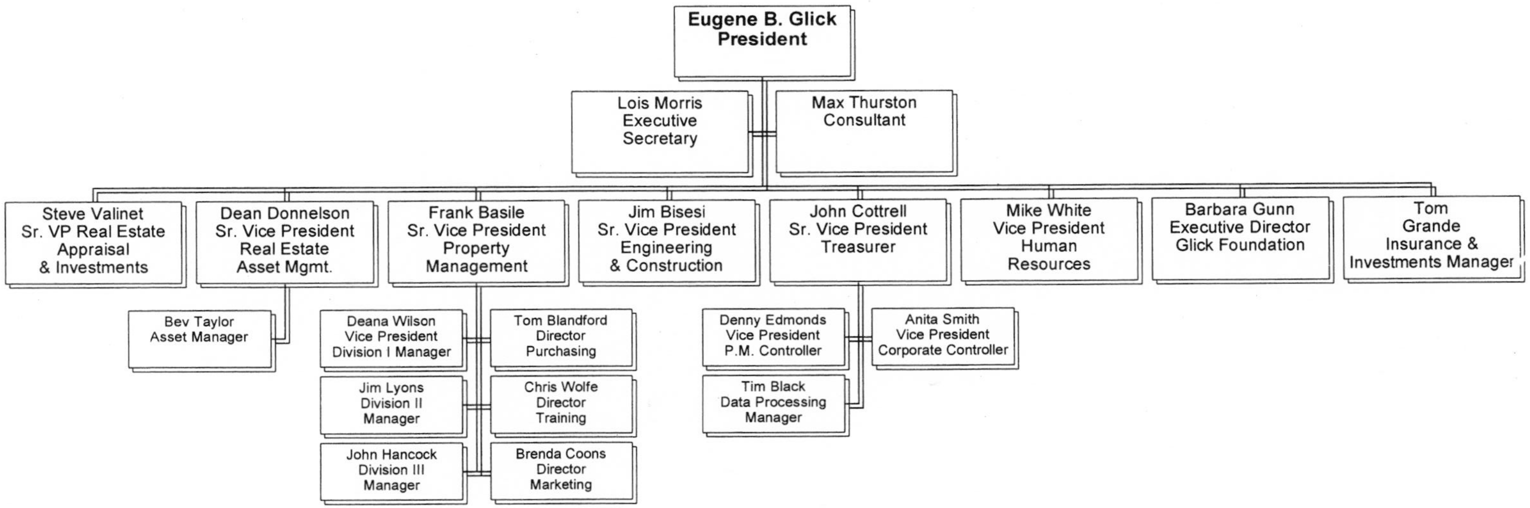
Eugene B. Glick
President
Lois Morris
Executive
Secretary
Max Thurston
Consultant
Steve Valinet
Sr. VP Real Estate
Appraisal
& Investments
Dean Donnelson
Sr. Vice President
Real Estate
Asset Mgmt.
Frank Basile
Sr. Vice President
Property
Management
Jim Bisesi
Sr. Vice President
Engineering
& Construction
John Cottrell
Sr. Vice President
Treasurer
Mike White
Vice President
Human
Resources
Barbara Gunn
Executive Director
Glick Foundation
Tom
Grande
Insurance &
Investments Manager
Bev Taylor
Asset Manager
Deana Wilson
Vice President
Division I Manager
Tom Blandford
Director
Purchasing
Jim Lyons
Division II
Manager
Chris Wolfe
Director
Training
John Hancock
Division III
Manager
Brenda Coons
Director
Marketing
Denny Edmonds
Vice President
P.M. Controller
Anita Smith
Vice President
Corporate Controller
Tim Black
Data Processing
Manager

FROM A SPARE BEDROOM TO WOODFIELD— A Chronology of the company's "homes"

Our "headquarters" were located in our home until about a year or so after Marianne was born in 1949. At that time we moved to a small portable building we had constructed in the vicinity of 13th Street and Ritter Avenue. This office could be hauled on skids to the various sites where we were putting in streets off of Lesley or Layman, between 10th and 13th streets.

In addition to this office we also had offices at the subdivisions we were developing, beginning with the National Homes Cadets in 1954 and 1955. For many years our entire office staff occupied five or six spec homes that we built in the different subdivisions but had not yet sold.

Eventually we consolidated our entire office staff operation, except for accounting, in an office building called Executive North, located on the south side of 82nd Street between College Avenue and Westfield Boulevard. The accounting department was housed in an office building at Fort Harrison.

In 1976 we moved to 9102 North Meridian Street, Suite 200, where for the first time since the company began all home office employees were housed in the same facility. Moving everyone to one location helped to create a more cohesive one-company feeling.

In 1986 we relocated to our present quarters at 8330 Woodfield Crossing Boulevard, Suite 200. A photograph of that building and its pleasant surroundings, including a lake, is included in the color photo section of this book.

Dear Mr. Glick . . .

. . . it should be brought to your attention . . . the wonderful care our manager, Renée, her associate, plus Roman and his maintenance help have given to Carriage House North.

The complex is just beautiful. . . . if your employees are caring people . . . you can have an apartment complex where people are proud to live.

Sincerely, Frank and Martha Jane Thomas
Indiananapolis, IN

. . . I want to express my gratitude to you for your constant efforts to maintain and improve your Cambridge Square Apartment complex. I feel blessed to be living here.

. . . it can be quite a challenge dealing in public housing [but] *you realize the importance of dignity, regardless of one's income, religion, or race.*

Sincerely, Maryellen Pound
Blasdell, NY

You've put up with me for eight years, and I can't help but express how happy I am to live here.

Don't know how you manage to do it. You've always had great managers and maintenance people here. They have a great understanding of people, always willing to help when in need. . . . Keep up the good work.

Yours, Doris R. Seiler
Beech Grove, IN

. . . my two-year stay at University Park Apartments has been the most pleasant experience which I have ever had in either rental or condominium living. . . . Your management and maintenance crew have been attentive and available at all times, as well as always pleasant and helpful. It is clear in every respect that you all take great pride in your work here. Because my new husband now works and lives in Chicago, I will be joining him there. . . .

. . . I am a bit sad to leave, even though my reason for doing so is a joyous one.

Sincerely, Elizabeth Ann Dively
Mishawaka, IN

Grace Rose was a wonderful resident at Cambridge Square, living alone there from the age of 85 until she died at 103. I went to her 100th, 101st, 102nd, and 103rd birthday parties. At the party for her 102nd birthday I said a few words to the forty or fifty residents gathered to celebrate their friend's special day.

In 1995 I went to Cambridge Square again to celebrate the birthdays of two ladies who turned 100. "People come over here and live long, healthy lives," I said to them. "The environment must be good for you!"

Grace Rose and I at her 102nd birthday celebration.

Mayor Stephen Goldsmith, a dedicated Pro-100 supporter, joined the festivities for the company's forty-fifth anniversary at Williamsburg North Apartments in 1992.

Marilyn and I met senators Birch Bayh and Ted Kennedy in the mid-seventies.

Indiana Senator Dan Coates (*right*), Marilyn, myself, and Jack Kemp, who was at the time the head of HUD, in the mid-eighties.

Marilyn stood by my side when I received an honorary degree from Butler University, May 1989.

Family and friends posed for this photo when I was inducted into the National Association of Home Builders Hall of Fame in 1988. *(From left)* Mark Schwartz and his wife, our daughter Lynda, Marilyn, myself, daughter Marianne, and Frank Basile.

I'm very proud of this beautiful award for my participation in Israel Bonds in the 1980s. The plaque symbolizes the links of the Twelve Tribes of ancient Israel to the rebirth of the nation.

(*Right*) Pictured with Marilyn and me at our office open house in 1987 are my secretary, Lois (*second from left*) and her daughter, Connie, and Connie's baby.

At Alice and Lu Palma's fiftieth wedding anniversary celebration in June 1993: (*from left*) Jack Dickhaus, Alice, Marilyn, Barbara Dickhaus, Lu, and myself.

THOUGHTS

On the Business of Business

Unless a deal is beneficial to all parties, it is not a good deal.

The opportunity for entrepreneurs today is greater than it has ever been in the history of our country.

I always try to set a standard for integrity, objectivity, enthusiasm, compassion and insight that would be difficult to surpass and everyone in our company would follow.

The soldier does best what the colonel checks.

Top priority: Meet with your key people regularly to plan and set goals and most important of all, make certain the plan is being followed and goals achieved. Our weekly meetings over 30-plus years, possibly more than anything else, are responsible for whatever success we may have achieved.

Listen to your customers but, above all, care about your customers. Do everything possible to employ people who care about people.

If you must criticize, do it face to face; put compliments in writing.

Our most successful associates all possess one great human trait—they care. Caring comes from the heart and produces great achievements; without it there is almost always failure.

Assigning the task to someone is 5 percent of the job; making certain that the assignment is completed is 95 percent.

Health is our most important asset. Exercise, eat, and drink in moderation, and take time to meditate; for the road to success is long and arduous and favors those who are strong, both mentally and physically.

Next to health, time is our most important and irreplaceable asset; employ it well so that "Every yesterday will be a dream of happiness and every tomorrow a vision of hope."

I believe that God's chosen people are those whose love and work are one and the same.

In your marketing and advertising promotion, emphasize Rosser Reeves' USP—*Unique Selling Proposition.* Distinguish why your product or service is superior to that of your competitors—and then deliver on that proposition.

Always remember that things are much easier to get into than out of.

What you make it a person's interest to do, they will do. Therefore, provide bonuses and other incentives which relate to your people.

Find the best in the marketplace and then improve on it.

Glick in German means "luck"; no matter how creative or intelligent the entrepreneur, almost without exception he or she will tell you that luck played a role in their success.

Treat your customers, business associates and all those whose paths cross yours just a tad better than you would like to be treated.

Learn early the art of listening.

Every man, woman, or entrepreneur who knows the ecstasy of success also is acquainted with the pain of failure; winners in the end are those who having failed, pick themselves up from the dust, learn from their mistakes and forge ahead to greater achievement.

Stick with what you do well. I'm like the old sage who said he was no genius but was smart in spots and always worked around those spots.

It is never too late to start dreaming and always too early to quit. Never stop trying to make your dream come true.

Young entrepreneur, if you love your work you are on the road to success. If love is not present you have already failed.

It is the daring, creativity, and ingenuity of the American entrepreneur that will enhance the lives of the people of the earth in the next century.

Recognize good work and give an employee the will to do better work. Don't recognize it and you feed one of the biggest gripes employees have—lack of recognition.

On the Business of Life

Set your sights on something worthwhile that will make a contribution to society and that you love to do, then work will all your heart, soul, and mind for that commitment.

Never hurry, never worry, and don't get mad.

Never hold a grudge because as the philosopher and comedian Buddy Hackett said: "The person against whom you are holding a grudge is out dancing and having a good time."

I have written many letters in anger, which were never mailed, for which I am grateful; I have remained silent when sorely angered, and have never been sorry. I often think of the sage who said, "Ye shall know the truth and the truth shall make ye mad."

Marry a pretty girl who is smarter than you, but who convinces you that you're the one with the brains.

Set aside time to write to thank, congratulate, compliment, and console those whose paths have crossed yours; a phone call ends in a moment, a letter is forever.

I believe with all my heart that helping others to become educated is the ultimate contribution to mankind.

A childhood hunger leads to a lifelong appetite.

Positive thinking lies at the heart of success, but you've got to get out there and make it happen.

Accept the cards you have been dealt and play them well.

When a person plants a tree under which he knows he will never sit, one can know that hope springs eternal within the human breast.

It is in the vital interest of our nation, and all nations, to want for all their children a quality education, for only then can any traveler plant his foot in any land and say, "I am home."

If you teach a child to do one thing well, that child will do everything better.

Real achievers get to the mountain top and immediately start looking around for another mountain to climb.

Of all the handicaps that can stand in the way of success in a person's lifetime, perhaps the biggest handicap of all is economic disadvantage.

Inherited wealth may be a major drawback to achievement. It may be the opiate that dulls ambition and destroys happiness.

Most of us take a lifetime to grow up and few completely succeed. Nonetheless in our executives we always seek people of excellence who are patient, calm, empathic, resolute, positive, courageous, and dependable.

To amass a sum of money is in any man's power; to give it away intelligently is very difficult.

I believe I have not done enough; that I have never done enough so long as it is still possible that I have something to contribute.

The greatest of gifts you can give are the time, wisdom, and opportunity you give to children. A hundred years from now material possessions will not matter, but the world may be better because I was important in the life of a child.

FAVORITE QUOTATIONS

Perfection is not obtainable, but if you chase perfection you can catch excellence.

—Vince Lombardi

We are happier in many ways when we are old than when we were young. The young sow wild oats. The old grow sage.

—Winston Churchill

If you value life, do not squander time, for that is the stuff life is made of.

—Ben Franklin

To be what we are and to become what we are capable of becoming, is the only end of life.

—Robert Louis Stevenson

Surplus wealth is a sacred trust which its possessor is bound to administer in his lifetime for the good of the community.

—Andrew Carnegie

My deeds must be my life.

—Stephen Girard

The best is yet to be. The last of life, for which the first was made.

—Robert Browning, on growing older

I long to accomplish a great and noble task, but it is my chief duty to accomplish humble tasks as though they were great and noble. The world has moved along not only by the mighty shoves of its heroes but also by the aggregate of the tiny pushes of each honest worker.

—Helen Keller

What we learn from history is that we do not learn from history.

—Benjamin Disraeli

The people part of management is the hardest part, but the most important; making people feel like human beings, with a purpose in life.

—Fran Tarkenton

Faced with the choice between changing one's mind and proving that there is no need to do so, almost everybody gets busy on the proof.

—John Kenneth Galbraith

Nothing will content him who is not content with a little.

—Greek proverb

You can never do a kindness too soon, because you never know how soon it will be too late.

—Ralph Waldo Emerson

The capacity to care is the thing that gives life its deepest meaning and significance.

—Pablo Casals

The pure and simple truth is rarely pure and never simple.

—Oscar Wilde

'Tis an old maxim in the schools, that flattery is the food of fools; yet now and then your men of wit will condescend to take a bit.

—Unknown

Mankind can bear only a little of reality.

—T. S. Eliot

Luck is not chance, it's toil. Fortune's expensive smile is earned.

—Emily Dickinson

Excellence is an art won by training and habituation. We do not act rightly because we have virtue or excellence, but we rather have those because we have acted rightly. We are what we repeatedly do. Excellence, then, is not an act but a habit.

—Aristotle

Anyone who is truly successful, continuously successful, must engage in thinking time and study time with regularity. Unfortunately, most people won't do that, and that's why they don't succeed.

—W. Clement Stone

Our business in life is not to get ahead of others, but to get ahead of ourselves—to break our own records, to outstrip our yesterday by our today, to do our work with more force than ever before.

—Stewart B. Johnson

If you have built castles in the air, you need not be lost; that is where they should be. Now put the foundations under them.

—Henry David Thoreau

Life does not come again. If you have not lived during the days that were given to you, once only, then write them down as lost.

—Anton Chekhov

Walk a mile in the other person's moccasins to understand their problems, motivations and actions.

—one of my mother's favorite adages

Businesses planned for service are apt to succeed; businesses planed for profit are apt to fail.

—Nicholas Murray Butler

The rewards in business go to the man who does something with an idea.

—William Benton

One right and honest definition of business is mutual helpfulness.

—William Feather

We believe that there is one economic lesson which our twentieth-century experience has demonstrated conclusively—that America can no more survive and grow without big business than it can survive and grow without small business . . . the two are interdependent. You cannot strengthen one without weakening the other, and you cannot add to the stature of a dwarf by cutting off the legs of a giant.

—Benjamin Franklin Fairless, president of U. S. Steel.

I like business because it is competitive, because it rewards deeds rather than words. I like business because it compels earnestness and does not permit me to neglect today's tasks while thinking about tomorrow. I like business because it undertakes to please, not reform; because it is honestly selfish, thereby avoiding hypocrisy and sentimentality. I like businesses because it properly penalizes mistakes, shiftlessness and inefficiency, while rewarding well those who give it the best they have in them. Lastly, I like business because each day is a fresh adventure.

—R. H. Cabell

Truly there is a tide in the affairs of men; but there is no gulf stream setting forever in one direction.

—James Russell Lowell.

Business demands faith, compels earnestness, requires courage, is honestly selfish, is penalized for mistakes, and is the essence of life.

—William Feather

Few things are harder to put up with than the annoyance of a good example.

—Mark Twain

What we obtain too cheap we esteem too lightly; it is dearness only that gives everything its value.

—Thomas Paine

In Military, as in other human affairs, will is what makes things happen. There are circumstances that can modify it or nullify it, but for offense or defense its presence is essential and its absence fatal.

—General Stillwell

Since a major obstacle to success is a fear of failure, which often means the fear of looking ridiculous, the ability to laugh—if not at fate at least with it—is vital for anyone who would really roll the dice. Humor bridges the gap between the perfection we seek and the imperfections we are stuck with. It also allows us to change perspective and take a detached view of situations whose gravity might otherwise engulf us. Given the tincture of time, all tragedy becomes comical—and the cliché that sometime we will look back on this and laugh, tends to be true—accordingly, why wait?

—Unknown

Health is a precious thing . . . the only thing, indeed, that deserves to be pursued at the expense not only of time, sweat, labor, worldly goods, but of life itself; . . . since without health, pleasures, wisdom, knowledge, lose their color and fade away.

—Montaigne

Spend your time getting even with the people who help you in life—and you won't have time to get even with the people who hurt you.

—Bill Carson's grandfather

To laugh often and love much; to win the respect of intelligent persons and the affection of children; to earn the approbation of honest citizens and endure the betrayal of false friends; to appreciate beauty; to find the best in others; to give oneself; to leave the world a bit better, whether by a healthy child, a garden patch or a redeemed social condition; to have played and laughed with enthusiasm and sung with exultation; to know even one life has breathed easier because you have lived—this is to have succeeded.

—Ralph Waldo Emerson

I was gratified to be able to answer promptly. I said I don't know.

—Mark Twain

Running a company is easy when you don't know how, but very difficult when you do.

—Price Pritchett

Things will get better despite our efforts to improve them.

—Will Rogers

I was going to buy a copy of the Power of Positive Thinking, and I thought, "What the hell good would that do?"

—Ronnie Shakes

More than anytime in history, mankind faces a cross-road. One path leads to despair, and utter hopelessness, and the other to total extinction. Let us pray that we have the wisdom to choose correctly.

—Woody Allen

As you're the only one you can really change, the only one who can really use all your good advice is yourself.

—Peter McWilliams

In a fight between you and the world, bet on the world.

—Frank Cothca

Never become irritable waiting for things to get better. If you'll be patient you'll find that you can wait much faster.

—Unknown

The things you learn in maturity aren't simple things such as acquiring information and skills. You learn not to engage in self destructive behavior. You learn not to burn up energy in anxiety. You discover how to manage your tensions. You learn that self pity and resentment are among the most toxic of drugs. You find that the world loves talent, but pays off on character. You come to understand that most people are neither for you nor against you, they are thinking about themselves. You learn that no matter how hard you try to please, some people in this world are not going to love you, a lesson that is at first troubling and then really quite relaxing. There are things that are hard to learn early in life. As a rule you have to have picked up some mileage and some dents in your fenders before you understand. As Norman Douglas said, "There are some things you can't learn from others. You have to pass through the fire."

—John Gardner

Show me a young idealist who is demanding the right to change a world he hasn't lived in long enough to know anything about, or contribute anything to, and I'll show you a pest. But show me a student who "merely wishes to make a good living," and I'll show you a kid who's going to be of service to his fellow men, because that's the only way he can make a good living.

—Al Capp

Human beings can alter their lives by altering their attitudes.

—William Jennings

Those who see the needs of the world—the helpless children, the hungry children, the unclothed children, the unhealed children, the uneducated children, the unloved children of every age—will find God.

—Unknown

Every great man, every successful man, no matter what the field of endeavor, has known the magic that lies in these words: Every adversity has the seed of an equivalent or greater benefit.

—W. Clement Stone

Praise is well, compliment is well, but affection—that is the last and most precious reward that any man can win, whether by character or achievement.

—Mark Twain

He has achieved success who has lived well, laughed often and loved much; who has gained the respect of intelligent men and the love of little children; who has filled his niche and accomplished his task; who has left the world better than he found it, whether by an improved poppy, a perfect poem or a rescued soul; who has never lacked appreciation of earth's beauty or failed to express it; who has looked for the best in others and gives the best he had; whose life was an inspiration; whose memory is a benediction.

—Mrs. A. J. Stanley

Make each day useful and cheerful and prove that you know the worth of time by employing it well. Then youth will be happy, old age without regret and life a beautiful success.

—Louisa May Alcott

We at the Glick Company follow these commandments, in addition to the Original Ten:

11—Thou shalt not inventory land

12—Thou shalt not commence construction without permanent financing.

13—Thou shalt always remember if a proposal sounds too good to be true, it is invariably good for the proposer and invariably bad for the proposee.

14—Thou shalt commence construction on a home or apartment only after thou hast carefully arranged furniture and accessories in every room.

15—Thou shalt plant beautiful trees, shrubs and flowers in the developments under supervision of a master landscape architect.

16—Thou shalt employ people of excellence to serve thy flock well, and with tender, loving care.

17—Thou shalt inspect thy dwellings regularly to make certain thy policies and procedures are being followed and that thy customers are content.

Greenbrier Photography

This photo was taken of the family in July 1996, when we were all together at Greenbrier. Seated to my right is grandson Ben Grande, and Katie Eynon is on Marilyn's left. Standing (*left to right*) are Alan Ellison (Marilyn's nephew), Tom and Arlene Grande, their daughter Laura, Jackie Barrett and her husband Dave, Mike and Brian Grande, Marilyn's niece Barbara Crystal and her husband Joel (brother of comedian Billy Crystal), Jason Basile (Katie Eynon's friend), Karyn Meshbane, Marianne Glick, Lauren Schwartz, Mark Filipow, Alice Meshbane, and Lynda Schwartz.

FAMILY MEMORIES

AS I LOOK at this picture of our family the memories come flooding back, and there is a vivid scene in my mind of how proud and happy we were when we brought our first child, Marianne, home from the hospital. Each of our four wonderful daughters has brought so much happiness into our lives. I believe if I had been asked before Marianne was born, "Would you rather have four boys or four girls?" I'd have emphatically replied, "If I have to make that specific choice, four girls!" And since that's the way it turned out, I can confirm that no man could have been happier with that preference.

We're proud of what the various members of our family have achieved and, I believe, justly so. Although Marilyn and I were as inexperienced in child-rearing as any young couple, we have tried our best to instill love of family in our daughters and we're thrilled with what they and their families have accomplished. I am reminded of a study by a prestigious university which cited the most important four factors which determine success in school and later in life: Both parents living at home, the quantity and quality of books in the home, the amount of television the children are allowed to watch, and the amount of homework the parents insist must be done. We think that's right on the mark.

Friday night has always been our family dinner night with the children, and has continued so through the years, adding sons-in-law and grandchildren—whenever they're in town and can come. It has become a great tradition enjoyed by every member of the family from the youngest—and I can say with absolute certainty—to the oldest.

THE MARVELOUS LITTLE BUNDLE we brought home that memorable day was Marianne, who became a bright, engaging , and a bit mischievous tot with her own mind, and who is that same person today. As a child she questioned and challenged the way things were done, and Marilyn had quite a few conferences with teachers who were enchanted and amused by this little girl who presented such strong cases for her ideas. She loved to play practical jokes and she reminded me of a little character in the comics named Miriam Kooperman, so I nicknamed her Koopie. We still call her that.

Marianne has always been outgoing and gregarious with the marvelous ability to quickly relate to others and put them at ease. From an early age she always had the ability to set goals and would strive to reach them, allowing nothing to stand in her way. And she never forgot a promise, as I found out one evening: Marilyn and I wanted to go out to dinner and we asked her to baby-sit, setting down some rules and knowing we could rely on her. I promised that if everything went well I'd take her out dancing after we got home, regardless of the time. So, after we returned about 11:30 or so, Marianne held me to that promise. I found a place where we could dance, and the two of us enjoyed the compliments from those around us.

Her independence and pursuit of goals has led her to form her own management and consulting firm. She is an excellent motivational speaker and does training and consulting for major firms. Marianne worked in our office after college and over time advanced to the position of regional property manager. But she came to me one day and said she wanted to go off on her own; she believed that no matter how good she was, everyone would attribute her success to the fact that her father owned the company. Ultimately she made her own mark and nothing pleases Marilyn and me more than having friends and business associates remark on Marianne's capability and success.

ARLENE—Li'l Arly, that is—appeared next on the scene, and I recall how a woman at the hospital remarked what a pretty baby she was—correctly, of course!. No little girl could have been more feminine, but Arlene always loved sports and was a real athlete. A genuine tomboy, she always wanted Marilyn to buy her boy's clothing and gear, explaining that "boys are more tougher."

She always excelled in sports and never backed away from participating, whether sledding down the big hill at Riverside Park or in mock battles with other kids. That athletic ability really came to the fore (pun intended) when Arlene took up golf. She has been a three-time women's champion at Broadmoor. It's a family joke that given the way Marilyn and I play golf, we must have brought the wrong kid home from the hospital!

Her mothering instinct was strong and she'd bring in injured critters and nurse them back to health. Now, married to Tom Grande, an executive with our firm, she's the daughter who seems ideal to have the most children. Arlene and Tom are raising five wonderful kids: daughter Jackie, the eldest, is a teacher, and was married in July of 1996 to David Barrett. Mike (Mickey) is nineteen; Brian (Mo), seventeen; another beautiful daughter, Laura (Laurakins) is ten; and Ben (nicknamed BenBoy—and we'll save that story for another book) is five.

It's always a tremendous source of satisfaction for parents to get compliments on their children, and praise from others constantly comes back to us from those who know Arlene well. She is so warm and loving that everyone who knows her holds her with affection. In her own quiet, efficient way serves her family, friends and the community well. Arlene's sense of family tradition is also strong; she is our "historian," working on the family genealogy.

DAUGHTER ALICE has always been the most studious of the children: I can remember her remarking once after bringing home wonderful grades, "That's not bad for my age." She was always a calm and easygoing child—today the term would be "laid-back," I believe.

"Al Baby," in her own calm fashion, was a great listener. When they were very young I instructed the girls not to gossip at the dinner table, but to bring a current event to discuss, and Alice always came prepared. Evidently she passed that along to her daughter Karyn, who asked me out of the blue at lunch one day, "Grandpa, what does God look like?" When I replied that no one knows, she immediately came back with, "Not even you, Grandpa?" So it's a fair assumption that Karyn—"Happy" to us—has inherited her share of smart genes!

Alice loved school and when she was at Indiana University would spend only a week or two at home between semesters and summer classes. She was never one to brag about her accomplishments, so we were unaware of her election to Phi Beta Kappa until we were congratulated by a neighbor. When we asked why she hadn't told us, she said it was "no big deal. I love learning and that was what was really important to me, not any recognition."

With the equivalent of a Ph.D. in research on how humans learn, Alice now teaches statistics to graduate students at Florida Atlantic University. Her love of learning and the passion to instruct others remains strong and she spends many hours after classes helping her students.

She and her husband Andrew are raising two fine daughters, Karyn and Dora ("Mona Lisa"), Andrew's child by a former marriage. We find them a delight, as we do all our grandchildren.

OUR YOUNGEST DAUGHTER, Lynda, is known affectionately as "Chocolate Sundae." She lives in California with her husband, Mark, a manufacturer's representative, and their two children, Johnny A., eleven, and Lauren (Gigi), seven. Two great kids, even if their grandfather says so; Johnny is becoming a fine athlete, with great hand/eye coordination. And Lauren, like her mother, is a beauty; when shown pictures of her, people want to know who the "starlet" is.

From the time she was a little girl Lynda has had a great taste in clothing and decorating and I'm convinced she could have had a brilliant career as a clothing designer or interior decorator. However, she made her choice early, and a career of raising children who will be a notable asset to our society is arguably the most noble of all.

Her compassion for others was shown one day in Florida. An elderly neighbor in our condominium left his table at the restaurant at which we were dining to tell us how he appreciated Lynda's kind words on the death of his wife. She had become acquainted with him slightly at the pool, and had heard of his loss and made a point of going to him and expressing her condolences. He said it was one of the nicest things that had happened to him since his wife's death, to have this lovely young girl talk with him about it.

I remember walking with her in Yellowstone Park, when she was about three. She grew tired, so I left her by a small brook while I walked on, after giving her my watch and showing her where the hands would be when I'd be back. On my return, she was in tears. She had amused herself by throwing stones into the stream and my watch had slipped off her wrist and gone into the water. But it was retrieved and the tears were dried.

There's also the story about how Lynda was asked by a top security officer in an Israeli airport to help check security . . . but that will have to be told in another book, or I'll run on too long!

FROM READING these reminiscences and memories of our life with our four lovely daughters, you will glean some sense of our love for them and how we were dedicated to doing our best to raise them to be contributing members of society.

Several thoughts come to mind in closing which speak of the philosophies of life which we tried to emphasize over the years. At Lynda's wedding I recited from the ancient Hindu poet, Kalidasa—

Look to this day!
For it is life, the very life of life.
In its brief course
Lie all the verities and realities of your existence:
The bliss of growth
The glory of action
The splendor of beauty,
For yesterday is but a dream
And tomorrow is only a vision,
But today well lived makes every yesterday a dream of happiness
And every tomorrow a vision of hope.
Look well, therefore, to this day!

And these lines from our prayer book—

Birth is a beginning
And life is a journey,

From childhood to maturity,
A sacred pilgrimage.

Marilyn and I both like this thought on success—

You can use most any measure
when speaking of success.
Measure it in the fancy home,
expensive car or dress.
But the real measure of your success
is one you cannot spend.
It's the way your child describes you
when talking to a friend.

And finally, the moving words of General Lucius Clay—

No one ever achieves all his hopes and aspirations. No one is ever sure, in looking back, that he has played his full part in making a better world. But as we live again in our children and our children's children, we do not need to be afraid. For we can touch the future with our children's hands. We can look to them to correct our failures, to achieve many of our hopes and aspirations which never came true for us.

Much is being said of the present crisis in the world and the need to do something about it. But to play a part and do our duty, we do not need to be the principal actors. We have only to be good citizens, good neighbors, and most of all—good parents.

Thanks to the following, who allowed themselves to be interviewed for this book:

Rex Arnett
Frank Basile
Jim Beatty
Jim Bisesi
Bob Bruce
Howard Campbell
Bill Carter
Josiah Child
John Cottrell
Jack Dickhaus
Marianne Glick
Marilyn Glick
Arlene Glick Grande
Barbara Gunn
Marge Bauer Harper
John Hart
Frank Hill
Bill Hudnut
Jack Kline
Mickey Maurer
Alice Glick Meshbane
Tom Miller
Syvaline Miller
Lois Morris
Andy Paine
Lu Palma
Fred Pratt
Tom Ringer
Henry Ryder
Lynda Glick Schwartz
Jack Shaw
Edith Shelton
Nick Smyrnis
Hans Steilberger
Max Thurston
Steve Valinet
Bob Whipple